Professionalism and Accounting Rules

The recent history of accounting has been marked by the rapid escalation of a vast array of accounting standards and other technical rules. In spite of this enormous regulatory activity, sudden corporate collapses and other associated financial reporting failures persist. In such a climate, audited financial reports are among the most highly regulated yet also the least reliable of commodities. This book investigates this issue from the perspective of accounting as a professional occupation.

The author argues that the accounting profession is beset by an inferior and incomplete notion of quality in its work, emphasizing only compliance with processing rules rather than the correspondence with commercial phenomena necessary to make accounting information a reliable guide for financial decision making. It is revealed that the discourse of accounting researchers is largely unconcerned with improving the technical quality of financial statements and that the emphasis in accounting education is on simply the mastery of a rule-book. Accounting practice itself has degenerated into a ritual of rule-compliance. Building from a consideration of the function of accounting, the nature, roles and responsibilities of professions, and the features and effects of accounting rules, it is concluded that the professional warrant of the accounting occupation remains to be validated by the cognitive authority expected of a professional occupation.

Professionalism and Accounting Rules will be essential reading for the academic accounting community.

Brian P. West is a Senior Lecturer in Accounting at the University of Ballarat, Victoria, Australia. Prior to commencing his academic career he worked in the audit division of an international accounting firm. Dr West is the author of several articles published in professional and academic journals.

Routledge New Works in Accounting History
Series editors: Richard Brief, Leonard N. Stern School of Business, New York University, USA; Garry Carnegie, Deakin University, Australia; John Richard Edwards, Cardiff Business School, UK; Richard Macve, London School of Economics, UK.

Professionalism and Accounting Rules

Brian P. West

Routledge
Taylor & Francis Group

LONDON AND NEW YORK

First published 2003
by Routledge
11 New Fetter Lane, London EC4P 4EE

Simultaneously published in the USA and Canada
by Routledge
29 West 35th Street, New York, NY 10001

Routledge is an imprint of the Taylor & Francis Group

© 2003 Brian P. West

Typeset in Garamond by
Florence Production Ltd, Stoodleigh, Devon
Printed and bound in Great Britain by
Antony Rowe Ltd, Chippenham, Wiltshire

British Library Cataloguing in Publication Data
A catalogue record for this book is available from the British Library

Library of Congress Cataloging in Publication Data
West, Brian P., 1961–
   Professionalism and accounting rules / Brian P. West.
      p. cm.
   Includes bibliographical references and index.
   1. Accountants—Professional ethics. I. Title.
   HF5635.W516 2003
   657—dc21   2002190864

ISBN 0–415–28569–0

Contents

Contents

Acknowledgements

This book is based upon my doctoral thesis completed at Deakin University. Foremost among those whom I wish to acknowledge are my supervisors. Professor Peter Wolnizer, my principal supervisor, was the source of much encouragement and wise counsel and his scholarship and standards of intellectual inquiry provided a model that I was motivated to strive to emulate. It was also my great privilege to have Raymond Chambers as an associate supervisor. Chambers' extraordinarily productive life came to an end while my thesis was under examination, and before I had conveyed to him my profound gratitude for all that he taught me. The publication of this volume grants me the consolation of an opportunity to acknowledge this indebtedness. To the staff and my fellow graduate students in the School of Accounting and Finance at Deakin University, many thanks for welcoming me into your scholarly community. In particular, I wish to acknowledge Professor Garry Carnegie for his advice and encouragement. Miss Grace Kit-Yee Tam kindly and competently responded to my queries regarding the regulation of accounting in Canada. These parties all helped to make this work better than it otherwise would have been. None bears any responsibility for its deficiencies, interpretations or conclusions as that burden rests exclusively with the author.

Finally, acknowledgement is due to the editor of *Accounting History* for permission to reproduce, in Chapter 3, a revised version of a substantial portion of the following article published in that journal in 1996: West, B.P. (1996) 'The professionalisation of accounting. A review of recent historical research and its implications', *Accounting History*, 1(1): 77–102.

Abbreviations

AAA	American Accounting Association
AARC	Accounting and Auditing Research Committee (Canada)
AARF	Australian Accounting Research Foundation
AAS	Australian Accounting Standard
AASB	Australian Accounting Standards Board
AECC	Accounting Education Change Commission (United States)
AIA	American Institute of Accountants
AICPA	American Institute of Certified Public Accountants
APB	Accounting Principles Board (United States)
ASA	Australian Society of Accountants (subsequently ASCPA)
ASB	Accounting Standards Board (United Kingdom)
ASCPA	Australian Society of Certified Practising Accountants (subsequently CPA Australia)
ASRB	Accounting Standards Review Board (Australia)
CAP	Committee on Accounting Procedures (United States)
CICA	Canadian Institute of Chartered Accountants
CLERP	Corporate Law Economic Review Program (Australia)
FASB	Financial Accounting Standards Board (United States)
FRS	Financial Reporting Standard (United Kingdom)
IASB	International Accounting Standards Board (previously International Accounting Standards Committee)
ICAA	The Institute of Chartered Accountants in Australia
ICAEW	The Institute of Chartered Accountants in England and Wales
ICAS	The Institute of Chartered Accountants of Scotland
SEC	Securities and Exchange Commission (United States)
SSAP	Statement of Standard Accounting Practice (United Kingdom)
UIG	Urgent Issues Group (Australia)

1 Matters in conflict

Professionalism, accounting rules and the function of accounting

> ... in no other established professional field is a stultifying, rigid book of rules the boss.
>
> (Paton 1971: 43)

The issue addressed in the study

The recent history of accounting – encompassing the last three decades in particular – has been marked by the rapid and continuing promulgation of accounting standards and other technical regulatory statements. There is a widespread belief that these accounting rules are necessary to improve the quality of accounting information and have been effective in achieving that end. In contrast, the central theme of this study is that this preoccupation with accounting rule-making and rule-compliance has distracted attention from the essential criterion of 'quality' in financial reporting. Compliance with rules per se is not what determines the reliability and usefulness of accounting information. The essential criterion of quality in accounting abides in the very meaning of the word itself. To provide an account of an event or circumstance is to describe that event or circumstance. A reliable and objectively useful account will be characterized by a correspondence between the description and the event or circumstance it purports to describe.[1] Correspondence with commercial phenomena is the determinant of the serviceability of financial reports. Compliance with accounting rules is only functional to the extent that it enables such correspondence. To elevate rule-compliance to the apex of accounting – as is now common in accounting practice, discourse and education – is to elevate the means over the end they purport to serve; to privilege process over purpose.

Specifications of the function of accounting reflect this distinction. Rather than emphasizing compliance with prescribed procedures, the function of financial accounting is said to subsist in ascertaining the dated, monetary magnitudes of the elements of financial position and performance of firms and communicating them to interested parties for the purpose of informing resource allocation decisions and accountability evaluations. In this way accounting is a technology that, like all other technologies, arises from a need for devices or procedures that serve a specified function (Chambers 1991a: 3). Building on this theme, Chambers (1992: 441) likens accounting to an instrument: 'a device for making more clear and precise some feature of objects and events'. As a specialized instrument, an accounting system is concerned only with financial matters: amounts of money received and paid, or receivable and payable, and measurements of the money equivalent of things that are not money. Reliable financial instrumentation is 'as necessary for the safe and profitable conduct of business as technical instrumentation is necessary for the safe control of its vehicles, its technical processes and the quality of its products' (Chambers 1992: 440).

The fruitfulness of this instrumentation analogy extends beyond helping to make clear what accounting is. It also draws attention to the conditions that determine the serviceability of accounting information and, therefore, how that serviceability might be advanced. The usefulness of any system of instrumentation derives from the extent to which two fundamental conditions are satisfied. First, the system must be concerned with variables that are relevant to the particular function at hand. Thus, the instrumentation system in a motor vehicle is concerned with phenomena that are of significance to the operation of a motor vehicle; for example, oil pressure, speed, engine temperature and the amount of fuel remaining. Extraneous information that would involve unnecessary cost and might distract or confuse the driver is excluded. Second, the instruments must give accurate and timely readings. That is, the information conveyed by the instruments must at all times correspond with the phenomena they represent. A speedometer that shows the speed of a motor vehicle to be markedly different from its actual speed at any time will not assist the driver to control the vehicle in a safe manner. Indeed, in many circumstances there may be a better chance of proceeding safely with no instrument rather than with one that is seriously misleading.

When functioning as properly calibrated instruments, financial statements describe in money terms the position of an entity relative to its external environment and how that relationship has changed over a specified period of time. Therefore, the essential inputs to these statements are periodic readings of the phenomena that determine an entity's capacity to interact with other entities through commercial exchange: the amounts of cash and claims to cash it has, the cash equivalents of its severable means, and the magnitudes of its existing financial obligations.

As instruments, financial statements can only provide *representations* of the phenomena that guide the decision-making processes of investors, creditors and other interested parties. The serviceability of these statements will be dependent on the extent to which they depict accurately the phenomena they purport to represent. This notion has been explained under a variety of guises in the accounting literature. Solomons (1978: 70) invokes a cartographic analogy: 'Accounting is financial map-making. The better the map, the more completely it represents the complex phenomena that are being mapped.'

Sterling (1989: 85) describes a 'correspondence concept': 'the need for correspondence of a calculated numeral to an independent observation (measurement) of the phenomena that the numeral purports to represent'. Wolnizer (1987: 56, emphasis in original) pursues the theme in terms of the need for financial reports to have an isomorphic quality:

> Financial statements may be viewed as descriptive accounts of the financial relationships between an entity and its environment from time to time, and changes in that relationship over time. Accordingly, a system of accounting may be viewed as a *model* of the system of financial relationships between an entity and its environment. The function of the accounting system is, therefore, to represent the financial consequences of an entity's actions and the financial consequences of the endogenous and exogenous factors which determine an entity's financial status in relation to all other entities. When the laws underlying the accounting model have the same syntactical structure as a corresponding set of laws which govern the phenomena of financial position (or state of affairs) and financial performance (changes in financial position), financial statements may be considered syntactically isomorphic with the actual financial position and financial performance of firms.

It is this isomorphism that provides financial statements with functional fitness for use or 'technical ophelimity': 'The technical ophelimity of accounts derives from their technical capacity as instruments to correspond with a company's actual state of affairs at a point in time' (Wolnizer 1987: 89). Only when this correspondence is achieved can financial statements permit meaningful assessments to be made of a firm's rate of return, solvency and capacity for adaptation: the crucial variables that inform financial decision making.

Following from this specification of accounting as a system of instrumentation is the matter of how to control or regulate the design and operation of that system. The consequences of faulty financial instrumentation, whether the result of neglect or intent, may be severe. Where the decision-making processes of individual investors are misguided, economic inefficiencies with broader social repercussions are likely to ensue. To protect against these adversities, accounting, in common with other systems of instrumentation, needs to be subject to some form of governance or discipline. Consistent with this, Chambers and Wolnizer (1991) show that qualitative standards for accounting information have a long history. They appeared in early bookkeeping manuals and were written into the constitutive documents of commercial ventures and a variety of statutes in the United Kingdom during the eighteenth and early nineteenth centuries. Their purpose was 'to signify the duty to ensure that accounts were properly kept as a basis for representing the financial affairs of public bodies and business firms' (Chambers and Wolnizer 1991: 198). This need for accounting information to be of a certain quality was also recognized in the first statute having general application to incorporated entities: the *United Kingdom Joint Stock Companies Act of 1844*. This legislation required that company balance sheets be 'full and fair'. General qualitative standards of this kind have persisted in the law applying to companies. The term 'true and correct' was introduced in the Joint Stock Companies legislation enacted in the United Kingdom in 1856. In the *Companies Act of 1948* the qualitative standard of 'true and fair' was implemented and subsequently adopted and retained by a number of British Commonwealth countries, including Australia.

However, a general qualitative standard does not of itself ensure the serviceability of financial reports. That outcome can only be achieved when the technical practices required to be applied to satisfy the standard have been specified and enforced. During the past hundred years, the onus for discharging this responsibility has been substantially placed with accounting practitioners. Both individually and through their formal associations, accountants have played the major role in designing accounting procedures and overseeing their application. As a distinct occupational group, accountants have thereby exercised significant authority in connection with the technical aspects of accounting practice. This is evidenced by the success of various associations of accountants in obtaining for their memberships an exclusive right to pronounce independently on the truth and fairness (or other similar general qualitative standard) of company financial statements (Lee 1979). Underlying these arrangements is the presumption that accountants possess special and exclusive expertise in connection with accounting matters.

This elevated occupational authority of accountants has parallels across a restricted range of other occupations. These occupations are commonly described as professions and the authority vested with them constitutes a particular form of social control. Professions are relied upon to be self-regulating: to exercise responsibly their specialist expertise with proper regard for the public interest. 'Professionalism' is characterized by the pursuit of these outcomes. In accounting it involves seeking to acquire and apply knowledge that improves the serviceability of accounting information; that is, the pursuit of a more reliable and informative system of financial instrumentation. 'Professional accounting knowledge' must thereby encompass an understanding of the nature of commercial activity and how the outcomes of that activity can be summarized in reports that serve as reliable guides in financial decision-making processes.

However, rather than seeking to ensure that accounting information corresponds with the actual financial features of firms as at their date – and that the function of accounting is therefore served – there is evidence that the accounting profession has been, and continues to be, concerned only to ensure that financial statements have been prepared on the basis of prescribed technical accounting rules.[2] Were these rules to prescribe an effective system of financial instrumentation, they would provide the means by which the function of accounting would be better served. But, as will be demonstrated in this study, the rules do not deliver that outcome. Instead, compliance with rules per se has become the end in itself. The serviceability of the information resulting from this compliance does not appear to be the focus of professional endeavour nor academic inquiry in accounting. Instead, as Lee (1990b, vol. 1: 33) suggests, accounting standards are now widely perceived as *constituting* accounting. Brown and Howieson (1998: 5) embrace this perspective explicitly: 'we take the . . . view that "accounting practice" means "accounting standard setting"'.

Acceptance of this 'rule-book accounting' is also evident in the discourse of accounting researchers where it is the *rule-making* – rather than the rules – that has been the favoured subject of inquiry. Thus, accounting standard setting processes have been subject to extensive examination (Aranya 1974; Benston 1976; Booth and Cocks 1990a; Brown and Tarca 2001; Collett 1995; Feller 1973; Fogarty 1994; Fogarty, Hussein and Ketz 1994; Gavens, Carnegie and Gibson 1989; Gibson 1980; Gillian 1995; Harding and McKinnon 1997; Hines 1987; Hogler, Hunt and Wilson 1996; Hope and Gray 1982; Hunt and Hogler 1993; Klumpes 1995; Laughlin and Puxty 1983, 1984; Miller 1995; Ogan and Ziebart 1991; Rahman 1992; Rahman, Ng and Tower 1994; Schipper 1994; Tutticci, Dunstan and Holmes 1994; Walker 1987; Walker and Robinson 1994; Watts and Zimmerman 1978; Weetman, Davie and Collins 1996; Willmott 1984; Willmott *et al.* 1992; Young 1995; Young and Mouck 1996). This has been extended to include examination of the interface between accounting standards and other regulatory frameworks, including the law (Committe 1990; Gangolly and Hussein 1996; Lowe, Gallhofer and Haslam 1991; Merino and Neimark 1982; Parker, Peirson and Ramsay 1987; Peirson and Ramsay 1983; Puxty *et al.* 1987; Turner and Jensen 1987). 'Culture' has been said to determine the form and content of standards (Bloom and Naciri 1989; Harrison and McKinnon 1986; Jonsson 1991). Historical narratives have documented the development of standard setting institutions (Davidson and Anderson 1987; English 1988; Feller 1974; Gibson 1971, 1979; Henderson 1993; Kessler 1972; Larson and Holstrum 1973; McGregor 1995; Nobes 1991; Zeff 1972, 1973, 1984). Comparison of the rules applying in different jurisdictions has now emerged as a favoured mode of inquiry, driven by an apparent belief that accounting will advance if the rules are 'harmonized' (Hegarty 1997; Humphrey 1997; Parker and Morris 2001; Sharpe 1998).

The discourse pertaining to accounting rule-making is therefore significant and extends across legal, economic, cultural, institutional, political and historical frameworks. However, when attention has been directed to the rules themselves the worth of the whole process is brought into question. The prescriptions contained in accounting standards have been shown to be technically deficient (Chambers 1973b, 1975, 1979; Chambers, Ramanathan and Rappaport 1978) and their application has failed to curb financial reporting failures (Briloff 1972, 1981; Chambers 1973b; Clarke, Dean and Oliver 1997; Margavio 1993; Sykes 1994). The observation of Clarke, Dean and Oliver (1997: 260) is instructive:

The only regulatory defence for compulsory Accounting Standards is that they would improve the serviceability of accounting information. One would pursue that line with the expectation that the more Standards, the less the complaint and criticism of accounting from consumers, and the fewer the instances of creative accounting. We have more prescribed procedures now than at any time in our history, nationally and internationally. One would have thought that there would be evidence of a decline in the dissatisfaction with the data accountants are producing – evidence of less creative accounting. The opposite has occurred (nationally and internationally).

Accounting rule-making, however, continues unabated and generally unquestioned: 'Oddly this proliferation of rules as a phenomenon, *per se*, has not attracted much attention as something to be explained' (Williams 1987: 176). As a result, and in spite of their dominance, technical accounting rules are commonly justified only by a variety of casual and often contradictory asides: they are associated with the progress of accounting as a profession; they are needed to 'standardize' financial reports; they originated as a response to public criticism of accounting; they allow participation in accounting policy making; they provide necessary guidance for practitioners; they redress deficiencies in conventional accounting. Other explanations derive from a notion that accounting information can be characterized as an 'economic good' and the 'market' for this 'good' analysed. On the basis of this analysis, prescriptions for accounting rules are either made (to correct 'market failures'; for example, May and Sundem 1976; Okcabol and Tinker 1993; Solomons 1983) or challenged (an unregulated 'market' would be more efficient; for example, Benston 1980, 1982a, 1982b; Leftwich 1980; Stigler 1964a, 1964b; Watts and Zimmerman 1986). A variation in the debate has originated from those who have questioned the public interest rationale for accounting regulations and adopted a private interest or 'economic theory' perspective (Peltzman 1976; Posner 1974; Stigler 1971) expressed in the form of 'regulatory capture' (Walker 1987). The majority view, though, has been that accounting regulations – including accounting standards and related rules – are explained and justified by disequilibrium in the 'market' for accounting information (Laughlin and Puxty 1983: 453).

Yet, no demonstration has been made of how extant accounting rules redress the alleged 'market failures'. Indeed, examination of these rules reveals that they do not embrace any coherent quality specification for accounting information. Nor has any robust explanation been offered for why the 'market failures' should necessitate a continuing expansion of the number of rules. Contrary to the expectations established by the 'market failure' rationale, a distinguishing feature of present accounting rules is their tendency to perpetuate accounting conventions that pre-date the standard setting era. That these conventions are sustained only by an increasing array of specific rules imposed by fiat appears to speak of a different kind of failure than that relating to the 'market' for accounting information. Witness, for example, how present accounting standards deal repeatedly with the issue of allocating costs between assets and expenses. The proliferation of these rules derives from these allocations not having empirical (commercial) referents. They are matters that can *only* be 'resolved' by prescribed methods of calculation. That is, the impetus for this rule-making is accounting technique, not failures in the 'market' for accounting information.[3] Moreover, the clue is thereby given that these rules do not contribute to enabling more reliable financial instrumentation as they are not concerned with describing commercial phenomena.

However, the accounting profession has typically responded to criticisms of its technical practices by promulgating more of the same kind of rules.[4] Textbook writers incorporate the provisions of technical pronouncements in their publications without subjecting them to critical scrutiny. The actual practice of accounting appears increasingly to terminate in an assurance that prescribed rules have been followed. Underlying these circumstances appears to be a widely held presumption that compliance with accounting rules is of itself functional and that the promulgation of more rules paves the path of progress in accounting. In short, compliance with rules – rather than correspondence with financial facts – has become the substance of contemporary accounting.

It is contended in this study that the accounting profession has been – and continues to be – preoccupied with rule-making and rule-compliance rather than the serviceability of the financial information yielded by the application of those rules. In addition, it is argued that this preoccupation has stifled the pursuit of the cognitive authority expected to characterize a profession: the holding of demonstrably reliable knowledge that provides the foundation for professional practice. Sporadic references that reveal an unease over the accounting profession having contented itself with the role of interpreting and enforcing accounting rules may be found in the accounting literature. Before the advent of accounting standards as they are known today, Byrne (1937: 378) emphasized that financial statements should be governed by 'principles' agreed upon by accountants:

> Accountants of the highest abilities and reputations are willing to give their considered opinion, after due examination, that the financial statements under review fairly present the position of a company based upon accounts determined in accordance with accepted principles of accounting. It follows that these fundamental truths upon which such opinion is based, and which may be properly dignified with the term principles, are known to the accountant and are matters with respect to which, by their very nature, there can be no general disagreement.

Such a theme is still evident in an observation of Chambers (1993: 16) more than half a century later: 'Regulation in other fields does not concern itself with technical knowledge and procedures; it presupposes the possession by practitioners of knowledge, based on scientific and practical grounds, of demonstrated and agreed merit.' Baxter (1994/1979: 16)[5] similarly questions the accounting profession's reliance on technical regulations: 'If standards confer such patent benefits, we should perhaps ask why most other professions fail to produce them.' Stamp (1980: 62) argues that professional accountants cannot discharge their duty just by following rules: 'If all that accountants are expected to do is to follow the prescriptions contained in a book of rules, they are not acting as professionals.' Clarke, Dean and Oliver (1997: 259) are also led to 'question whether compulsory compliance with prescribed processing standards is compatible with the notion of a profession'. Schuetze laments that accounting rules are 'too voluminous, too detailed, too complex and too abstruse' (2001: 1) with the consequence being that 'accountants are doing accounting for accountants' sake' (2001: 4). Sprouse (1988: 121) encapsulates the fundamental concern that motivates this study:

> It is my strong conviction that, for accounting to be a legitimate field of study in colleges and universities and for accountancy to be acknowledged as a legitimate learned profession, something more fundamental and enduring than facile application of an increasingly comprehensive set of detailed rules and procedures must be at its foundation.

The explanation and evaluation of accounting rules and their implications that is pursued in this study is guided by ideas about the nature, roles and responsibilities of professional groups. This is a distinctive emphasis. Despite the range of theoretical frameworks applied in the study of accounting rules, inquiries emanating from the perspective of accounting as a professional occupation have been lacking.

The aims of the study

The primary aim of this study is to demonstrate that present accounting rules do not yield serviceable financial information and that expertise in interpreting and applying those rules does not substantiate a cognitive authority of the kind expected of a professional occupation. Underlying this thesis is the notion that the quality of accounting information is not determined by the extent to which it complies with the requirements of prescribed rules, but by the extent to which it corresponds with commercial phenomena. For this reason, accounting rule-making cannot of itself be presumed to be functional; it is so only if it enables the development of a more useful and accurate system of financial instrumentation. As it is the responsibility of accounting professionals to ensure that accounting information is functionally fit for its intended purpose, their duty cannot terminate simply with an assurance that particular rules have been complied with.

This study also has three subsidiary aims. First, it seeks to draw attention to a gap in the literature on accounting regulation. As indicated above, this literature has sought to justify present accounting rules on the ground that they are needed to remedy 'failures' in the 'market' for accounting information. However, how present rules achieve this end has not been demonstrated. It will be argued in this study that the continued promulgation of these rules, without any demonstration of their fitness for use, speaks more of an adherence to conventional and unserviceable accounting practices than failures in the 'market' for accounting information. In particular, a persistent focus on such abstract notions as 'cost allocations' and 'future economic benefits' has made accounting dependent on the prescriptions of formal pronouncements. The inherently disciplined techniques of a system of instrumentation – the observation and measurement of phenomena – are rendered inoperable.

Second, the study attempts to show that the proliferation of accounting rules has had an adverse impact on intellectual activity within the accounting discipline. Several decades of promulgating accounting standards have failed to curb financial reporting failures. Yet, the conviction with which the accounting profession stands by present accounting rules is such that it routinely assumes that the blame for accounting failures must rest with other parties: the misjudgements of company managers and the misunderstandings and unjustifiable expectations of the users of financial reports. Similarly contented, accounting researchers have turned their attention away from the subject matters of accounting in favour of examination of the behaviour of accountants. Underlying this complacency appears to be a belief that the continued promulgation of technical rules constitutes, and is evidence of, the progress of accounting as a profession. In rejecting this conventional perspective it will be argued that, by settling for institutional rather than cognitive sanction of its technical practices, the accounting profession has been sapped of intellectual vitality. The evidence and consequences of this are examined in this study within the contexts of accounting discourse, education and practice. The purpose of this is to demonstrate that the implications of present technical rules extend beyond their direct failure to deliver serviceable financial reports. By perpetuating deficient means of accounting these rules have constituted a barrier to reform rather than a mechanism of reform, and thereby retarded, rather than advanced, the cognitive authority of accountants.

Third, the study seeks to contribute generally to enhancing understanding of the nature of professional groups. Critiques of the sociology of the professions' literature (Abbott 1988; Freidson 1983; Saks 1983) have called for empirical work that maps the case histories of individual professions. Accounting has been nominated for special attention in this regard:

> the jurisdiction of money requires the kind of attention long received by health. Perhaps sociologists and historians, as biological individuals, concern themselves more with the profession of life and death than with the profession of loss and profit, but surely accounting is today far more socially important than medicine.
>
> (Abbott 1988: 325)

This study responds to such calls (see also Cooper and Hopper 1987; Lee 1991; Willmott 1986) by examining the role of technical accounting rules in the shaping and controlling of the accounting jurisdiction. By so doing the study also examines the nature of professional expertise. While specialized knowledge has long been stated to be the core feature of professions, the sociology of professions literature contains various admissions that its pronouncements about such knowledge have often proceeded from assertion rather than investigation (Baer 1986; Boreham 1983: 695; Goldstein 1984: 183–4; Parkin 1979: 103). This appears to have been the case in accounting where, without being subject to critical scrutiny, formally stated rules have often been represented as a codification of accountants' professional knowledge. By drawing attention to how these rules lack a unifying and functional quality specification, insights are provided to apparent anomalies concerning the nature of accountants' professional claim and the consequences of this for the quality of accounting information.

The method employed in the study

While the origins of accounting rule-making lie in the first half of the twentieth century it has been during the last three decades that this activity and its outputs have achieved their dominating status. During this period the volume, variety and status of rules have increased and the accounting profession's dependence upon them become resolute. It is this recent history of accounting that is under scrutiny in this study, proceeding on the basis of observation (perceiving phenomena in a systematic manner) and analysis (critical examination in pursuit of enhanced understanding). The analysis is concerned with explaining the origin, nature and consequences of accounting standards and related rules and is informed by ideas about the nature, roles and responsibilities of professional groups. An impediment to the construction of this analysis is the lack of theoretical closure within the sociology of professions literature. As will be outlined in Chapter 2, different authors have viewed professions in different ways and there is no universally accepted 'theory of professions'. In order to transcend this discord a pragmatic understanding of professions is adopted which de-emphasizes purely theoretical issues. In particular, debates that are ideologically based or that emphasize conjectures about the motives of professional groups are avoided on the ground that they are beyond empirical resolution. Instead, an emphasis is placed on the concept of occupational authority. That is, professions are characterized as occupational groups that have socially conferred mandates to oversee particular domains for the purpose of enhancing social order. In this study, an investigation of the discharge of these mandates is advocated and pursued.

Social order is dependent on means for mediating interactions among the actors that constitute a society. Laws and regulations imposed by government and its agencies are an example of such means. Customs and social mores also play roles in contributing to the maintenance of social order. In unregulated markets, consumer knowledge is relied upon to mediate mutually beneficial exchanges between buyers and sellers. The authority vested with professionals – both individually and collectively – constitutes another and quite distinct form of mediation. The members of a profession, according to Carr-Saunders (1966/1928: 6), 'mutually guarantee not only their competence but also their honor'. Thus, the provider of professional services – whether in a market situation such as between lawyer and client, or a non-market situation such as may arise between teacher and student – carries primary responsibility for ensuring the quality and suitability of those services. The essential justification for such a structure of authority is the special knowledge and skills claimed by the members of the professional group. It is, however, an authority that is usually endowed without formal accountability mechanisms. Faith is placed in professional expertise. The bridging of this accountability gap requires that professional knowledge claims be investigated rather than taken for granted. In the context of accounting it requires an examination of whether an ability to understand and apply accounting rules – the prerequisite expertise for contemporary accounting practice – accords with the need for serviceable financial reports.

The structure of the study

The study has two main themes. The first is concerned with *explaining* the nature and existence of technical accounting rules. This is developed in Chapters 4 and 5, building from a discussion of professions generally in Chapter 2 and accounting as a profession in Chapter 3. The second deals with the *consequences* of present accounting rules within the contexts of accounting discourse (Chapter 6), education (Chapter 7) and practice (Chapter 8). The final chapter (Chapter 9) recapitulates the main argument: that a professional accounting jurisdiction cannot be defended legitimately by just the promulgation and enforcement of accounting rules. Instead, professionalism in accounting is contingent upon the technical quality of the information that accountants produce. Expertise in achieving compliance with rules – no matter how great their numerosity or complexity – cannot be offered as a substitute for expertise in devising a reliable system of financial instrumentation and the ongoing tasks of operating, monitoring and refining that system.

Accordingly, the study culminates in a call for an invigorated search for a cognitive grounding for accounting practice. This would mark a fundamental transition from the present reliance on processing rules that are not derived from any coherent specification of the required technical qualities of financial reports. However, it is a transition that is essential if accountants are to validate their claim to professional status and its accompanying privileges. Progress in this direction demands the willingness of accountants to engage in the intellectual struggle necessary to free their discipline from the torpor presently inflicted by the minutiae of the 'accounting handbook'. It requires a recognition that the function of accounting is not served by perfunctory processes of calculation that generate financial statements which may comply with a set of technical rules but which fail to correspond to commercial facts as at their date. Rather, the function of accounting is to provide factual information that corresponds with what is determinative and indicative of the actual dated financial position of firms and their progress from time to time. Only through such a reorientation can some seemingly modest expectations concerning the technical qualities of accounting information be met. These include that financial statements be descriptive of, and relatable to, real-world commercial activity, respect fundamental principles of arithmetic and the reliable findings in other fields of knowledge, be factual rather than conjectural, and be capable of independent corroboration. Financial statements having these qualities would have the capacity to serve as reliable financial instruments.

2   Professions

Their nature, roles and responsibilities

The professions dominate our world. They heal our bodies, measure our profits, save our souls. Yet we are deeply ambivalent about them.

(Abbott 1988: 1)

Introduction

The study of professional groups is well-established within the discipline of sociology, but has developed in a fragmented manner.[1] As Turner (1995: 131) states:

Sociological theory appears to develop through the contradiction of paradigms, whereby traditional frameworks are constantly rejected in favour of paradigmatic revolutions. . . . The sociological analysis of professions is no exception.

Consistent with this view, the sociology of professions literature is marked by descriptions such as 'highly confused' (Freidson 1973b: 19), 'widely divergent' (Trebilcock 1978: 3), 'in turmoil' (Rueschemeyer 1983: 38), 'vague and chaotic' (Freidson 1983: 36), 'fragile' (Halliday 1985: 421), 'theoretically unproductive' (Atkinson and Delamont 1990: 90), and 'an intellectual shambles' (Freidson 1994: 149).[2] Research on professions is said to have been guided by 'a shifting and diverse range of theoretical frameworks' (Saks 1983:1), with the outcome that 'there is no single theory of the professions; rather, there are competing theories, no one of which has become completely hegemonic' (Meiksins and Watson 1989: 561).

This dissonant character of the sociology of professions literature means that it does not offer a generally accepted theory of professions that is 'ready made' for application in explaining and evaluating the circumstances of particular occupational groups. Hence, it is the objective of this chapter to establish an understanding of professions that transcends the current discord in the literature and which will inform this study. Towards this end, the next section of the chapter reviews the historical development of the sociology of professions literature. This is followed by a critique of the literature and approaches that have been employed in the study of professions. Emanating from this, the understanding of the nature, roles and responsibilities of professional groups that will be adopted in this study is described. This emphasizes that professions are occupation-based structures of authority and vested with responsibility for overseeing specific domains within society. It is argued that the justification for the endowment of this authority must be found in the exclusive and specialized expertise that an occupational group possesses and demonstrates a commitment to apply responsibly. On account of its centrality in connection with professions generally, and this study in particular, the subject of professional knowledge is then elucidated. It is shown that sociologists of the professions – despite their many disagreements – have been united in regarding specialist expertise as a universal and distinguishing feature of professions. However, it is a feature that has rarely been the subject of systematic examination, with sociologists placing the constitution of professional knowledge outside their field of inquiry. It is argued in this chapter that understanding and evaluating professions as significant social institutions requires that this failure to examine the nature of professional knowledge be redressed – if not by sociologists, then by academics as independent holders of professional expertise.

Development of the sociology of professions literature

As Abbott (1988: 3) notes, while 'the professions derive from medieval or in some cases ancient origins', systematic attempts to study them did not commence until the twentieth century. Thus, Carr-Saunders (1966/1928: 4) would observe: 'The story of the evolution of the professions is ... an unwritten chapter in the social history of the last two centuries.' Early contributions to overcoming this lack of understanding were generally reverential in their descriptions of professions.[3] *The Acquisitive Society* by Tawney (1920: 94) stresses the altruistic nature of professional service:

> The difference between industry ... and a profession is, then, simple and unmistakable. The essence of the former is that its only criterion is the financial return which it offers to its shareholders. The essence of the latter, is that, though men enter it for the sake of livelihood, the measure of their success is the service which they perform, not the gains which they amass. They may, as in the case of a successful doctor, grow rich; but the meaning of their profession, both for themselves and for the public is not that they make money but that they make health, or safety, or knowledge, or good government or good law.

In the case of Whitehead's *Adventures of Ideas* (1933: 72–3), the ideal emphasized is the theoretical grounding of professional knowledge:

the term profession means an avocation whose activities are subjected to theoretical analysis, and are modified by theoretical conclusions derived from that analysis. . . . Thus foresight based upon theory, and theory based upon understanding of the nature of things, are essential to a profession. . . . The antithesis to a profession is an avocation based upon customary activities and modified by the trial and error of individual practice.

Such was Durkheim's faith in professional groups that he saw them as primary sources of moral and ethical responsibility within society (1957: 7),[4] and envisaged a continuing and deserved elevation of their roles (1957: 96–7):

> The permanent groups, those to which the individual devotes his whole life, those for which he has the strongest attachment, are the professional groups. It therefore seems indeed that it is they which may be called upon to become the basis of our political representation as well as of our social structure in the future.

These idealized portrayals persisted in what is widely acknowledged as the first comprehensive and systematic examination of professional groups: Carr-Saunders and Wilson's ground-breaking study *The Professions*, published in 1933. In the preface to this work Carr-Saunders and Wilson lamented that the study of professional associations had been 'almost entirely neglected' and that this was 'all the more astonishing' on account of the 'greater skill and responsibility of professional men' (1933: iii). In order 'to examine and evaluate all that is characteristic of professionalism' the authors surveyed 26 occupational groupings, being 'the established professions and those other vocations which for any reason throw light upon professional organization and activity' (1933: 3). Their evaluation depicted associations of professionals as crucial but under-recognized sources of social cohesion:

> Professional associations are stabilizing elements in society. They engender modes of life, habits of thought, and standards of judgement which render them centres of resistance to crude forces which threaten steady and peaceful evolution. But the service which they render in so doing is not sufficiently appreciated. It is largely due to them and to other similar centres of resistance that the older civilizations stand firm. . . . The family, the church, the universities, certain associations of intellectuals, and above all the great professions, stand like rocks against which the waves raised by these forces beat in vain.
>
> (Carr-Saunders and Wilson 1933: 497)

Significantly, Carr-Saunders and Wilson (1933: 3–4) eschewed the closely related issues of definition and demarcation: 'It is no part of our purpose to attempt to draw a line between professions and other vocations . . . and we shall not offer, either now or later, a definition of professionalism.' Attempts to fill this lacuna would preoccupy writers on the professions for the next several decades, guided by Carr-Saunders and Wilson's (1933: 4) suggestion that 'the typical profession exhibits a complex of characteristics'. Thus was ushered in what has been variously labelled the 'trait', 'attribute' or 'taxonomic' model of professions. Cogan's (1953: 49) attempt at definition is typical of this work and describes a particular set of characteristics intended to permit professional and non-professional occupations to be distinguished:

> A profession is a vocation whose practice is founded upon an understanding of the theoretical structure of some department of learning or science, and upon the abilities accompanying such understanding. This understanding and these abilities are applied to the vital practical affairs of man. The practices of the profession are modified by knowledge of a generalized nature and by the accumulated wisdom and experience of mankind, which serve to correct the errors of specialism. The profession, serving the vital needs of man, considers its first ethical imperative to be altruistic service to the client.

Subsequent writers tended to be even more explicit in their advocacy of the trait model, electing simply to provide a list of discrete features rather than an integrated definition. Greenwood's (1966/1957: 10) list is often cited: 'Succinctly put, all professions seem to possess: (1) systematic theory, (2) authority, (3) community sanction, (4) ethical codes, and (5) a culture.' Barber (1963: 672) enumerated four 'essential attributes' of professional behaviour:

> a high degree of generalized and systematic knowledge; primary orientation to the community interest rather than to individual self-interest; a high degree of self-control of behavior through codes of ethics internalized in the process of work socialization and through voluntary associations organized and operated by the work specialists themselves; and a system of rewards (monetary and honorary) that is primarily a set of symbols of work achievement and thus ends in themselves, not some end of individual self-interest.

In contrast, for Wilensky (1964: 138, emphasis in original) there were only two fundamental traits:

> In the minds of both the lay public and professional groups themselves the criteria of distinction seem to be two: (1) The job of the professional is *technical* – based on systematic knowledge or doctrine acquired only through long prescribed training. (2) The professional man adheres to a set of *professional norms*.

Attempts to define professions by reference to a checklist of attributes reached their pinnacle with Millerson's (1964) survey. Although noting that 'a mass of confusion stems from all analyses which attempt to determine the occupational characteristics of a profession' (1964: 4), the following six 'essential features' of a profession were nominated:

(a) A profession involves a skill based on theoretical knowledge.
(b) The skill requires training and education.
(c) The professional must demonstrate competence by passing a test.
(d) Integrity is maintained by adherence to a code of conduct.
(e) The service is for the public good.
(f) The profession is organized.

(Millerson 1964: 4)

Explicitly trait-based models of professions persisted in the sociology literature until at least 1970, with the publication of *The Professions: Roles and Rules* by Moore (1970).[5] In this work the author stressed full-time occupation, commitment to a calling, organization, esoteric but useful knowledge and skills derived from specialized training or education, service orientation, and autonomy as the 'defining characteristics' of a profession (Moore 1970: 5–6).

Emerging from among the later contributions to the trait genre was a structural–functional model of professions developed from the anthropological theory of functionalism. Under this theory, 'society is seen as an entity all the parts of which function to maintain one another and the totality, the disruption of one part provoking readjustment among others' (Freedman 1988: 337). The existence of professions was thereby taken to provide evidence of their social utility, as indicated in the writing of Elliott (1972: 11):

The professional group controls a body of expert knowledge which is applied to specialised tasks. This poses special problems of social control. Such problems can be seen in the relationship between the unskilled client or, more generally, in the tension between values developed within the profession and the values of the wider society. Social control in the professional group takes two forms. The professional institutions oversee all the functions of the profession. They lay down standards controlling entry to the group. Through the training necessary to achieve these qualifications, and through associations with professional peers, the individual acquires the norms and values of the group. Through these, mechanisms of social control become internalised. Such internalisation is peculiarly necessary because of the opportunities which exist for exploitation in professional practice and because of the loose control which can be exercised by institutions, especially in individual practice situations.

The structural–functional interpretation thus depicted professions as being party to a social contract:

the professions 'strike a bargain with society' in which they exchange competence and integrity against the trust of client and community, relative freedom from lay supervision and interference, protection against unqualified competition as well as substantial remuneration and higher social status.

(Rueschemeyer 1983: 41)

The extension of trait-based descriptions of professions into a structural–functional model offered the advantage of providing some rationale for the items included in trait listings. For example, codes of ethics were no longer just a benign item in a checklist for evaluating occupational status, but a necessary social control device to counter what was deemed to be the inherently unequal relationship between the suppliers and consumers of professional services. In spite of such theoretical support, the trait and structural–functional models of professions came under sustained attack from the early 1970s.[6] The attack was launched by writers identified by a variety of labels – 'radical', 'critical', 'monopolist', 'Marxist', 'Weberian' – and featured two central and closely related themes. The first comprised an often scornful critique of the sociology of professions literature, including allegations that it was bound by a subservience to the interests of professional groups.[7] The second involved a persistent questioning of the legitimacy of the privileges enjoyed by professions, amid sustained attempts to investigate the process of professionalization which provided access to such privileges.

Pivotal in this redirection of the sociology of professions literature was Johnson's *Professions and Power*, in which the author regretted 'a widening gap between research and the theoretical problems suggested by the phenomenal growth of the professions and the implications of this growth for the changing distribution of power in industrial societies' (Johnson 1972: 12). Persistent focus on the 'largely sterile attempt to define what the special "attributes" of a profession are' (1972: 12) was criticized. Instead, a call was made for inquiries designed 'to understand professional occupations in terms of their power relations in society – their sources of power and authority and the ways in which they use them' (1972: 18).

Roth's critique was especially caustic, contending that preoccupation with trying to establish criteria for distinguishing professions and non-professions had 'decoyed students of occupations into becoming apologists for the professionalism ideology, justifying the professionals' control over the work situation' (Roth 1974: 6). The pursuit of an attribute-based model of professions was denounced:

The trouble with the attribute approach is that it does not focus on this process [of professionalization], but on its product, and typically even this focus is contaminated with the ideology and hopes of professional groups rather than an independent assessment of what they achieve. Various occupations play the attribute rating game in an effort to increase

their relative standing in the occupational world and to reap the attendant rewards. Sociologists who focus on lists of attributes do not study
this process, but participate in it. They have become the dupe of the
established professions (helping them to justify their dominant position
and its payoff) and arbiters of occupations on the make, keeping score
instead of observing and interpreting the behaviour involved in the
process of scoring. . . .

    The listing of attributes and the rating of occupations on a profes-
sionalism scale are objectionable not only because they have proved a
theoretical dead-end, but also because they have deflected concern from
the more crucial problems caused by professionalization, such as the
avoidance of accountability to the public, the manipulation of political
power to promote monopoly control, and the restriction of services to
create scarcities and increase costs.

(Roth 1974: 17–18)

The study of the historical development of professions was offered as 'the best
antidote for the attribute rut' (Roth 1974: 18).

    Having noted that profession is 'a concept which is notorious for the
diversity of its definitions and usage by sociologists', Dingwall (1976: 331)
also eschewed concern with the pursuit of a precise definition. Such efforts,
it is claimed, are destined to fail: 'We cannot . . . define what a profession is.
All we can do is to elaborate what it appears to mean to use the term and to
list the occasions on which various elaborations are used' (Dingwall 1976:
335). As with other writers during this transitional phase, Dingwall
(1976: 331) offered his own proposal for furthering understanding of professions:

> we should . . . proceed to the empirical investigations of socially distrib-
> uted commonsense knowledge of social structures, abandoning any claim
> to legislate a correct use of the term 'profession', but treating it as a
> concept invoked by members of particular collectivities and seeking to
> describe its practical usage.

    Klegon (1978: 260–7) offered a further critique of the trait-based approach
to studying professions, and recommended another 'new' approach that would
be of a social constructivist character. The 'real issue' for Klegon involved
identifying 'the social conditions that allow a particular occupational group
first to claim, and then perpetuate their claim to holding special expertise'
(1978: 268). Researchers were called on to:

> examine the relationship of the occupation and its practitioners to other
> aspects of the social structure. Such a new approach towards the profes-
> sions also requires the adoption of a more critical ideological orientation
> and the abandonment of the very notion of particular occupations as
> something inherently distinct from other occupations and requiring

a separate framework for analysis. Occupations may differ along such factors as status, degree of control, organization, influence and so forth. However, just because an occupation may become idealized and reified in the social consciousness, there is no reason for sociologists to do the same.

(Klegon 1978: 268)

The seeds of a paradigm shift in the sociology of professions were sown. The important issue was no longer one of delineating professional and non-professional occupations. Instead, 'theories of action as opposed to those of structure' (Macdonald 1995: 1) were favoured, with the dynamics of *professionalization* – broadly defined as the process by which occupational groups ascend the occupational hierarchy – supplanting the static hermeneutics of *profession*. The recommended mode of inquiry was social constructivist, focusing on how and why certain occupations gained enhanced status and privileges, as '*power* became the key word for both academic and nonacademic writers on the professions' (Freidson 1986: 29, emphasis in original). Underlying this new direction in research on the professions was an increased level of scepticism about the rationales traditionally advanced in defence of the privileges enjoyed by professional groups. Indeed, the new mood was described as 'radically and bitterly anti-professional' (Halmos 1973: 6).

Earlier writers on the professions had tended to associate status acquisition simply with the accumulation of particular traits. Greenwood (1966/1957: 19), for example, claimed that his trait-based 'model of the professions' could be used to 'illuminate the goal' of aspiring professions. Other writers adopted an almost Whig-like interpretation in which professionalization was viewed as a corollary of social progress. Goode referred to 'a natural line of development' (1960: 906) and suggested that 'An industrialising society is a professionalising society' (1960: 902). Attempts were also made to map out a 'sequence' of professionalization, with Caplow (1966/1954: 20) concluding that 'The steps in professionalization are quite definite, and even the sequence is explicit.' That sequence was said to comprise the establishment of a professional association, changing the name of the occupation, promulgation of a code of ethics, and political agitation concurrently with the development of training facilities under the control of the occupational group. In a similar vein, Wilensky (1964: 142) asked if there was 'an invariant progression of events' that paved the way to professional status. The conclusion was again affirmative:

In sum, there is a typical process by which the established professions have arrived: men begin doing the work full time and stake out a jurisdiction; the early masters of the technique or adherents of the movement become concerned about standards of training and practice and set up a training school, which, if not lodged in universities at the outset, makes academic connection within two or three decades; the teachers and activists then achieve success in promoting more effective organization, first local, then national – through either the transformation of an existing occupational association or the creation of a new one. Toward the end, legal protection of the monopoly of skill appears; at the end, a formal code of ethics is adopted.

(Wilensky 1964: 145–6)

Early attempts to describe professionalization were thus analogous to the trait-based method then in vogue for defining professions. However, as the lack of congruence in the sequences described respectively by Caplow and Wilensky indicates, they suffered from similar deficiencies.

The literature that emerged during the 1970s radically changed the way in which professionalization was viewed. Adam Smith (1952/1776: 55) had warned some 200 years earlier that 'People of the same trade seldom meet together, even for merriment and diversion, but the conversation ends in a conspiracy against the public, or in some contrivance to raise prices.' It was this sentiment that appeared recurringly in the sociology of professions literature as images of altruism, ethical service and self-regulation were supplanted by a portrayal of professions as self-interested collectives. Employing Weberian notions of closure and collective social mobility, Larson's (1977) work was seminal in this new wave of literature. Closure has been defined as 'the process of mobilizing power in order to enhance or defend a group's share of rewards or resources' (Murphy 1984: 548). Collective social mobility encompasses the process of attaching status and social standing to occupational roles (Larson 1977: 66). Professionalization was thus depicted as 'an attempt to translate one order of scarce resources – special knowledge and skills – into another – social and economic rewards' (Larson 1977: xvii). The key to extracting such rewards was an ability to exert market control: 'To maintain scarcity implies a tendency to monopoly: monopoly of expertise in the market, monopoly of status in a system of stratification' (1977: vii). Professionalization was not a natural and inevitable form of occupational development, it was a 'project' aimed at achieving social and economic ascendancy and involving the adoption of a particular ideology. Duman (1979: 114) explains its development in nineteenth-century England as:

> a unique ideology based on the concept of service as a moral imperative. This provided doctors, lawyers, clergymen and the members of an ever growing number of other occupations with an article of faith with which to justify their claim to superior social status and special privileges, such as self-discipline. The ideal of service allowed the professions to reconcile the concept of the gentleman with the necessity to work for a living and to formulate a definition of their relationship with clients and with society.

The 'attributes' articulated by earlier writers as the defining features of professions were thereby largely supplanted by more abstract notions about the presumed motives of professionals, namely achieving elevation through class and economic strata (Collins 1979; Duman 1979; Larson 1977; Parkin 1979). Many of the traits commonly associated with professions – for example, codes of ethics, formal associations, a public interest avowal – were not to be understood as endogenous features but simply some of the 'tools' that might be employed in the pursuit of enhanced status. The existence or importance of a knowledge base remained unchallenged, but professionalization was said to be 'as much established through social and political processes' (Boreham 1983: 694).

Against this background, relations between aspiring professional groups and the state emerged as a focus for theoretical development, particularly within the United Kingdom (Johnson 1973, 1980, 1982; Macdonald and Ritzer 1988: 260–3; Miller 1990). While the state has authority to exert considerable influence over the outcome of professionalization projects (for example, through licensing arrangements which create professional monopolies), Johnson (1982: 207–8) constructed a theoretical model stressing the interdependency of professions and the state:

> Professionalisation, where it occurs, is indicative of a particular form of articulation between the state and those occupations which have been of particular significance in the state's historical formation. . . .
>
> In Britain . . . the power of the professional colleague association . . . was reinforced and sustained by the extension of professional activity throughout the empire during the period of imperial state formation. It was the adoption of this imperial role with its quasi-official functions which allowed a number of professional bodies to assume a degree of authority and independence of action which the professions in many other countries have never attained.

The dominance of writings dealing with the location of professions in class and economic strata, and which characterized professionalization as a means of achieving elevation through such strata, led Saks (1983: 5) to conclude that 'The new orthodoxy in the sociology of professions in the contemporary Anglo-American context is now rooted in the contributions of neo-Weberian and Marxist writers.' Such explicitly ideological approaches prompted some concerns of bias, as the mood in the sociology of professions was described as 'becoming progressively more hostile to privileged occupational groups' (Saks 1983: 9). Parkin (1979: 58), for example, described professions as an additional vehicle for capitalist exploitation:

> the dominant classes under modern capitalism can be thought of as comprising those who possess or control productive capital and those who possess a legal monopoly of professional services. These groups represent the core body of the dominant or exploiting class by virtue of their exclusionary powers which necessarily have the effect of creating a reciprocal class of social inferiors and subordinates.

In spite of their stridency, the perspectives offered in this new wave of literature attracted significant support. Torstendahl (1990: 60) has written of 'The enormous leap forward that was taken in the development of the theory of professionalism in the late 1970s.' For Macdonald (1995: 8) it was 'a new and rewarding theme'. Saks (1983: 16) was even prepared to excuse the anti-professional bias he perceived in such literature:

> This tendency . . . to engage in swingeing implicit, and often explicit, attacks on professions and professionals without adequate analysis is perfectly comprehensible as a reaction to the lengthy domination of the trait and functionalist perspectives stressing the virtuous aspects of professionalism.

However, the call was made for more empirically oriented study of professions:

> The way forward . . . is not difficult to discern. Although there is no universal agreement about the precise definition of a profession amongst neo-Weberian and Marxist contributors, they do largely concur that they are at root occupational groups characterised by some configuration of concrete, usually legally sustained privileges. This restricted conceptualisation carries important advantages over the outmoded taxonomic model in that it creates the possibility of opening up to rigorous empirical analysis the historical conditions under which professionalisation has occurred and the current nature and role of professions in society. Sociologists of the professions should grasp this opportunity with both hands for only in this way will deeper insights be gained into such pressing issues as the explanation of state involvement in supporting strategies of professionalisation, the role of specialised knowledge in both securing and maintaining professional status and the extent to which an altruistic orientation does indeed distinguish professions from other occupational groups.
>
> (Saks 1983: 17)

Evidence of some response to calls for more empirically oriented studies (Freidson 1983; Saks 1983; Torstendahl 1990) can be observed across a variety of occupational groups; for example, in nursing (Chua and Clegg 1990; Turner 1986), engineering (Makkai 1991; Meiksins and Watson 1989), law (Tomsen 1992), medicine (Dent 1993; Kerr, Cunningham-Burley and Amos 1997; Turner 1995), science (Gieryn, Bevins and Zehr 1985), and accounting (see Chapter 3). However, the evidence adduced from such studies has not yet been sufficient to resolve debates about the nature of professions that were previously contested on ideological and theoretical grounds.

The increasing emphasis on empirical studies evident since the mid-1980s has not been at the complete exclusion of further theoretical developments.

These have added to the already considerable range of perspectives on professions and continued the familiar pattern of challenging existing theory. Freidson (1986) is one of few authors who have endeavoured to make the nature of professional knowledge a central focus for inquiry. His study characterizes professionals as 'the agents of formal knowledge' (1986: 16), but found that their agency is influenced by practical concerns: 'Formal knowledge is systematically transformed by professionals with differing perspectives created both by the particular demands of the work they do and by the demands of their particular clients' (1986: 210). A challenge was thereby issued to the assertion of Elliott (1972: 133) that professional bodies of knowledge are not available for 'amendment' by the individual professional.

Abbott (1988) challenges one of the fundamental contentions of those writers who emphasize the anti-competitive tendencies of professions. Instead, competition is posited as the crucial force that shapes the 'system of professions', albeit *inter*-profession rather than *intra*-profession competition:

> The professions . . . make up an interdependent system. In this system, each profession has its activities under various kinds of jurisdiction. Sometimes it has full control, sometimes control subordinate to another group. Jurisdictional boundaries are perpetually in dispute, both in local practice and in national claims. It is the history of jurisdictional disputes that is the real, the determining history of the professions.
>
> (Abbott 1988: 2)

According to this thesis there is a force operating to regulate professions which extends beyond conventionally ascribed *self*-regulatory mechanisms (such as codes of ethics) and the possibility of state intervention. A profession's 'jurisdictional claim . . . is based on the power of a profession's abstract knowledge to define and solve a certain set of problems' (Abbott 1988: 70). That claim must be protected and renewed by continuing development of the knowledge base. To fail in this regard is to invite 'jurisdictional incursions' and, ultimately, a loss of status. Abbott's 'system of professions' is thereby a constantly evolving one in which professions that stagnate and fail to satisfy rising societal expectations will suffer a loss of status. However, the view that professions are primarily shaped by competition over jurisdictions has in turn been modified by Selander's (1990) theory of 'associative strategies'. Under these strategies, occupations are said to '*cooperate* with others until they are strong enough to make social and occupational demarcations, to enclose a certain area of interest' (Selander 1990: 140, emphasis added).

In common with Abbott (1988), Perkin (1989) infuses his analysis with a theme of competition, but with a more pessimistic outcome. His argument is that while the rise of professions marks the triumph of scientific rationality, it threatens to deliver a 'professional society' in which different kinds of expertise precipitate a persistent quarrelling among experts. Important social and political issues are thereby put beyond resolution. In *Beyond Monopoly*,

Halliday (1987) seeks, in part, to reinstate an ideal that had been stressed by earlier writers but firmly dismissed by those pursuing more critical inquiries: altruism. While noting that 'it is unlikely that professions will serve the state without any consideration of cost to themselves', the author argues that it would be 'equally implausible to believe that the only driving motivation of professions is an unbridled bid for collective gain' (1987: 370).

Diversity in the way in which professions have been comprehended extends to predictions about their future. The literature contains no shortage of references to the 'proletarianization' of professionals and their increasing tendency to occupy salaried positions of employment (Belkaoui 1991; Brewer 1996; Child and Fulk 1982; Dent 1993; Derber 1982; Engel and Hall 1973; Orlikowski 1988; Prandy 1965; Shaw 1987). While acknowledging 'a widespread tendency in contemporary societies to adulate the professions', Collins (1990: 39) also asserts that 'the potential seems to be building up for a serious crisis of the professions' (1990: 42). However, Brewer's (1996: 36) portrayal is of a secure future: 'Professional culture, knowledge and practical skills protect employee professionals from routinisation of their labour and loss of control over their work.'

In summary, the twentieth century witnessed a persistent effort by sociologists to forge greater understanding of what professions are and what roles they play. However, agreement on these matters has proven elusive. The literature on the professions is 'Janus-headed' (Johnson 1972: 17; see also Atkinson and Delamont 1990: 98). It has provided professions with adulation as the altruistic saviours of modern society, but also depicted them as self-interested cartels concerned only with furthering the economic and social status of their members. Not surprisingly then, offerings in the literature that claim some consensual basis are inclined to be general. Turner (1995: 139) concludes:

> professionalization is now regarded as an occupational strategy in which social groups attempt to control their place within the market. However, these market strategies also depend upon the acquisition of an esoteric body of knowledge via the university system under the general regulation of the state.

Collins (1990: 25) offers a similar portrayal:

> Instead of merely responding to market dynamics, as in the model of class conflict stemming from Marx, occupations attempt to control market conditions. Some occupations are relatively successful at this, others less so. Those which are especially successful we have come to call 'the professions'.

However, aside from their generality, these conclusions leave several matters unresolved. They exclude from consideration groups, such as the clergy and the military, that are commonly included in discourse on the professions but can hardly be said to operate within markets.[8] The definition of a profession offered by Collins also invites a questioning of how, if it all, professions are to be differentiated from industry associations or trade unions.[9]

While Hall's (1983: 11) pronouncement that 'the nature of the professions appears to be a dead issue in the sociology of work and occupations' may have been premature (see, for example, Macdonald and Ritzer 1988), there is some evidence that continuing difficulties in achieving theoretical closure in the study of professions may have led to the 'confused exhaustion' feared by Rueschemeyer (1983: 38). Collins (1990: 26) writes of a 'malaise' and according to Atkinson and Delamont (1990: 91) the sociological study of professions has 'ceased to be innovative and exploratory'. Chua and Poullaos (1993: 691) similarly draw attention to allegations of an 'unexciting routine', while Roslender (1992: 19) suggests that the sociology of professions 'may have become a little less productive'. Parallel to these concerns has emerged a questioning of the notion that professions exhibit sufficient commonalities to constitute a discrete social phenomenon. Thus, Freidson (1983: 34) has urged that professions be studied 'as individual empirical cases rather than specimens of some more general, fixed concept' (see also Child and Fulk 1982; Johnson 1980: 367, 1982: 208; Shaw 1987: 778). Abbott (1988: 84) expresses a similar view, but more forcefully: 'the fundamental assumption of the professionalization literature is incorrect; there is no fixed limit of structure towards which all professions tend'. Thus, the tendency of current responses to the 'problem' of the professions has been to deny the possibility of resolution:

> The debate surrounding the professions . . . has been anything but satisfactorily concluded. The only conclusion seems to be negative – i.e. that professionalism is neither inevitable, universal, nor of any single type.
>
> (Crompton 1987: 106)

Critique

Despite the frequency and fervour with which they have been debated, fundamental issues relating to professions – what they are, how they come into being, what role(s) they play, and whether they are socially and economically beneficial – remain equivocal. The unsatisfying nature of this situation is magnified by the fact that it concerns one of the most powerful of social institutions:

> The professions dominate our world. They heal our bodies, measure our profits, save our souls. Yet we are deeply ambivalent about them. For some, the rise of professionalism is a story of knowledge in triumphant practice. It is the story of Pasteur and Osler and Schweitzer, a thread that ties the lawyer in a country village to the justice on the Supreme Court

bench. For others it is a sadder chronicle of monopoly and malfeasance, of unequal justice administered by servants of power, Rockefeller medicine men.

(Abbott 1988: 1)

The ambivalence referred to by Abbott is testimony to a lack of progress in understanding professions. There are surely few social phenomena that have been the subject of such sustained inquiry without yielding more concrete results. A complex of factors appears to lie behind this outcome. In partial defence of the efforts of sociologists of the professions, there is little doubt that the nature of occupational groups commonly described as professions has rendered them a difficult subject for examination. Sociologists wishing to study such groups must confront the difficult task of accessing complex work environments in which technical languages and unique cultures predominate, and where admission is normally only granted after long periods of formal study and induction. The preparedness of sociologists to write generally about 'the professions' has thus masked the reality that 'it is difficult for any one person to know much about more than one profession in any great and secure detail' (Freidson 1973a: 7). Carr-Saunders and Wilson (1933: iii–iv) were explicit in acknowledging the problem:

> Every profession lives in a world of its own. The language which is spoken by the inhabitants, the landmarks so familiar to them, their customs and conventions can only be thoroughly learnt by those who reside there. . . . There is no excuse for inaccuracy in the reports of what we have seen, but we realize that we may not have learnt the native idioms. We may call things by unfamiliar names and in a thousand ways betray our foreign origin. We would plead with those of our readers who belong to one of these worlds to be indulgent when we describe it, and fail to speak as though we also resided there.

Contrasting inferences about the workings and status of particular professional groups which are scattered through the sociology of professions literature bear further testimony to the difficulty of overcoming these barriers.[10] In connection with the knowledge base of professions the problem of access is of such magnitude to have qualified the whole literature (Goldstein 1984: 177, emphasis in original):

> Sociologists of the professions are not intensive sociologists of knowledge. They recognize that professions must have knowledge bases, but they treat them as givens, placing the *constitution* of professional knowledge outside the purview of their investigation.

Hence, the sociology of professions literature has largely left unexamined the very item that it constantly affirms as the central feature of professions.

The alternative to inquiries undertaken by sociologists are those initiated by the professionals themselves. Here another, and potentially more troublesome, impediment to understanding emerges as group affiliations and roles introduce bias (Millerson 1964: 3). At worst, stories of professional groups related by members of those groups have seen the selective use of literature in a thinly disguised attempt to bolster professional claims: 'The emotion-laden identification of men with their occupation, their dependence on it for much of the daily meaning of their lives, causes them to defend it vigorously and to advance its cause where possible' (Goode 1960: 902).[11] In sum, the very nature of élite occupational groups has compromised the success of research efforts directed towards understanding them. Sociologists engaged in such studies have been hindered by problems of access and comprehension. The resulting dissonance in the literature has aided, and been compounded by, its ripeness for exploitation by members of particular occupations endeavouring to justify professional claims.

According to Dezalay (1995: 336), 'More than any other discipline, the sociology of the professions merits Perkin's [1989: 397] harsh judgement likening social science to "organized prejudice".' Behind this criticism lies the explanation that progress in the sociology of professions literature has been significantly impeded by the extent to which it has been influenced by ideology; that is, the propagation of beliefs held on a priori grounds. Larson (1977: xi) characterizes the very concept of 'profession' as 'fraught with ideology' (see also Duman 1979; Jamous and Peloille 1970: 116–17; Johnson 1972: 57) and it is therefore not surprising, and perhaps inevitable, that the literature debating such a concept will itself have been significantly influenced by the preconceived policy stances of contributors.[12] The intensity of the self-interests that attend debates over what a profession is, and especially which occupations have achieved that status, have further accentuated the tendency towards predetermined perspectives. While ideologically inspired views on the professions are not without importance, their tendency to dominate has been at the cost of more scholarly exposition. Thus, while Roth (1974: 17) accused earlier writers of being 'the dupe of established professions' and 'helping them justify their dominant position and its payoff', Saks (1983: 17) found it necessary to rebuke more recent contributors in a similar manner. They were requested to 'remove their blinkers' and accused of having 'little improved on the traditional practice of reifying elements of professional ideologies and turning them into objective definitional attributes of professions'.

Another factor retarding progress in the study of professions has been a preoccupation with unobservables, particularly attempts to attribute motives to professionals. Not surprisingly, the results of these endeavours are most notable for their diversity. Cogan (1953: 49) states that a profession 'considers its first ethical imperative to be altruistic service to the client'. According to Millerson (1964: 4), a distinguishing feature of a profession is that its 'service is for the public good'. Larson's (1977: xvi, emphasis in original) perspective is of 'producers of special services' who seek to 'constitute *and control* a market for their expertise' and reap the consequent rewards. Boreham (1983: 714) describes professions as 'the dominating elements in the reproduction of the hegemonic strata of the bourgeoisie'. Variously then, professions are said to serve their clients, broader society, professionals themselves, or particular class interests. Hall (1983: 11) adds 'the employing organization' as another candidate for being the primary beneficiary of professionals' loyalty. The contradictions among these claims expose their conjectural nature and the likelihood that they are beyond empirical validation. Another, more specific, example of this tendency to make conjectures about motives of professionals concerns codes of ethics. According to Barber (1963: 672), such codes are indicative of 'a high degree of self-control of behavior', consistent with a 'primary orientation to the community interest rather than to individual self-interest'. But, as Abbott (1983: 864) notes, other theorists 'attribute to professional ethics the function, not of control, but of aggrandizement'.

The study of professional groups, then, has been hampered by difficulties of access, a tendency toward inferences based on ideology, and a distracting emphasis on unobservables. The consequence of these matters is that the study of professions has not proceeded on a firm empirical basis, a situation regretted by Saks (1983: 16–17):

> if sociology is to amount to anything more than armchair theorising, its central activity must be the generation and examination of theories which can, in principle, be disconfirmed by evidence. Herein lies the central problem of the history of the sociology of professions in the Anglo-American context. One conventional wisdom has simply been allowed to succeed another without either being subject to adequate empirical research or even, in some cases, leading to the satisfactory formulation of problems for empirical inquiry.

As well as this lack of empirical study there has been a reluctance to elucidate what *should* be expected of professional groups. The important issue of defining the circumstances in which an occupational group should be given a legislatively protected monopoly not only remains unclarified by the sociology of professions literature, but generally unexamined.[13] Lacking both empirical input and a normative framework, the sociology of professions literature has often resorted to tautology as its main method of inquiry. Attempts to define professions have almost invariably proceeded on the basis of predetermined views regarding what occupations are entitled to that description. That is, definitions have been crafted not for use in identifying professional groups, but rather to justify classifications already made. The origins of this fault can be traced back to Carr-Saunders and Wilson (1933: 289), and their willingness to accept that 'By common consent certain vocations now rank as professions.' The basic circularity thus introduced has permeated the literature. Contributors to the trait-based genre invariably constructed their lists by reference to the particular occupations they had *already* decided were professions and variations in these lists appear to be explained by a tendency to draw general conclusions from specific observations. Other writers have been accused of drawing their conclusions not from observation at all, but simply accepting 'professional rhetoric itself' (Johnson 1972: 26). Circularity is also evident in attempts to define the process by which occupations 'professionalize'. Stages identified in this process (for example, formation of an association of practitioners and adoption of a code of ethics) are also nominated as defining features of professions, 'and are therefore both cause and effect of the developments' (Johnson 1972: 30). The study of professions has thus been caught in a circle in which a lack of theory and a lack of empirics prey on each other, as Torstendahl (1990: 45) explains:

> It is impossible to find out empirically which are the characteristics of professions without having a stipulation or enumeration of which are the professions. And it is equally impossible to identify which groups act in a professional manner without deciding first which kind of action is to be considered professional. Likewise, it is impossible to analyse the changes in professional groups without first being able to pick out the professional groups which may be subject to change.

Even the very subject of the sociology of professions literature remains ambiguously defined, and managed only by a tendency towards even greater generality (Abbot 1988: 3–9; Dezalay 1995; Freidson 1983; Klegon 1978).[14]

Professions and occupational authority

In pursuit of escape from the discord that has characterized the sociology of professions literature, this study advocates and adopts a method for studying and understanding professions that has a different emphasis from the majority of those previously employed. The main themes in studies of professions have been definitional and explanatory; that is, what professions are and how they achieve their status. This is most evident in the trait-based models which list various 'ingredients' that are required in order to 'make' a profession. However, the later studies guided by Weberian and Marxist perspectives have a similar structure, with the ideology of market control replacing a list of traits as the essential 'ingredient' for the construction of a profession. That is, the concern of these writers has been with 'what professions actually do in everyday life to negotiate and maintain their special position' (Larson 1977: xii).

However, more practical issues relating to the consequences of the professionalization of occupations have usually not been directly examined. Instead, judgements about professions have typically been inferred from conclusions about the presumed motivations of professionals. Having noted the reproachless nature of the features they listed, the attribute theorists invariably concluded that the existence of professions was socially desirable. Society was presumed to make the 'right' choice in elevating occupations to the status of professions because of the special qualities they possessed, including an altruistic intent. The critical theorists concluded differently. Their claim that professions are formed through the pursuit of an ideology oriented towards acquiring elevated economic and social status led to a questioning of whether professionalization yields social benefits. Instead, the impounding of benefits within the professional group was emphasized.

Common to both approaches is a presumption that the social worth of professions can be inferred from the motivations that underlie their development. That is, it is presumed that professions can be evaluated collectively from a conclusion about whether their members are motivated by altruism or concerns about economic and social status. The difficulty with this approach is that the motivations of professionals are likely to be beyond reliable empirical determination and, in any case, might reasonably be suspected to vary between individuals. More pointedly, it is not the attitude of a professional practitioner that provides the means to cure illness, resolve a legal dispute, or that otherwise determines the adequacy of a professional service. While there is clearly an ethical dimension associated with the provision of professional services – and indeed the provision of commodities generally – it does not supplant the importance of the technical quality and reliability of those services.[15] There is little comfort to be drawn from knowing that the provider of a technically inferior service was acting honestly and selflessly.

In order to avoid the limitations that have been described, this study advocates a focus on the actual outcomes of professionalization rather than conjectures about the motivations that precipitate those outcomes. Depictions of professions that derive from primarily ideological premises are also avoided in order to escape 'the rarefied theoretical atmosphere' (Hall 1983: 13) that has accompanied so many studies on the professions. Instead, the concern is with what professionals deliver and the crucial issue in the evaluation of the worth of professions as social institutions is deemed to pertain to professional competency and the technical quality of the services provided.

This form of analysis commences from the observation that within certain occupations the members, both individually and collectively, are vested with enhanced levels of *authority*.[16] This authority will typically comprise two main elements: an exclusive right to perform certain tasks and the right to define the nature of those tasks. For example, registered medical practitioners have exclusive authority to prescribe specified drugs (authority to perform a task) and have responsibility for determining the circumstances in which such prescriptions are made (authority to define the nature of a task). Medical practitioners also collectively exert influence over policy debates related to matters such as public health. Authority of this kind is not universal among occupations. Truck drivers perform a socially useful service. However, they neither appear to be in a position of significant authority with respect to their employers or clients nor exert any obvious influence over government with respect to matters of transport policy and the like. On the contrary, their work environment is significantly influenced by the constraints of externally imposed regulations (restricted driving hours, speed limits, the need to maintain logbooks and such).

Authority, then, is differential among occupations. Occupational groups having the privilege of high levels of authority also have the capacity to influence significantly particular domains within society and for this reason constitute a class that is of particular interest. This study uses the term 'professions' to describe this class. That is, the members of professional occupations have significant authority within the particular domains in which they operate.[17] This notion of occupational authority has the potential to unify the variety of definitional perspectives contained in the sociology of professions literature. It is consistent with the notions of community sanction and self-regulatory power emphasized by the attribute theorists. However, it also accords with the more recently espoused view that professions are characterized by a capacity to exert control over the markets for their services.

That professions carry special authority in the domains in which they operate has been alluded to by other writers. Richardson (1987a: 341), for example, describes professions as 'occupational groups which have gained a social mandate to define what is right and wrong within a specific sphere of activity'. Halliday (1985: 421) notes that professions 'have had substantial influence on areas of public policy'. In a similar vein, Kerr, Cunningham-Burley and Amos (1997: 300) state that professions are characterized by 'cognitive authority'. As well as providing a necessary response to the problem of definition, this focus on occupational authority serves to highlight the primary concern of this study. As with other structures of authority (for example, those vested with the police, government, a university council) the justification for the authority endowed upon particular occupational groups rests with its contribution to enhancing social order. Social order is dependent on means for mediating interactions between the actors that constitute a society. The occupational authority vested with professions constitutes a particular form of such mediation. The provider of professional services – whether in a market situation such as between lawyer and client, or a non-market situation such as may arise between a university lecturer and student – has primary, and often exclusive, authority to provide certain services and define the nature of those services.

This occupational authority can be distinguished from other means by which human interactions are mediated. One example is the imposition of regulations by government or its agencies. In such circumstances the primary mediating force is sourced externally to the interacting parties. For example, in the case of certain manufactured goods government imposed regulations take precedence in mediating the market interaction of buyers and sellers. In other circumstances, most notably unregulated markets, it is the knowledge of consumers that is relied upon to facilitate socially useful interactions in the form of market exchanges.

In the case of economic interactions, three broad forms of mediation can be discerned and illustrated by reference to a transaction for an unspecified service. First, the supplier of the service, typically vested with special authority encompassing an exclusive right to provide the service, may be expected to assume primary responsibility for ensuring its quality and suitability (reliance on the authority of the party supplying the service). This study deems this kind of authority to be distinctive of professions. Second, externally imposed regulations may operate to specify and enforce prescribed technical bounds for the service (reliance on the authority of a third party). Third, the parties acquiring the service may be presumed competent to make their own inquiries, and through their choices call forth from suppliers the particular features and quality they seek (reliance on the authority of the party acquiring the service).

These means of mediating interactions are not mutually exclusive and are rarely absolute. In the purchase of a simple household commodity, for example, a consumer may rely on the advice of the seller, take comfort from knowing that the good complies with regulations imposed by government, and also exercise discretion that is based on personal knowledge. However, some interactions clearly display a tendency towards a particular mediating force. For example, a person seeking medical treatment may be expected to rely to a very significant extent on the skill and knowledge of the medical practitioner who is consulted. There are unlikely to be externally imposed technical regulations that govern the interaction and the party seeking medical services may be unable to identify confidently what treatment is required, nor assess the quality of the treatment administered. The primary mediating influence relied upon in such a circumstance is the prerogative of the practitioner.

Professions, then, are characterized by a particular kind of authority and the justification for this authority must be found in its contribution to enhancing social order. As with other structures of authority, it is appropriate to investigate and analyse professions on empirical grounds. At issue in the conception of professions that has been adopted are two fundamental questions. First, to what extent is occupational authority relied upon as a mediating device within particular domains? Licensing or other arrangements that restrict to members of prescribed associations the right to provide complex services in an environment largely free of other externally imposed regulations would be indicative of such authority. Second, how effective are professions in mediating interactions between actors within those domains where their authority is relied upon as the primary mediating influence? The concern here is whether the elevated occupational authority of professions 'works' in particular domains and whether reliance on it should be increased or decreased, or even supplanted by an alternative mediating device such as government regulation.

These questions guide this study in the pursuit of an understanding of the status and functioning of accounting as a profession and the role of technical accounting rules within that context. Despite the apparent importance of the issue, few studies in the sociology of professions literature have grappled with the question of whether or not professional authority has functioned as an effective mediating device within those domains in which it is relied upon. As Boreham (1983: 705) states, 'Arguments concerning the dominance of professionalization as a mode of occupational control . . . have rarely been the object of detailed analysis and critique.' The existence of this lacuna is to be regretted particularly because of the fact that professional authority is not usually accompanied by any formal mechanism of accountability. The academic community, as independent holders of professional expertise, has a crucial role to play in bridging this accountability gap: 'academics have a responsibility to critically evaluate professional claims, not to treat them as unproblematic "facts" ' (Robson and Cooper 1990: 369).

Of central importance in such evaluations are the knowledge bases of those occupational groups privileged with special authority.[18] The prerequisite for the proper functioning of a profession is that its members possess special knowledge and skills sufficient to justify their authority and qualify them to discharge their responsibilities properly. That is, professions are presumed to have an '*epistemological* warrant for public influence' (Halliday 1985: 422, emphasis added). Professionalism is therefore characterized by the self-directed application of knowledge to some function that serves a particular human need and an ongoing search for means by which that need might be better satisfied. In short, the fundamental responsibility of a professional group is to ensure that its practices are technically sound – serviceable or fit for their purpose. As outlined in Chapter 1, the function of accounting focuses on the preparation and authentication of dated reports that describe the financial position and performance of an entity from time to time and – serving as reliable financial instruments – inform financial decision making. Evaluation of the 'professionalism' of the accounting occupation must encompass an examination of its technical practices rather than be centred on conjectures about the motives of accounting practitioners.

Professional knowledge

That the enhanced occupational authority enjoyed by professions derives from and is justified by their exclusive expertise is perhaps the only consistent and uncontentious theme in the sociology of professions literature. Without equivocation the contributors to this literature assert that professions possess bodies of 'specialized knowledge'. This is illustrated by the quotations contained in Box 2.1 which have been drawn from a broad spectrum of the sociology of professions literature.

'Knowledge', often described in the relevant literature by a range of adulatory adjectives, is deemed to play a twofold role in the professionalization process. First, it is deemed to be the agent that binds practitioners together into a distinct group (Goldstein 1984: 175; Larson 1977: 40). Second, it

Box 2.1

Statements describing the knowledge base of professions:

. . . what we now call a profession emerges when a number of persons are found to be practising a definite technique founded upon specialized training. A profession may perhaps be defined as an occupation based upon specialized intellectual study and training.
(Carr-Saunders 1966/1928: 3–4)

It has emerged that special competence, acquired as the result of intellectual training, is the chief distinguishing feature of the professions.
(Carr-Saunders and Wilson 1933: 307)

The crucial distinction is this: the skills that characterize a profession flow from and are supported by a fund of knowledge that has been organized into an internally consistent system, called a *body of theory*.
(Greenwood 1966/1957: 11, emphasis in original)

. . . professional fields emerge from a parent body of knowledge.
(Goode 1960: 906)

Any occupation wishing to exercise professional authority must find a technical basis for it . . . the success of the claim is greatest where the society evidences strong, widespread consensus regarding the knowledge or doctrine to be applied.
(Wilensky 1964: 138)

The professional group controls a body of expert knowledge which is applied to specialised tasks.
(Elliott 1972: 11)

. . . professional bodies of knowledge cannot simply be regarded as conglomerate accretions of raw facts and theories ready for indiscriminate use or amendment by the professional. They are already ordered, sorted and interpreted within the theoretical position currently shared within the profession.
(Elliott 1972: 133, footnote reference omitted)

The main instrument of professional advancement . . . is the capacity to claim esoteric and identifiable skills – that is, to create and control a cognitive and technical basis.
(Larson 1977: 180)

In short, then, the 'professions' are occupations which provide highly valued services based upon a complex body of knowledge.

(Johnson 1980: 342)

. . . 'profession' refers to an exclusive occupational group possessing a specialized skill that is based in some way on esoteric knowledge.

(Abbott 1983: 856)

Of the [attributes of professions] the absolutely necessary one – which may deliberately stressed or simply taken for granted – is the body of knowledge.

(Goldstein 1984: 175)

[Professionals are] the carriers of formal knowledge.

(Freidson 1986: 13)

A [profession's] full jurisdictional claim . . . is based on the power of the profession's abstract knowledge to define and solve a certain set of problems.

(Abbott 1988: 70)

. . . we may define knowledge-based groups as the groups which may develop professionalism.

(Torstendahl 1990: 54)

Legitimation of professional authority involves three claims: that the knowledge and competence of the professional have been validated by a community of peers, that this consensually validated knowledge rests on scientific or scholarly grounds, and that professional judgement and advice are oriented toward important social values.

(House 1993: ix)

Both apologists for, and critics of, the professions have been united in stressing the importance of a profession's knowledge base. The power and status of professional workers depend to a significant extent on their claims to unique forms of expertise, which are not shared with other occupational groups, and the value placed on that expertise.

(Eraut 1994: 14)

> The origins of any profession lie in the existence of an area of knowledge which those who possess it are able to isolate from social knowledge generally, and establish a special claim to.
>
> (Macdonald 1995: xiii)
>
> The specialized knowledge of the professional creates the basis for prestige and social distance between the expert and the client, since the client by definition is excluded from the esoteric knowledge of the professional association. The basis of professional knowledge is cognitive rationality whereby the privileged status of the profession is grounded in a scientific discipline.
>
> (Turner 1995: 133)

provides a foundation for procuring authority and negotiating state-endowed privileges (Larson 1977: 69; Moore 1970: 15; Rueschemeyer 1983: 41; Tuohy and Wolfson 1978: 113). Such notions are so entrenched as to have prompted a statement that, in a literature notable for its heterogeneity, is surprisingly conclusive: 'an emphasis on knowledge "as a core generating trait" of professionalism is entirely correct' (Halliday 1985: 423).

In spite of such assertions, the sociology of professions literature contains various admissions that its proclamations about the knowledge base of professions have been derived from assumption rather than examination. Examples of these statements are provided in Box 2.2.

The consequence of this failure to examine the nature of professional expertise is evident in descriptions of the form that professional knowledge takes. Crompton (1987: 105) states that a professional claim is 'based on a codified body of theoretical knowledge'. According to Elliott (1972: 129), however, the expertise of professionals cannot be codified: 'although professional knowledge is universally applicable, it cannot be reduced to a codified expertise'. Consistent with this proposition, professional knowledge is often said to be 'abstract' rather than codified: 'Only groups which have acquired a considerable amount of "abstract knowledge" . . . are accepted as professionals' (Torstendahl 1990: 53). Indeed, according to Klegon (1978: 278) it is the codification of occupational tasks that may precipitate the 'proletarianization' of professionals. Child and Fulk (1982: 161), however, argue that the inherently indeterminate nature of professional work protects against such an outcome. Developing this theme further, Boreham (1983: 697, emphasis in original) suggests that professions may deliberately pursue the 'creation of an aura of *indetermination* about their activities that denies the possibility of rationalization and codification'.

The contrasting nature of these claims provides further evidence that – in spite of its apparent importance – the sociology of professions literature has

Box 2.2

Statements acknowledging a failure to examine the knowledge base of professions:

> . . . the knowledge of engineering, medicine, social work and other professions, both can and should be examined from the outside rather than being taken for granted.
>
> (Freidson 1973a: 14)

> . . . the case for a complex and codified 'knowledge base' as an indispensable prerequisite for professional closure is taken as self-evident rather than as a case to be argued. That is, the proposition is never formulated in such a way as to encourage dispassionate judgement of those elevated claims made by the professions themselves concerning their command of specialized knowledge. In particular, no distinction is made between forms of knowledge that might be thought to constitute the operational core of professional work, and those various accretions that have scant practical application but are more in the way of ritual embellishments that prolong the period of training, thereby protecting market scarcity.
>
> (Parkin 1979: 103)

> Professional knowledge claims and, in particular, construction of professional ideology based on the exclusive determination of expert knowledge have not been the subject of significant evaluation. The literature evidences few attempts to separate claims of knowledge as an ideological mechanism for building public and political support and the effectiveness of that knowledge as it is applied to everyday practice of the professions. . . . Failure to critically examine the knowledge base of the professions lies at the core of the inability of much sociological work to adequately account for the conflict exhibited within many professional occupations.
>
> (Boreham 1983: 695)

> [Sociologists of the professions] have always asserted that the social role and status of professionals is legitimated by their esoteric expertise.
>
> (Goldstein 1984: 183–4)

> Other than objective elements enter into what is a matter of choosing to regard, rather than merely recognising, as a skill. This raises the interesting but as yet unstudied question whether the

> virtualities, the qualities which cannot be taught and routinised, and are so jealously guarded as the distinguishing feature of professional skills, are not also, partly or even largely socially constructed. If so, they may be vulnerable to demystification.
>
> (Shaw 1987: 778)

> It is often stated that expertise and specialized knowledge are at the core of professions. Yet there has been comparatively little discussion about them. . . . The lack is unfortunate. A thorough analysis would throw more light on a number of issues besetting the sociology of the professions.
>
> (Baer 1986: 532)

> . . . in the literature of the sociology of professions the intellectual core, the knowledge base of the professions, is . . . taken as given factor around which professionalisation takes place.
>
> (Loft 1986: 140)

> The literature on the development of occupations and professions has rarely seriously considered the knowledge base of the activity in question: how the knowledge emerges; the claims it makes, and the changing sites to which it is applied.
>
> (Robson and Cooper 1990: 386)

not made significant progress in describing the nature of professional expertise. In a similar manner to the clients of professionals, sociologists of professions have placed their faith in 'what professionals do'. In contrast, this study posits that conclusions about the nature of knowledge base of particular professions should proceed from investigation rather than assumption. Accountants, for example, routinely perform and sanction aggregations of financial quantifications that represent different attributes (for example, cost, present value, realizable value) and are expressed in different monetary units (that is, without adjustment for changes in purchasing power). This, unquestionably, is what accountants 'do', but it is a practice without cognitive foundation. It defies a basic principle of arithmetic. The origins and persistence of the practice must be explained by custom, ignorance, convenience or some other factor.

Résumé and conclusion

This chapter has noted the difficulties evident in attempts to forge an understanding of professions. Guided by a variety of theoretical frameworks, the sociology of professions literature has offered an array of different and often contradictory perspectives on professional groups. Part of the explanation for this dissonance may be attributed to the peculiar features of élite occupations that render them difficult targets for study. However, the tendency of the sociology of professions literature to often elevate ideology, tautology and conjecture over empirical investigation has done much to compromise the development of a more robust understanding of professions. In particular, the contribution of professions to enhancing social order has rarely been subject to direct systematic examination, but only inferred from perceptions about the underlying motives of professionals. In a similar vein, representations about professional knowledge have largely been based on assertion rather than investigation.

In pursuit of an escape from these limitations, this chapter has emphasized the need to study the outcomes rather than just the processes of professionalization. Elevated occupational authority was nominated to be the most important evidence and consequence of the professionalization of occupations. That is, the members of professionalized occupations enjoy largely exclusive authority to provide certain services and define the nature of those services. This stress on occupational authority was found to unify rather than contradict existing definitional perspectives on professions.

As with other structures of authority, the justification for that vested with professional groups must be found in a contribution to enhancing social order. Evaluation of this contribution is warranted. This necessitates examination of the special knowledge that is traditionally offered as providing the key rationale for the authority ceded to professional groups. In the context of accounting, therefore, the primary concern is not with conjectures about the motives of accountants but with the technical quality of the accounting information they produce. That is, the public interest is deemed to be served – and the professional authority of accountants justified – when accounting information serves its stated purpose and functions as reliable financial instrumentation. Consistent with this concern, two pertinent questions are posed. First, to what extent is professional authority relied upon as a device for regulating the quality of accounting information? Second, if professional authority is relied upon as a regulatory device, what is the nature and efficacy of the knowledge that is applied in this role and how does it discipline accounting practices and the technical rules that underpin them? It is the first of these questions that guides investigation of the extent and origins of accountants' occupational authority in Chapter 3.

3 Accounting as a profession

The extent and origins of occupational authority

... we need to go beyond the triumphal march of progress depicted by conventional accounting history.

(Miller and Napier 1993: 644–5)

Introduction

In the preceding chapter, professions were characterized as occupational groups that enjoy largely unchallenged authority in connection with the technical aspects of the services they deliver. Rather than responding to the preferences of consumers or the directives of external agencies, the nature of professional services is determined in substance by professionals themselves. This is not to imply that professional work necessarily proceeds in an undisciplined manner according to the whims of individual practitioners. On the contrary, a cognitive oversight is presumed to operate, with the bounds of acceptable technical practice defined by the knowledge base of the profession. It is on this ground that responsibility for ensuring the serviceability and quality of professional services is turned over to the providers of those services. The authority vested with professionals thereby constitutes a particular means by which human interactions are sought to be mediated and social order enhanced.

This chapter turns attention from consideration of professions generally to the specific occupation that is the focus of this study: accounting. Its purpose is to provide a necessary background to the matters that are explored in subsequent chapters. These are concerned with explaining and evaluating technical accounting rules and their consequences within the context of the specifications of the function of accounting and the onus of professional groups that have been provided in Chapters 1 and 2 respectively. Before proceeding to such matters it is appropriate to clarify the extent to which the accounting occupation is characterized by professional authority. This issue is the focus of the next section of this chapter. The chapter then proceeds to outline the historical background to the development of this authority. A synthesis of the findings regarding the extent of occupational authority and its origins is then provided. This draws attention to how the elevated occupational authority enjoyed by accountants did not develop from a systematic body of knowledge that linked technical accounting practices to a clear specification of the function of financial reporting. Instead, a range of social and environmental factors are identified that contributed to enhancing the social status of accounting work and from which a broader occupational credibility was inferred. The standing of accounting as a professional occupational is thereby shown to have a predominantly social rather than cognitive origin.

The extent of occupational authority

Evidence that is indicative of the extent to which accountants individually and, through their formal associations, collectively exercise authority over accounting-related tasks is available from a variety of sources. First, there are the representations of accountants themselves. Second, reference may be had to the findings of independent parties, particularly sociologists, who have used indicators of occupational authority in the classification of occupations. Third, primary evidence that is indicative of occupational authority is available; for example, legislative provisions that place restrictions on who may perform particular accounting tasks. Each of these will be considered in turn.

Claims by associations of accountants and their representatives to professional status are abundant (for example, Carey 1968, 1969; Carey and Doherty 1966; Jeffery 1995; Roy and MacNeill 1967; Windal and Corley 1980). A President of the ASCPA has described accounting as 'an established, recognised and highly regarded profession' (Jeffery 1995: 3). Similar claims to professional status are evident within the United States, with the period from 1896 to 1936 described as that in 'which certified public accountants . . . advanced from a technician class to attain professional status' (Carey 1969: 4). After enumerating a list of attributes claimed to be indicative of such status, Roy and MacNeill (1967: 31) concluded that 'Certified public accountants share all of these professional attributes.' Windal and Corley (1980: 7) extend this claim by stating that it enjoys broader social recognition:

> Certified public accountants have for many years regarded themselves as professionals, equal in every respect to the more uniformly recognized professions of law, medicine and theology. In recent years, furthermore, they have come to be regarded by society as deserving of that appellation.

Within the academic accounting literature greater reservation concerning the entitlement of accountants to claim professional standing has been evident (Belkaoui 1991; Briloff 1990; Burns and Haga 1977; Chambers 1966b: 356–9; Cooper *et al.* 1994; Dyckman 1974; Gerboth 1978; Lee 1990a, 1990b, 1991, 1994, 1995b; Mitchell *et al.* 1994; Most 1993; Robson and Cooper 1990; Tweedie 1993; Willmott 1990; Willmott, Puxty and Cooper 1993; Willmott, Sikka and Puxty 1994; Wolnizer 1987: Ch. 7; Zeff 1987). The sentiments expressed in this literature generally do not challenge the notion that accounting is widely recognized as a professional occupation, but rather cast doubt on the extent to which the expectations accompanying that status have been satisfied. The typical nature of the reservations contained in this literature are concisely articulated by Lee (1991: 193) as encompassing:

> persistent and seemingly intractable problems such as the dubious meaning of reported accounting figures, inconsistencies in accounting rules, education orientated solely to training for current practice, a lack of research influence on practice, and managing the ethical behaviour of practitioners.

Concerns of the kind expressed by Lee and other academic accounting writers are less evident in the mainstream sociology of professions literature. In spite of the uncertainty over the definition of profession that pervades this literature, its contributors appear to endorse overwhelmingly a view of accounting as a highly professionalized occupation. Carr-Saunders (1966/ 1928: 3) includes accounting among 'the rise of numerous new professions' during the second half of the nineteenth century. Goode (1960: 906) lists 'certified public accountancy' as one of the 'major professions which have arisen over the past century'. In his survey of occupations within the United States, Wilensky (1964: 142) places accounting in the category of 'established' professions. Recurrent reference to accounting in general discourse on the professions further supports the claim that it is recognized as a professional occupation (Abbott 1988; Carr-Saunders and Wilson 1933; Elliott 1972; Freidson 1986; Larson 1977; Macdonald 1995; Millerson 1964; Moore 1970; Wilensky 1964). Occasionally, sociologists of professions have even made accounting the particular focus of their inquiries (Macdonald 1984, 1985, 1987, 1995; Montagna 1973, 1974a, 1974b, 1986, 1991; Roslender 1990a, 1990b, 1992, 1996). Johnson (1972: 18) has been singular in expressing reservation concerning the status of accounting, asserting without elaboration that it was 'not highly advanced in the process of professionalisation'. However, the same author apparently considered accounting sufficiently 'professionalized' to use it to illustrate his discussions of 'professional patronage' (1972: 65–74), professions as instruments of state control (1980: 354–62) and the profession–state axis (1982).

These observations of sociologists provide some evidence of recognition of accounting as a professional occupation. However, their significance is compromised by a lack of clarity in the sociology of professions literature concerning what a profession is. In response to this lack of clarity this study has identified occupational authority as the significant discriminating feature of professionalized occupations. That is, professions are occupational groups that have a predominance of authority in the performance of certain tasks and in defining the nature of those tasks. This emphasis on occupational authority and the presumption that it is underwritten by cognitively-based expertise unifies rather than contradicts the variety of definitional viewpoints contained in the sociology of professions literature.

Associations of accountants have been successful in acquiring for their members an exclusive right to perform some (but not all) accounting-related tasks. This exclusivity is clearly evident in respect of the auditing of company financial statements – the instruments of financial reporting. Within Australia, for example, the *Corporations Act* mandates that certain companies appoint an auditor to report on the truth and fairness of their accounts. The same legislation (section 1280) lists membership of a prescribed accounting association as criterion for registration as a company auditor. Similarly, in Canada (Richardson 1997: 641–4), the United States (Guy, Alderman and Winters 1996: 12) and the United Kingdom (Power 1997: 17) the right to provide company audit services is restricted, with the obtaining of qualifications administered and conferred by specified associations of accountants the usual prerequisite. In this way, these associations effectively control who is able to act as a company auditor. Additionally, they exert a substantive influence over the technical aspects of audit practice. The significance of this authority can scarcely be overstated on account of the importance of the audit function: 'The audit of accounts is a kind of quality control, control of the quality of information on which managers, investors and creditors will make judgements about the performance and prospects of companies' (Chambers 1973b: 144). The authority vested with registered auditors – as the exclusive purveyors of this quality control – is substantial.

Accentuating this authority is that auditors conduct their work almost entirely free of any externally imposed regulatory framework pertaining to how an audit is to be conducted. The law applying to corporations does specify the expected outcomes of an audit. Under section 308 of the *Australian Corporations Act* an auditor is required to express an opinion as to whether a company's financial report provides a true and fair view of its financial position and performance and complies with the law and applicable accounting standards. However, the legislation is silent on the procedures to be applied in formulating this opinion and, most importantly, the meaning of 'true and fair'. The resolution of crucial technical issues in auditing – such as what constitutes audit evidence, the amount of evidence required to support an opinion, and the interpretation of 'true and fair' – is largely left to those providing audit services and their professional associations. While auditors are appointed by, and required to report to, company shareholders, they do not take any instruction from them. Also, the ability of shareholders and other interested parties to evaluate the quality of audit services is significantly restricted: 'Quite often the only measure of audit quality comes from subsequent events that demonstrate that an audit was not performed at an acceptable level for a particular engagement' (Byington and Sutton 1991: 316). Power (1994: 305–6) emphasizes this inevitability of placing faith in auditors: 'audits are in fact a dead end of accountability, a process which terminates in the necessity of trusting experts'. Even when auditor performance is investigated within the jurisdiction of law, the usual practices adopted within the profession are likely to be presumed indicative of an acceptable standard of practice.[1]

The accounting profession also exercises substantial authority over the technical aspects of financial reporting practice. In part this authority derives from the audit function itself: 'financial auditors have had a decisive influence on the standards of performance to which the auditee is subjected' (Power 1994: 302). However, it has also been more directly expressed through the regulations governing financial reporting.[2] Within Australia, the professional accounting associations 'have achieved a dominant position in the regulation of external financial reporting through control of the setting of legally backed accounting standards' (Cooper 1996: 179). This perception persists in spite of efforts to make the standard-setting process more independent (Brown and Tarca 2001; Miller 1995; Walker 1987). Within Canada, the status of the CICA is such that its handbook of technical statements is recognized as authoritative under the *Business Corporations Act and Regulations* (Part V, section 44). In the United Kingdom and the United States the institutions now responsible for the setting of accounting standards are formally separated from professional accounting bodies. However, as is the case in Australia, such arrangements have not prevented accounting associations from exerting significant influence over standard-setting processes (Committe 1990; Fogarty 1994; Fogarty, Hussein and Ketz 1994; Gangolly and Hussein 1996; Hunt and Hogler 1993).

Supporting these general observations that accountants, as an occupational group, have substantial authority in connection with financial reporting practices are the conclusions drawn by other writers. Montagna (1986: 104) testifies to the wide-ranging extent of accountants' influences:

> In political democracies, extensive financial control requires legitimation. Accountants provide that legitimation through theory and practice. They apply 'generally accepted accounting principles', rules which define what is fair presentation of financial transactions to shareholders and the public, as agreed upon by both accountants and the business community. Bank loans to support Third World development, inventory stockpiling to prepare for anticipated market surges, new capital investment in plant and equipment, distribution of profits to shareholders – all these and other financial management decisions fall under the auditor's review of capital planning and use.

Richardson, in a similar vein, characterizes accounting as a 'legitimating institution', noting that accounting information 'gains its credibility, and hence its potential for motivation and control, in part through its association with independent professionals' (1987a: 341). Likewise, Lee (1989: 249) describes accounting as 'a legitimated institution in society'. According to Roslender (1992: 39), 'what accountants say usually goes is a truism of modern corporate life'. Johnson's (1995: 485) view is that accounting 'has gained, and is continuing to gain, prominence as a warranted means of regulating many aspects of our lives'. Matthews, Anderson and Edwards (1997) describe accountants as 'the most prominent professionals active in British management today' (1997: 407). Cooper and Hopper (1987: 408) further testify to the self-regulatory privileges that accountants enjoy:

> The image of accountants as powerful money men (rarely women!) would suggest governments and society would take an interest in their activities. Aside from occasional Congressional forays since the mid 1970s, this has hardly been the case. The activities of accountants in the U.K. and U.S.A. have been subject to self-regulation rather more than any form of direct public control.

The preceding observations support the notion that accountants, as an occupational group, exercise substantial authority over accounting-related matters. In particular, they have been vested with largely exclusive authority as the providers of 'quality control' in connection with corporate financial reports and have, at least, significant roles in influencing the prescribed form and content of those reports. In aggregate, accountants enjoy significant authority in the determination of what is 'right', 'wrong', 'acceptable' and 'unacceptable' within the accounting domain. Associations of accountants are legitimated institutions with legitimizing powers. This study concurs with Lee's (1991: 193) assessment:

> The accountancy profession ... has expanded rapidly worldwide to become one of the leading professions in terms of the number of people it employs, the quantity and variety of services it offers and renders, the size and pervasiveness of its public firms, the extent of its provision and use of educational and research resources, the degree of influence it has in its relations with the state, and the social status and economic rewards enjoyed by its members.

Consideration will now be given to explaining the origins of this elevated occupational authority.

The origins of occupational authority

Adding to the observations already made in Chapter 2 concerning diversity in the way in which professions are perceived, historical studies of professions can be divided into two distinct categories. There is 'official history' (Dingwall 1976: 346) and, by implication, 'unofficial history'. The former is usually recounted under the auspices of professional associations and is alleged to have an ideological function, being the 'legitimation of the present state of affairs by selective attention to historical events' (Dingwall 1976: 346).

Official histories of accounting include those published by the American Accounting Association (AAA) (1966), the Australian Society of Accountants (ASA) (1962), Brown (1968/1905),[3] Burrows (1996), Carey (1969), The Institute of Chartered Accountants in England and Wales (ICAEW) (1966), The Institute of Chartered Accountants of Scotland (ICAS) (1984/1954), Linn (1996), and Olson (1982). Tinker (1985: xxi) is particularly dismissive of the contribution of such histories to providing an understanding of accounting:

> Accounting is one of the few bastions of the establishment that still lingers in the twilight of social comprehension: it is immature in terms of the state of its social consciousness, fairy tales pass for its history.

Loft (1986: 138) criticizes official accounting histories on the grounds that they 'tend to assume not only that accountants are supremely necessary to society but also that the major factor enabling their current success has been their form of professional association'. According to Sikka and Willmott (1997: 158):

> the accountancy profession has surrounded itself with narratives of even-handed public behaviour, professional ethics and discipline through which it rehearses and sustains the dominant fable of 'progress' embedded in accounting history. In this fable, heroic professional bodies and their leaders battle against the odds and, amidst the chaos, introduce order to protect the public from diverse troubles and dangers.

Linn's (1996: 202) history of the accounting profession in Australia, commissioned by the ASCPA, exemplifies the often adulatory tenor of official accounting histories:

> Those men who founded the first professional institutes of accountants in Australia in the mid-1880s would find the modern world unrecognisable. The organisations which they created have been part of the ebb and flow of national life. In so many ways, accountants have contributed to the progress and profit of the nation through their use of powerful tools and incisive thought. There are many issues raised by the founders, though, that remain at the centre of the thinking of the Australian Society of Certified Practising Accountants: the search for excellence; due regard for integrity and ethics; a profound and enduring education and professional development; high quality of service.

The notion that the history of accounting is marked by a preoccupation with matters such as excellence, integrity, ethics and a 'profound' educational experience is less evident outside of the profession-sponsored literature. Heralding a 'new accounting history', Miller, Hopper and Laughlin (1991: 395) emphasize the role of historical inquiries in providing insights to 'the institutional forces that shape actions and outcomes and the rationales that set out the objects and objectives of accounting'. Within this context, accounting researchers have responded to a call to 'explore the origins and development of the accountancy profession – that is, to discover the reasons why it came into existence and the means by which it has prospered despite its long-standing problems' (Lee 1991: 193; see also Burchell *et al.* 1980; Willmott 1986: 555).

Contributions to explaining the professionalization of accounting can be divided into two main themes.[4] First, the *incentives* that caused accountants to organize into associations and seek to advance the status of their occupation have been identified. Second, explanations for the apparent *success* of accountants in achieving occupational ascendancy and closure over accounting work have been presented. Each of these will be considered in turn.

The first associations of accounting practitioners in English-speaking countries were formed in Scotland; in 1853 in Edinburgh and Glasgow (Carr-Saunders and Wilson 1933: 209) and 1867 in Aberdeen (Kam 1990: 28). This process of organizing into associations continued in England in 1870 (Willmott 1986: 566), Canada in 1879 (Richardson 1987b: 598), the United States in 1882 (Kam 1990: 29) and Australia in 1885 (Parker, 1961). Identification of the incentives that prompted accountants to organize into associations appears to have generated little controversy and supports the notion that 'professional formation is a sociopolitical process which may be motivated by the desire for economic rewards and occupational ascendancy' (Walker 1995: 287). Expansion of the economic rewards available to providers of accounting services in the mid-nineteenth century has been attributed to 'industrialization, management information needs, company failures, court actions, regular reporting and auditing requirements and taxation' (Lee 1990a: 92). Changes in the legislative environment, in particular, have long been cited as providing a primary impetus for the formation of the first associations of accountants (Brown 1968/1905: 209; Carr-Saunders and Wilson 1933: 210; ICAS 1984/1954: 25) and this has been reinforced by more recent research: 'an impending change in bankruptcy legislation . . . prompted the formation, first of the Edinburgh society, and then the Glasgow society' (Briston and Kedslie 1986: 124). Similar circumstances applied in England and Wales, where 'the profession derived a large part of its initial rationale from those extensions to the accounting domain which had been created by successive companies and bankruptcy acts and legislation which provided for the regulation of sectors such as railways, building societies and municipal utilities' (Burchell *et al.* 1980: 7). In the United States, claimed excesses arising from a laissez-faire attitude towards business 'incited the calls for an independent accounting profession which were so central to the formation of the profession' (Preston *et al.* 1995: 516). Rapid growth in the number and size of corporations has also been described as an important change in the commercial environment that provided a rationale for accountants to pursue professionalization strategies (Moore and Gaffikin 1994).

Given the expansion in the market for accounting services during the nineteenth century it is perhaps not surprising that manoeuvres intended to deliver an enhanced share of the consequent economic rewards would ensue. This necessitated a strategy of stratification; the creation of an élite by differentiating the 'professional accountant' from those who were merely bookkeepers or clerks. This incentive to stratify accounting-related work has been associated particularly with attempts by accounting associations to seek royal charters: 'A Royal Charter denoted some degree of exclusiveness if not sanction' and 'marked off a self-selected elite who distinguished themselves from others' (Chua and Poullaos 1993: 700).

Opportunities emerging from a changing legislative and economic environment, prompting a desire by some accountants to stratify their occupation, provide cogent rationales for the pursuit of professionalization. But how and why did such endeavours succeed? Merely organizing into associations does not create a profession; following Larson (1977) there is a need to achieve 'collective mobility' and 'closure'. That is, the organized members of the occupation must succeed in elevating the social standing of their field of work and then achieve a privileged status within the market or other purlieu in which they operate. In endeavouring to explain the *success* (rather than just the motivation) of early accountants' professionalization strategies, significant research effort has been expended in identifying the resources harnessed in the pursuit of closure and collective mobility. Dominated by the critical outlook of the 'new accounting history' (Miller, Hopper and Laughlin 1991), these studies have seen 'scholars reject mainstream economic rationales for accounting's past, and argue that social, political and ideological factors may be chiefly responsible for accounting events' (Tyson 1995: 17). Contrary to conventional depictions of the nature of professionalization, accounting knowledge has not been emphasized within this research. Instead, attention has been drawn to factors such as the social class, gender and political acuity of aspiring professional accountants.

Macdonald's (1984) examination of the social background of Scottish accountants who practised over the period 1853 to 1879 prompted the conclusion that the rapid rise of the Scottish accounting profession could be attributed to the fact that 'its leaders were associated with the gentry, the legal profession and the more respectable (commercial, as opposed to manufacturing) part of the bourgeoisie' (1984: 174). In reaching this conclusion, Macdonald considered the education of the Scottish chartered accountants and the occupations held by their fathers. Other roles undertaken by members (such as church elder, Justice of the Peace, company director, stockbroker, and in charity and education) were also identified that served to enhance their status (1984: 183). The essence of Macdonald's contribution is to suggest that the customary claims of a professional group (for example, of training, specialized knowledge and altruism) were more likely to be accepted by the public and other established professions if they were 'made by men of acceptable middle class characteristics, who could vouch for the other members admitted to the professional body' (1984: 187). Indeed, Macdonald even hypothesizes that the likely explanation for the earlier rise of the accounting profession in Scotland than England was that the 'English accountants contained within their ranks far fewer of the established middle class than in Scotland and lacked the connection with the legal profession so important to their Scottish counterparts' (1987: 188; see also Walker 1988: 18–20).

Macdonald's work has been criticized by Briston and Kedslie (1986: 122) who question his use and interpretation of source materials and data. However, Macdonald (1987) has in turn sought to counter these criticisms. The differing conclusions of these writers appear to be explained in large part by their emphases on different aspects of the professionalization process. Macdonald focuses on how status was given to an 'occupational collectivity' (1984: 187). Briston and Kedslie, on the other hand, emphasize the 'pure economic stimulus' (1986: 128) that motivated the adoption of professionalization strategies. Common ground is found in Kedslie (1990b: 13) with her acknowledgement that 'the early members of the Edinburgh society were predominantly upper to upper-middle class' and that the 'legal profession, the Church, and landowners' were present among the Glasgow accountants (although to a lesser extent than in Edinburgh) (1990b: 15). In both cases the founders were 'concerned to ensure that the new societies had a recognized status in their respective communities, which they accomplished by inviting membership only from men of proven social and professional standing' (1990b: 18). Importantly, the use of a variety of instruments 'to ensure that the societies were elitist' (1990b: 15) served not only to establish a power base, but also to perpetuate it as the status 'would be imputed to future members' (1990b: 18). Further support for the apparent importance of social class is available from Stewart (1975) who notes that the Glasgow Institute initially expressly excluded accountants engaged in business as merchants or manufacturers from membership. However, 'second jobs' with higher social status were tolerated and 'many of the early members had other occupations, such as stockbroking, banking, insurance or estate factoring' (1975: 114). Selective membership is also suggested by the procedures for admission to membership of the Glasgow Institute, with only some applicants being required to sit examinations (Stewart 1975: 114), and in Edinburgh where 'there were for many years examples of candidates being examined in a very informal manner' (Kedslie 1990a: 196). Lee's (1996a: 334) study of the formation of the Institute of Accountants in Edinburgh (IAE), incorporated as the Society of Accountants in Edinburgh (SAE) under royal charter, concludes that it was:

> effectively the organization of a very special type of club. It was formed by stages in a very élitist way. A small number of influential individuals laid the groundwork and introduced a further few persons of considerable stature within the Edinburgh accounting community to form the governing élite. The initial membership was restricted to approximately one half the total community of accountants. Selection appears to have

been based on a mixture of social background, legal connection, and professional reputation . . . Thus the formation of the IAE/SAE, so often characterized as the creation of a work monopoly with respect to court-related work, can also be characterized as the creation of a social élite.

However, subsequent to their initial establishment there is evidence to suggest that the Edinburgh accountants relied on increasing membership in the pursuit of 'occupational pre-eminence' (Walker 1988: 54). In contrast, some other early associations appeared to persist with a strategy of building exclusivity through a tightly controlled rationing of new memberships. This is alluded to by Preston *et al.* (1995: 516) with reference to the United States in the early part of this century: 'While established accountants achieved their designation by waiver, potential new entrants faced an examination with failure rates around 90%' (see also Young 1988). A strategy of social exclusivity is also revealed in Richardson's (1989a: 15) study of Canadian accountants during the period 1880 to 1930:

> In the late 1800s, accountancy was disorganized, subject to frequent scandals and generally held in low repute. The early accounting associations sought to improve their position in the profession by differentiating themselves from the mass of practitioners. The exclusiveness of the early associations was in part based on competence but the effectiveness of this program of status enhancement was also due to the social characteristics of members.

At issue in these observations is the 'dilemma of exclusiveness versus market control' (Macdonald and Ritzer 1988: 257).[5] That is, should an aspiring professional group rely on recruiting an élite (thereby constructing an aura of exclusiveness) or endeavour to recruit a substantial majority of existing practitioners (thereby increasing the likelihood of market control)? The research referred to above suggests that the strategies adopted by different associations of accountants were influenced and subject to change according to the particular circumstances they faced. In the case of the accountants in the United Kingdom the issue proved to be a contentious one: 'While chartered accountants were united in their conflict with the state . . . they were seriously divided over the best strategy for establishing control and monopoly over the market for accountancy services' (Macdonald and Ritzer 1988: 259). As a consequence, the failure of accountants to achieve occupational registration within the United Kingdom has been attributed to 'internecine quarrels between a number of [accounting] bodies' (Macdonald 1985: 346, emphasis omitted). Similar intra-profession rivalries have been deemed important in shaping the accounting profession within Canada (Richardson 1987b, 1989b) and Australia (Carnegie and Edwards 2001).

While superior social standing, mediated by a need to have sufficient members to exert market control, was likely to have been a positive force in the pursuit of professionalization, there seems little doubt that female membership would have been a significant encumbrance. Given that women have traditionally occupied a subordinate role within western society, an inverse relationship between the power of an occupational group and the extent of female membership has often been evident (Witz 1992). More specifically, while not all occupations are male dominated, those most commonly described as high-status professions traditionally have been (Perks 1993: 11). The female-dominated occupations of nursing (Turner 1986; Chua and Clegg 1990) and family day care (Saggers *et al.* 1994) have struggled to achieve professional status, while other occupations in which women were marginalized have more readily claimed a position in the highly professionalized section of the occupational continuum (Atkinson and Delamont 1990; Coutts and Roberts 1995). Researchers examining the professionalization of accounting have therefore sought to examine whether success in this endeavour might be at least partly attributable to gender.

Kirkham and Loft (1993) have analysed the role of gender in the professionalization of accounting within the United Kingdom. They conclude that in the early years of professional formation (prior to 1870), the tasks undertaken by clerks and accountants were established as work that 'was not fit work for women' and that 'this meant more than the exclusion of women, it was a way of signifying the contribution and social worth of such employments' (1993: 550). Subsequently, when clerical work became increasingly accessible to women, accountants sought to differentiate their work from that of clerks. The outcome was that the 'qualities demanded of a professional accountant were represented as being in opposition to the contemporary construction of what it meant to be a woman' (1993: 551), and 'by 1930 the term "professional accountant" had come to be constituted, in part, as something that is "not a clerk or bookkeeper" and, in part, as "something that is not a woman" ' (1993: 507).

The view that achieving and maintaining professional status was dependent on the exclusion of women is also expressed by Roberts and Coutts (1992: 389): 'For an occupation like accountancy, which was involved in a complex struggle to achieve professional status, the risk implied by feminization was too large a one to take.' That risk was a consequence of perceptions that women 'were not regarded as possessing the characteristics that make a good accountant; they were perceived as being too emotional and subjective, and not able to cope with figures' (1992: 388). Lehman (1992) identifies two additional factors compounding the extent of bias against women. Not only were females perceived as being inherently unsuitable for undertaking accounting work, their entry would increase competition – 'thus lowering the remuneration for all' (1992: 266) – and compromise the class standing of accountants: 'as . . . upper class British women never had to work, only women from the lower classes would enter the profession' (1992: 266). Possibly these were the grounds that lay behind the ICAEW, for example, expressly excluding women from membership for the first 40 years of its existence.

Abandonment of the policy was ultimately forced only by a change in legislation (Boys 1994: 14). Similar circumstances prevailed in Scotland (Shackleton 1999).

The extrication of social class and gender as discrete factors of importance in the professionalization of accounting still leaves an extensive and more general literature that depicts professionalization as a political struggle and emphasizes the political acuity of accountants within that struggle. The broad perspective of this literature is epitomized by Willmott's comment that 'professional bodies are *primarily* but not exclusively, political bodies whose purpose is to define, organise and advance the interests of (their most vocal and influential) members' (1986: 556, emphasis in original). As a consequence, the success of a professionalization project has been deemed to depend on:

> a range of conditions, including the structure of the relationship of professions with consumers of their services; their relationship with the agencies empowered to legitimate and extend their occupational domain and control; and, finally, the sections of their membership whose material position and social identity is affected by the activities of their association.
>
> (Willmott 1986: 561)

Among the political activities that have been linked with early associations of accountants are the establishment of a positive relationship with government and its related apparatus, the cultivation of strategic alliances with existing social institutions, and actions to denigrate those who sought to tread on the territory that accountants had claimed as their own.

According to Johnson's thesis (1980, 1982), success in the pursuit of professional status is likely to depend significantly on the state on account of its power to grant status enhancing appurtenances (such as royal charters) and legislatively imposed privileges (such as monopoly). Studies of the endeavours of Australian accountants to acquire a royal charter and elevate their status (Chua and Poullaos 1993, 1998; Cooper 1996; Poullaos 1993, 1994) shed light on these matters. The narratives contained in this research document a complex and sustained struggle and testify to the importance, and possible complexity, of interactions with the state (which is motivated by its own agenda – see Johnson 1980 and 1982) in the process of professionalization. An early attempt (1904) by the Incorporated Institute of Accountants in Victoria to obtain a royal charter was motivated by a concern 'to protect and expand its territory through an appeal to an Imperial agency' (Chua and Poullaos 1993: 722). Ultimately the attempt was defeated by the conspiracy of a complex set of forces:

> the compromises, detours, shifting alliances, trade-offs and deals that were struck by each group of actors as they sought to do that which was perceived to be feasible and beneficial at a point in time. There was no

stable intentionality or set of interests that guided the whole affair and determined its outcomes, beyond some vague concept of 'acting to protect one's own interests'.

(Chua and Poullaos 1993: 723)

A subsequent attempt by the Australasian Corporation of Public Accountants to acquire a royal charter, 'an incontrovertible sign of professional status' (Poullaos 1993: 198), was characterized by a similar political struggle, lost initially on account of diplomatic considerations, the self-interests of legislators who were concerned to preserve authority, and the opposition of other accounting bodies who were concerned about their 'possible loss of status and market positioning' (Poullaos 1993: 225–6). Eventually, however, after a complex set of struggles spanning four decades, a group of Australian accountants would succeed in acquiring a royal charter (in 1928) that was 'Born of struggle and compromise, not to mention dangerous and difficult liaisons' (Poullaos 1994: 219).[6] The importance of the state, and its lack of neutrality, in the professionalization process is also borne out, albeit in a vastly different context, in Bailey's study (1992) of an attempt to establish accounting as a profession in Russia. 'Lenin had held accounting to be within the grasp of any literate person and not a matter of expert knowledge' (1992: 14) and the Bolsheviks determined that accounting 'would undergo change in response to the new conditions in which there existed socialist means of production' (1992: 20). The outcome was that over fifty years of struggle to professionalize accounting in Russia would be brought to 'an ignominious end' (1992: 20). An unsympathetic state has also been shown to have retarded the development of an accounting profession within the Czech Republic (Seal, Sucher and Zelenka 1996).

In addition to relations with the state, the importance of 'associative strategies' (Selander 1990) based on alliances with other professions, particularly law, has been identified. Concerning the early Edinburgh accountants, Walker (1988: 15) suggests that their 'connections with those in the older professions of established standing threw a lustre of professional and social status over them'. The point is reinforced by Kedslie's assertion that strong links to the legal profession 'would be significant in establishing the social status of the members of the new society' (1990b: 13–14). Consistent with this theme, Macdonald (1984: 184–5) notes that connections with courts and the law were emphasized in the petitions for royal charters of the Edinburgh, Glasgow and Aberdeen societies, while accounting skills received only 'scant attention' (see also Lee 1996a: 329). Indeed, according to Sikka and Willmott (1995a: 554), the emergence of accountants as a distinct group of specialists owes much to 'the disdain of lawyers for accounting work'. However, proximity with the legal profession necessitated a careful balancing act. While the early Scottish accountants relied on a close association with the legal profession in order to *establish* their professional claim, later associations of accountants would downplay such a connection as they sought to emphasize the distinctive nature of their occupation. In the code of ethics promulgated by the Sydney Institute of Accountants in 1896, the sharing of profits, commissions or bonuses with a solicitor was deemed to provide grounds for the forfeiture of membership (Parker 1987: 123).

While studies of the kind cited emphasize the importance of interaction with the state and other influential institutions in the professionalization process, recent research has also drawn attention to internal political struggles among the providers of accounting services. Within this context, success in consolidating professional status is dependent on maintaining elitism by denigrating or excluding potential competitors. The early Scottish accountants have, again, been subject to analysis (Kedslie 1990a; Shackleton 1995; Walker 1988, 1991, 1995). Walker (1991: 271) concludes that 'entry to the chartered societies was conditional upon the ability to surmount exclusionary barriers rather than on individual merit'. The eventual outcome was that:

> not only had the chartered societies developed expanding, high standing professional organizations, they had also gained domination of the practice of their vocation, secured judgements which provided legal protection for the source of that dominance and, witnessed the demoralization and ineffectiveness of their competitors who had been weakened by the unsuccessful challenges to that domination.
>
> (Walker 1991: 281)

As the number of studies dealing with the professionalization of the accounting occupation expands, so too, it seems, expands the number of factors claimed to have played a role in the process. In addition to the factors already discussed, the literature makes reference to the construction of a 'mystique' concerning accounting knowledge (Moore and Cooper 1994) and the mechanisms by which accountants informally established their credentials in the absence of state registration (Macdonald 1985). Hines (1989) emphasizes the importance of being able to *claim* (rather than necessarily possess) a body of knowledge. During its formative years within the United States it has been suggested that 'the accounting profession sought to legitimize its activities and have conferred upon it the status and privilege of a profession by subscribing to political and moral ideals of the day' (Preston *et al.* 1995: 517). O'Leary and Boland (1987) specifically allude to the notion that accountants functioned as brokers of 'trust' within this context. In a similar vein, Ramirez (2001) highlights the importance of the 'cultural context' in shaping the outcome of the professionalization endeavours of accountants in France. Hoskin and Macve (1986, 1994) draw attention to the importance of the examinatorial system; not in terms of an objective assessment of the ability of candidates, but as a means of institutional legitimation. While much of the inquiry into the professionalization of accounting has been geographically specific, attention has also been given to the importing and exporting of professionalization strategies which evidence the origins of accounting's progress to becoming a global profession (Annisette 1999, 2000; Briston and Kedslie 1997; Carnegie 1993; Carnegie and Edwards 2001; Carnegie and Parker 1996, 1999; Gavens and Gibson 1992; Parker 1989; Poullaos 1994: 304).

Inquiries into the origins of accounting as a profession have uncovered a complex variety of strategies, influences and fortuitous circumstances. Early professional accountants were exclusively male and many were from privileged social backgrounds. They were politically astute, had connections to other powerful institutions such as the legal profession, and were not averse to denigrating and excluding those who sought to intrude on territory they had claimed as their own. Their work was rendered increasingly important by a changing legislative and economic environment. Collectively these factors, along with a variety of other strategies, were relied upon to construct an aura of élitism that permitted closure and the elevation of accounting within the occupational continuum. Strategies that proved successful in one location were often replicated in other parts of the globe. In summarizing the professionalization of accounting in the United Kingdom and the United States, Lee (1996b: 193) describes the process as 'essentially an economic text with a cover entitled the public interest'.

The importance of this understanding of the initial professionalization of accounting transcends the time-frame from which it originates. While the paths travelled by occupational groups to achieve professional status may be numerous and have been only partly mapped, there are grounds for suggesting that they define an essentially one-way journey. In the course of the last two centuries, members of the traditional learned professions of medicine, law and theology have been joined by engineers, architects, accountants, pharmacists, veterinary surgeons, actuaries and others. However, examples of occupations that achieved professional status and subsequently lost it are more difficult to find.[7] The implication is an important one; while professionalization may be a complex and arduous project in which specific strategies sometimes fail (Chua and Poullaos 1993; Macdonald 1985), once it is achieved it tends to deliver an enduring status. Thus, the influence of factors contributing to the initial professionalization of an occupation transcend the particular time-frame in which professionalization occurred as they construct a power base that ensures that the 'ongoing process of negotiating and renegotiating . . . status' (Allen 1991: 51) is conducted from a privileged position. The authority enjoyed by accountants within the contemporary setting is thereby inextricably bound to the factors that explain the initial elevation of the status of their occupation. It is for this reason that understanding of a profession's 'unique historical past may give insights into contemporary problems and concerns' (Tinker 1985: xxi).

Synthesis

'Accounting is an ancient practice with a distinctive modern power' (Hoskin and Macve 1994: 57). This statement encapsulates the fundamental quandary surrounding the professionalization of accounting. That accountants have been vested with significant authority within the domain of financial reporting is beyond doubt. But what caused the practitioners of an 'ancient practice' to be elevated, in a comparatively short period of time, to this position of authority? The preceding review of literature dealing with the professionalization of accounting provides abundant evidence of a *social* dimension to the process. This is partly in accord with Goldstein's description: 'the sociological conception of a profession posits a previously given *intellectual* core and a subsequent, multi-faceted *social* process which takes place around that core' (1984: 175, emphasis in original). But what of the 'intellectual core'? A basic premise of the sociology of professions literature is that it *must* be there: 'In sociological theory, the social process of professionalization is dependent upon the intellectual core; but the reverse is not true' (Goldstein 1984: 175). Contrary to this representation, accounting knowledge, far from being clearly identified as a factor contributing to the professionalization of accounting, has often been either implicitly or explicitly *excluded*, as revealed in the statements contained in Box 3.1.

Box 3.1

Statements critical of the knowledge base of the accounting profession:

[Early writers on accounting] made little showing of any systematic thought. . . . Like many another trade or occupational group, their dicta were amazingly positive and their argument as amazingly inconsequential. . . . the work of the accountant and the writings on accounting, until very recently, proceeded by a sort of patchwork and tinkering.

(Canning 1978/1929: 8–9)

It is a remarkable fact that there is in the world of accountancy, almost alone among the professions, no association having any study interests or activities. . . . nothing has yet been done by the profession in the way of organized study or research.

(Carr-Saunders and Wilson 1933: 226)

. . . in greater or lesser degree, ordinary accounting figures give bad advice. They say to expand or contract, buy or sell, hire or fire when sometimes the opposite should be done, and when usually the extent of such action should be modified or enhanced. They say that depreciation and costs are such and such when they are more or less, often decidedly more or less. They frequently say that income taxes should be paid when real income indicates that they should not be, and *vice versa*. They frequently say that dividends should be paid, when they should not be, and *vice versa*. Consequently, business uses a guide that is certainly not highly reliable when it uses accounting.

(Sweeney 1964/1936: xliii–xliv)

. . . the great majority of contemporary certified financial statements must necessarily be untrue and misleading due to the unsound principles upon which modern accounting methods are based. . . . For more than 400 years, since Pacioli's book on double entry bookkeeping in 1494, accounting methods, and hence accounting reports, have been based on expediency rather than on truth. Financial statements today are based on a bewildering mixture of accounting conventions, historical data, and present facts, wherein even accountants are unable to distinguish between truth and fiction.

(MacNeal 1970/1939: vii)

. . . accountants do not appear to have any complete system of thought about accounting. . . . There are unquestionably several systems of thought about the *practice* of accounting: systems which attempt to categorise the kinds of things accountants do in practice. These systems are almost all the subject can boast in the way of theory, and for this reason accounting lacks the sharpness, the progressiveness of other technologies.

(Chambers 1955: 17, emphasis in original)

It is true that accounting practices are not the results of logical and systematical developments.

(Ijiri 1972: 65)

Accountants' associations themselves have been marked by an apathetic attitude towards the development of basic accountancy knowledge through research. . . . Particularism in the development of knowledge has been recognised as a major problem for the development of a unified accountancy occupation in so far as procedures, ground rules, techniques, continue to vary.

(Johnson 1972: 71)

Accountants were not much more than specialized craftsmen, i.e. bookkeepers, when an almost overwhelming responsibility was rather suddenly thrust upon them. They switched from bookkeeper to independent auditor.

(Sterling 1973b: 61)

. . . nineteenth century accountants did not 'solve' most of the problems which they debated.

(Brief 1975: 296)

. . . it should be borne in mind that there is little in the development of accounting as practised that would lead one to describe its essential rationale in terms of the furtherance of economic efficiency or rationality.

(Burchell *et al.* 1980: 10)

. . . there is no evidence to suggest that the accounting profession has pursued, in a disciplined manner, the discovery and ongoing refinement of a coherent body of reliable (accounting) knowledge.

(Wolnizer 1987: 178–9)

. . . the history of accounting is interpreted as a complex web of economic, political and accidental co-occurrences that mirror neither technical rationality nor a necessary progress.

(Arrington and Francis 1989: 2)

. . . the absence of general agreement about which profit measurement and asset valuation procedures should be used provided ample scope for nineteenth-century corporate managers to prepare reports designed to meet particular managerial objectives rather than to portray fairly the underlying economic facts.

(Edwards 1989: 125, emphasis omitted)

It would seem that the success of the accounting professionalisation project cannot be explained by reference to the *substance* of a formal body of financial accounting knowledge.

(Hines 1989: 85, emphasis in original)

We need to see contemporary accountancy as nothing other than an assemblage of disparate components that has been put together in a piecemeal fashion.

(Miller and Napier 1993: 644)

Varieties of neglect have led accountants to concentrate on bookkeeping mechanics, to invent terms understood only among accountants themselves, to rationalize longstanding habits, to qualify freely what seem to be offered as reliable dicta or principles, to perpetuate and tolerate logical solecisms and practical absurdities – rather than to observe carefully and be guided strictly by the firm elements of financial and commercial intercourse.

(Chambers 1994: 87)

The accounting profession's power/knowledge initially did not lie in the formal claims of possession of special skills and knowledge. The skills and knowledge claimed by the profession were not unique, they belonged to other professions.

(Moore and Gaffikin 1994: 63)

. . . the attainment of professional status [in auditing] was achieved against a background of litigation, adverse publicity and critical judicial commentary.

(Chandler 1997: 61)

In comparison to the statements contained in Box 3.1, attempts to justify the professional status of accounting on the grounds of 'accounting knowledge' are lame. Roy and MacNeill (1967: 32) made the claim that 'as the traditional learned professions depend upon bodies of specialized knowledge, so also does accounting'. The authors listed 'Accounting, The Humanities, Economics and Behavioural Science, Law, Mathematics, Statistics, Probability, The Functional Fields of Business' as the 'major categories' of 'the common body of knowledge for beginning CPAs' (1967: 11). However, no attempt was made to articulate how the combination of items in this listing would manifest in a coherent body of professional accounting knowledge, and one reviewer suggested that the study was 'aimed more at edification than problem solution' (Zald 1968: 138). Indeed, this attempt to specify 'accounting knowledge' is notable for its hesitancy and contradictions. It is suggested that accountants are required to be 'objective', requiring the avoidance of 'personal bias' (Roy and MacNeill 1967: 205). However, simultaneously there is a perceived need for them to be 'conservative', to avoid the possibility of 'undue optimism' (1967: 206). Cost is to be used to measure assets (1967: 202), but the statement of financial position – said to have 'survived because it meaningfully presents information of use to investors and creditors' (1967: 203) – is claimed to indicate the resources available to meet debts and 'the relative ability of the entity to continue operations' (1967: 204).

Acknowledging that accountants' claim to a particular cognitive domain 'was quite problematic', Macdonald (1995: 201) concludes that their professionalization in Britain was a function of the *breadth* of knowledge they possessed:

In fact their 'esoteric' knowledge was less than esoteric on the face of it, because there was scarcely an aspect that they did not share with some other occupation. Bookkeeping, company law, insolvency, taxation, trust accounts – lawyers, company secretaries and a host of bookkeepers and clerks with modest qualifications could be found to deal with each of these. So the Chartered Accountants' case had to rest on the claim that they were the only group that could do them all. . . .

As the economic world which gave rise to accountancy became increasingly complex and the legislation required to regulate it followed suit, professional practice came to entail an esoteric collection of areas of knowledge, rather than a basis in esoteric knowledge.

Difficulties are again apparent with this perspective. Most importantly, it denies that there is a body of unique accounting knowledge by suggesting that the individual elements of accounting expertise are known to others.

Those writers who have endeavoured more explicitly to link knowledge development with the professionalization of accounting have had recourse to what is now usually described as management accounting. Loft (1986, 1994), for example, emphasizes the developments in cost accounting and according to Lee (1990a: 91) convenience saw these being adopted for the quite distinct role of financial reporting: 'Ideas from cost accounting with respect to allocations for matching purposes were available and slowly incorporated into accounting for external reporting.' In their investigation of 'the genesis of accounting's modern power', Hoskin and Macve (1994) draw attention to bookkeeping, and the role of accounting as a disciplinary device within organizations. Other rationalizations of financial reporting and auditing practices have been premised on ideological or self-interest grounds. Merino (1993), for example, explains the emergence of proprietary theory not in terms of an outcome of objective inquiry, but as 'an imaginative and creative response to conditions that threatened to undermine continued acceptance of private property rights' (1993: 178). Thus, 'proprietary theorists' were not disinterested proponents of what they considered to be a better form of accounting, they were 'partisan' (1993: 178). Lee's (1994) investigation of financial reporting quality labels emphasizes their social construction and utility as 'a considerable economic resource to the audit profession' (1994: 43), rather than their conventionally attributed role of protecting the users of financial reports. More generally, Miller and Napier (1993) emphasize the discursive construction of accounting calculations and the 'disparate events and processes' (1993: 644) which comprise their genealogies.

Concerns about accounting knowledge claims with respect to financial reporting exist, not just within the context of initial professionalization, but also in the contemporary setting. Most (1993: 1) has summarized the condition of the accounting profession: 'Their product, the financial report, is a costly mess; their generally accepted accounting principles in chaos; their signatures on audit reports suspect; and their education and training considered unacceptable.' Some degree of indeterminacy in professional knowledge has been said to provide a means of accentuating professional authority (Baer 1986; Boreham 1983; Jamous and Peloille 1970) as it 'allows secrecy and means that control over . . . professional skills remains in the hands of practitioners' (Perks 1993: 13). However, the strength of ongoing criticisms of accounting practice suggest that the professionalization of accounting has been achieved in spite of discord in accounting knowledge rather than because of it. Vague and inconsistent accounting practices have consistently been alleged to have diminished public confidence in accountants, and therefore impeded rather than aided the pursuit and retention of professional status (Birkett and Walker 1971; Briloff 1972, 1981, 1990; Cooper *et al.* 1994; Feller 1974; MacNeal 1977/1939; Mitchell *et al.* 1991; Shah 1996; Walker 1981).

The conclusion drawn is that while accountants have unquestionably achieved substantial occupational authority, it is an authority that has only a problematic origin in accounting knowledge. While the process by which accounting became professionalized is contrary to the expectations established by the mainstream sociology of professions literature, it is not necessarily unique. According to Collins (1979: 135), 'Many of the techniques by which the professions of today became organized and achieved their high status were based on mystification and secrecy regarding their real skills and use of their status background rather than their technique per se.' Even medicine – traditionally regarded as providing the example par excellence of a profession – has been described in such terms: 'What is striking about the traditionally high status of medicine is the fact that it was based on virtually no valid expertise at all' (Collins 1979: 139). As with at least some other occupations, the occupational authority enjoyed by accountants cannot be assumed to carry an epistemological vindication of that status. In this circumstance the legitimacy of a professional mandate is rendered problematic: 'If full professional status is systematically compromised by individual characteristics – e.g. gender or race – this must call into question the *real* salience of the knowledge and skills and thus the legitimacy of the claim to "professionalism"' (Crompton 1987: 107, emphasis in original).

Résumé and conclusion

This chapter has noted that accountants exercise a substantial degree of authority within the accounting domain. Through statutory provisions relating to company audits they are commonly vested with exclusive authority to attest to the truth and fairness (or other similar general qualitative standard) of financial reports. The technical procedures related to the conduct of such audits are substantially determined by those providing the services. Even when courts are called upon to assess auditor performance it is the standards widely accepted within the profession that are likely to be of prevailing influence. In addition, the processes of setting accounting standards and other technical regulations that govern financial reports are substantially influenced by associations of accountants. These circumstances are indicative of the kind of elevated occupational authority that this study has nominated to be the outcome of professionalization.

However, while it is clear that accountants exercise substantial authority within the domain in which they operate, it is not clear that the origin of that authority lies in cognitively based expertise. Instead, there is abundant evidence of a social process surrounding the professionalization of accounting. It reveals that the social class, gender and political acuity of early accountants contributed to the elevation of accounting within the occupational contin-uum, assisted by changes in the legislative and economic environments. Developments in accounting knowledge – particularly in connection with the financial reporting function where accountants' authority has been especially evident – are less easily identified as an explanatory factor. The development of a systematic process for *recording* accounting transactions, based on double entry accounting, preceded the formation of the first associations of accoun-tants in English-speaking countries by almost 400 years. However, the adoption of a coherent framework for *reporting* the financial position and results of firms – that is, a functional system of financial instrumentation – has not been in evidence at any time since 'professional' accountants ascended to a position of authority in connection with the preparation and authenti-cation of accounting information.

These circumstances depict an occupational group that succeeded in achieving an elevated level of authority over financial reporting practices that was not sourced from, or validated by, a coherent body of knowledge per-taining to those practices. In the continued absence of cognitive vindication of their mandate, it also creates an expectation that accountants would struggle to administer the occupational authority they had won. Without a robust theoretical framework and intellectual tradition, it would be necessary to resort to convention to define and justify technical practices. Instead of providing the means for enabling reliable financial instrumentation, those practices would become ends in themselves. These issues form the subject of the next two chapters.

4 The nature of accounting rules

> It is as if accountants were being directed to construct a machine the capacity and function of which is not known, or is secret.
>
> (Chambers 1975: 151)

Introduction

Professions are characterized by an elevated occupational authority, typically involving an exclusive and state-sponsored mandate to provide certain services and define the nature of those services. Both individually and through their formal associations, accountants exercise such authority over financial reporting matters. They have exclusive rights to provide company audit services and are largely unfettered by external regulations in the performance of this work. Their work processes are also hidden, preventing any confident evaluation of auditor performance: 'In the end auditors must be trusted about what it is they produce' (Power 1997: 28). The users of financial reports also lack the access and, in many instances, the expertise necessary to make their own direct assessments of the quality of information contained in those reports. Faced with a general lack of alternative information sources, investors and other decision makers are forced into a reliance on audited financial reports that must be taken 'as given'.

The authority of the accounting profession evident in these circumstances is accentuated by its ability to influence the processes that define accepted financial reporting practices. These processes include the development of accounting standards and other regulatory statements and systems of education that impart particular understandings of accounting. However, the genealogy of the professionalization of the accounting occupation does not emphasize that the authority exercised by accountants was derived from a demonstrable claim to specialized expertise. A multiplicity of factors appear to have contributed to the elevated status and authority enjoyed by accountants, but these are essentially of a social nature.

Following from these observations, attention is now directed to the matter of accounting technique. Since this is now largely defined by formally stated rules these are the principal subject of scrutiny. The purpose of the chapter is to demonstrate that despite the apparent enthusiasm with which these rules have been embraced by the accounting profession, they do not provide a cognitive justification for its mandate. The usefulness of any set of accounting rules – and the expertise of interpreting and applying them – is contingent upon those rules being systematically connected to the function of accounting. Indeed, their only justification is that they demonstrably serve that function by improving the capacity of financial statements to serve as reliable financial instruments. This outcome can only be achieved when the rules are internally consistent and not in contradiction of the various fields of knowledge relevant to accounting practice. This consistency – 'a condition of all logical discourse' (Chambers 1955: 22) – would provide evidence that accounting practice had gone beyond tradition, chance and convenience to be governed by disciplined reasoning. A system of accounting based on observations of specified commercial phenomena would have the capacity to inherit this quality of consistency from the coherence that abides innately within all factual information.

In the course of this chapter it will be demonstrated that present accounting rules lack any unifying function and are often disconnected from commercial phenomena. The evidence for this is the discretionary and calculational methods of accounting that are repeatedly prescribed and which are not derived from any robust theoretical framework. Greenwood's (1966/1957: 11) description of a profession's body of theory – 'a system of abstract propositions that describe in general terms the classes of phenomena comprising the profession's focus of interest' – is peculiarly inapplicable in the case of accounting. The various abstract propositions that underlie the accounting profession's technical practices are typically not invoked to define and categorize phenomena but to yield only further abstractions, such as unamortized costs, and profit figures and balance sheet totals that have no empirical connotation.

Accounting methods that are not based on the observation of phenomena do not yield outputs that can be independently verified. That is, the outputs have no truth-value independent of the rules that prescribe the manner by which they are calculated. A self-referential system of this kind cannot be claimed to provide an epistemological basis for accounting practice. When accounting is based on imaginary concepts – such as costs allocations, future economic benefits and the sums yielded by invalid aggregations – it is segregated from the realm of knowledge-based disciplines and the precepts they provide. By embracing the unknown and undiscoverable as their subject matter present, accounting rules perpetuate this divide, relegating accounting to the domain of personalized conjectures which belie the very notion of 'standards'. No matter how numerous accounting rules are, nor how stringent the attempts to enforce them, they cannot rigorously standardize or otherwise discipline financial statements while they prescribe calculations yielding outputs unable to be verified by recourse to independent evidence. A coherent and functional system of financial instrumentation can only obtain when the elements of financial reports have actual and discoverable counterparts within the commercial setting.

The next section of the chapter provides an analysis of the nature of accounting rules, illustrated with references to the AASB series of accounting standards. An evaluation is then made of the potential of concepts statements issued in connection with 'conceptual framework' projects to achieve their stated purpose of improving the quality of accounting rules.

The nature of accounting rules

Technical accounting rules now exert a dominating influence on the practice of accounting. The preparation of financial reports entails following the directives of these rules in what has been described aptly as a 'cookbook approach' to accounting (Clarke, Dean and Oliver 1997: 238). The role of auditors within this framework is confined largely to checking that the 'recipe' has been followed, with an absence of regulation on a particular issue increasingly interpreted as a sanctioning of 'anything goes' (Walker 1993; see also Cheung 1994; Deegan, Kent and Lin 1994).

These factors alone invite a questioning of professional knowledge claims within accounting as they are suggestive of a procedural activity without an intellectual foundation. However, more detailed consideration of how the reduction of accounting to a process of rule application has affected the intellectual vitality of the accounting profession is deferred until later in this study (Chapters 6, 7 and 8). The matter of immediate concern involves the technical quality of the information – audited financial reports – yielded by the application of present accounting rules. This investigation does not commence from any preconceived stance on the worth or otherwise of accounting rules per se. Rather, the foundational precepts are that accounting information has an important function in the conduct of human affairs and that it is the duty of an accounting profession to provide the specialized expertise that enables this function to be properly served.

As has been noted earlier in this study, the examination and evaluation of professional knowledge claims has been neglected within the sociology of professions literature. Redressing this neglect has the potential to contribute significantly to a better understanding of professions, both individually and collectively. In the context of this study, three interrelated questions are posed: What is it that accountants do? What knowledge is applied in this doing? What is the social utility of this knowledge? Collectively, these questions embody the pragmatic basis for comprehending and evaluating professions and professionalism that was outlined earlier in this study. They are directed at ascertaining the extent to which professional authority within accounting contributes to enhancing social order by providing a knowledge-based mediation of the interactions between actors engaged in reporting and using accounting information.

Specification of what accountants 'do' within a financial reporting context has already been described. Technical rules now dominate that context and accountants – whether in the preparation or audit of financial reports – are concerned primarily with interpreting and applying those rules. This observation also provides an answer to the question of what knowledge accountants bring to bear in their work. It is, of course, a knowledge of accounting rules. This conclusion can also be inferred from the emphasis placed on these rules in accounting textbooks and professional and university education programmes. But what is the social utility of this knowledge? The answer to this question must be searched for in the rules themselves. In this search there is particular concern with whether present accounting rules constitute the formal expression of a coherent body of reliable accounting knowledge. If they do, then accounting practitioners, as the agents of accounting rules, would deliver through their work a cognitively derived means of regulating the quality of accounting information: an outcome conforming to the commission of a professional occupation. However, if accounting rules do not embody reliable accounting knowledge, then the agency of accounting practitioners is singular: they bring to bear in their work only a knowledge of those rules.[1]

The description and evaluation of the nature of accounting rules that is developed in this section explores four issues that have 'consistency' as a unifying theme: consistency between accounting rules and the function of accounting; between accounting rules and the findings in a variety of specialist fields of knowledge; between individual accounting rules; and between accounting rules and commercial phenomena. This emphasis on consistency has an epistemological basis, being the key criterion for evaluating whether accounting rules are consonant with the features of knowledge-based statements.

'According to the most widely accepted definition, knowledge is justified true belief' (Quinton 1967: 345). Goldman's (1988: 22) definition is similar: 'a belief counts as knowledge when appeal to the truth of the belief enters prominently into the best explanation for its being held'. For Maddox (1993: 3) 'Knowledge is both true and verifiable.' The common element in these statements is that knowledge is associated with what is 'true' (see also Chisholm 1989: 90; Hamlyn 1970: 99; Lewis 1970: 18). That is, knowledge-based statements must be capable of being defended as true statements, as Maddox (1993: 3) explains:

> If we know something we should be able to justify it and explain why it is true, cite evidence for it and show how it can be verified. Even when a belief is true it is still not knowledge unless the believer can substantiate it and show why it is true.

The provision of criteria for distinguishing truth from falsehood – and by implication the demarcation of what constitutes knowledge – is one of the most fundamental and enduring of philosophical problems. Two theories about truth have achieved prominence. Under the *correspondence theory* truth consists in some form of correspondence between belief and fact: 'the truth of basic propositions depends upon their relation to some occurrence, and the truth of other propositions depends on their syntactical relations to basic propositions' (Russell 1973/1940: 272). Moore explains the theory in the following terms:

> To say that this belief is true is to say that there is in the Universe a fact to which it corresponds, and to say that it is false is to say that there is not in the Universe any fact to which it corresponds.
>
> (cited in Prior 1967: 226)

The second prominent theory for testing the truthfulness of statements emphasizes that true statements must be consistent with each other. This forms the basis of the *coherence theory*, which White (1967: 130) explains in the following terms:

> to say that a statement . . . is true or false is to say that it coheres or fails to cohere with a system of other statements; that it is a member of a system whose elements are related to each other by ties of logical implication as the elements in a system of pure mathematics are related. . . . To test whether a statement is true is to test for coherence with a system of statements.

The coherence theory of truth has been demonstrated by White (1967: 130) in connection with pure mathematics:

> It is characteristic of the parts of a logical system like that of pure mathematics that no part would be what it is if its relations to the other parts were different from what they are. Thus, 2 would not be the number we associate with the numeral two if it were the third of 4 instead of the half of 4 or the cube root of 27 instead of the cube root of 8. Hence, it is said, the meaning and the truth of, for instance, '2 + 2 = 4' are bound up with the meaning and the truth of all the other statements in the arithmetical system; and our knowledge of its meaning and its truth is bound up with our knowledge of their meaning and their truth.

Common to both the correspondence and coherence theories of truth is the principle that in circumstances where there are incompatible statements, then one or more of the statements must be false. Testing for the truthfulness – and epistemological vindication – of any set of statements involves assessing the consistency of those statements with known facts and other statements. As explained by Popper (1968: 91–2, emphasis in original), this consistency is the most fundamental attribute of a body of knowledge and has practical as well as theoretical significance:[2]

The requirement of consistency plays a special role among the various requirements which a theoretical system, or an axiomatic system, must satisfy. It can be regarded as the first of the requirements to be satisfied by *every* theoretical system, be it empirical or non-empirical.

In order to show the fundamental importance of this requirement it is not enough to mention the obvious fact that a self-contradictory system must be rejected because it is 'false'. . . . [T]he importance of the requirement of consistency will be appreciated if one realizes that a self-contradictory system is uninformative. It is so because any conclusion we please can be derived from it. Thus no statement is singled out, either as incompatible or derivable, since all are derivable. A consistent system, on the other hand, divides the set of all possible statements into two: those which it contradicts and those with which it is compatible. (Among the latter are the conclusions which can be derived from it.) This is why consistency is the most general requirement for a system, whether empirical or non-empirical, if it is to be of any use at all.

This requirement for consistency has application to accounting, being the quality that must be in evidence if a system of accounting – including that defined by present accounting rules – is 'to be of any use' and not rejected as 'false'. That is, the system must be able to withstand in substance the scrutiny of a search for inconsistent elements if it is to be defended as providing a cognitive grounding for accounting practice.[3] It is this criterion that is applied in the following discussion which examines individual accounting rules within the contexts of the function of accounting, the findings in various specialist fields, the provisions of other accounting rules, and the features of commercial phenomena.

Accounting rules and the function of accounting

While the practice of accounting now centres on achieving compliance with prescribed rules, this is unmentioned in definitions of accounting or specifications of its purpose. Instead, the reporting of information – variously described as 'financial' or 'economic' – for the expressly functional purposes of informing decision making and discharging accountability obligations has been stressed. This is illustrated by the statements contained in Box 4.1, which are drawn from a broad spectrum of the accounting literature.

On the basis of these statements which describe what accounting is, achieving compliance with accounting rules can be defended only as a means and not an end. The function of accounting pertains to the provision of information that facilitates informed human action. The justification for the existence and enforcement of accounting rules can only proceed from a demonstration of how those rules serve that function.[4] This requires that the prescriptions of individual rules enhance the overall quality and usefulness of the information reported in financial statements: 'Specific rules relating to

Box 4.1

Definitions of accounting and specifications of its function:

> Accounting is a means by which the complex data of the market, as they attach to the particular business, are translated into effective managerial criteria. It is the function of accounting to record values, classify values, and to organize and present value data in such a fashion that the owners and their representatives may utilize wisely the capital at their disposal.
>
> > (Paton 1962/1922: 7)

> . . . the primary duty of the accountant is to report information in the forms thought to be most useful to the persons who have legitimate interests in the enterprise affairs.
>
> > (Canning 1978/1929: 312)

> . . . the ultimate goal of accounting is to produce relevant, accurate, and complete information, especially on the balance sheet and the profit and loss statement; for successful and intelligent business management must rely upon being given such information.
>
> > (Sweeney 1964/1936: 101)

> The function of accounting is to record, collate, and present economic truths.
>
> > (MacNeal 1970/1939: 295)

> The purpose of accounting is to furnish financial data concerning a business enterprise, compiled and presented to meet the needs of management, investors and the public.
>
> > (Paton and Littleton 1940: 1)

> The committee defines accounting as the process of identifying, measuring, and communicating economic information to permit informed judgements and decisions by users of the information.
>
> > (AAA Committee to Prepare a Statement of Basic Accounting
> > Theory 1966: 1)

> Accounting is a systematic method of retrospective and contemporary monetary calculation the purpose of which is to provide a continuous source of financial information as a guide to future action in markets.
>
> > (Chambers 1966b: 102)

Accounting is a service activity. Its function is to provide quantitative information, primarily financial in nature about economic entities that is intended to be useful in making economic decisions, in making resolved choices among alternative courses of action.

(APB 1970: para. 40)

The preparation of financial statements (accounting) and auditing both the statements and the accounts from which they are prepared are means of achieving accountability in society.

(Tinker 1985: xvii)

Accounting [is] broadly conceived as the measurement and communication of economic information relevant to decision makers.

(Watts and Zimmerman 1986: vii)

General purpose financial reports shall provide information useful to users for making and evaluating decisions about the allocation of scarce resources.

(AARF and ASRB 1990: para. 43)

particular classes of assets, equities, revenues and expenses are useless unless they improve the exactness of the general indicators' (Chambers 1973a: 51).

Present accounting rules are not linked to any clearly specified notion of data serviceability and this is evident in three interrelated failings. First, valuation practices that have no discernible connection to decision-making processes are mandated. Second, choices in accounting method are sanctioned, meaning that the information communicated to financial statements users is not of a standard form. Third, calculations that do not yield independently verifiable magnitudes are prescribed, making the content of financial reports conditional on personal judgements. Each of these matters will be considered in turn.

The notion that published financial reports should aid the decision-making processes of shareholders and other constituent groups is uncontentious (see Box 4.1). So too is the notion that assessments of debt-paying capacity (solvency), the rate of return on invested funds (profitability) and financial flexibility (liquidity) are of recurring and primary interest to these groups.[5] However, the set of data that is relevant to making these assessments is restricted. In particular, historical costs have no capacity to inform evaluations of solvency or liquidity since they do not reveal the ability to access cash: the spending power that permits debts to be repaid and resources acquired. In addition, changes in the ability to access cash (including those arising from movements in market prices) are a determinant of the spending power increment – 'the financial object of economic activity' (Chambers 1991b: 12) – that is the essential input to measuring the rate of return on invested funds (profitability).

However, the accounting mandated by present rules does not just consistently endorse cost valuations, but perpetuates the idea that costs themselves may constitute a financial resource. Thus, for example, costs associated with the purchase of goodwill, borrowings, pre-production activities in the extractive industries, research and development programmes and incomplete construction projects are, in certain circumstances, permitted or required to be recorded as assets.[6] The lower of cost and net realizable value rule prescribed by AASB 1019 'Inventories' combines what is relevant for financial decision making (realizable value) and what is not (cost). A further example concerns the current and deferred 'tax assets' created through the application of AASB 1020 'Income taxes'. These can best be described as the anticipated savings on tax that has not yet even been levied; a bookkeeping contrivance resulting from items being recognized at different times for accounting and taxation purposes.

These examples demonstrate how present accounting rules compromise the functionality of financial statements by prescribing methods of valuation that do not contribute to revealing the financial stability and profitability of firms. At best, conventional indicators of these variables – such as the current ratio, debt to equity ratio, return on assets and return on equity – provide only crude approximations rather than the reliable readings that would characterize a properly functioning system of financial instrumentation. This failing does not pertain to only a few isolated accounting rules. It is a feature of the whole corpus of accounting standards and related regulations and a consequence of these rules not being derived from any clear technical specification of what is purported to be represented in financial statements and how it serves the information needs of the various parties who rely on those statements.

Compounding and further evidencing this failing is that accounting rules permit choices, making accounting method a matter of 'policy'. Yet the financial features of firms – their profitability, solvency and financial flexibility – are not constituted by arbitrary choices in calculational technique. They are constituted by facts to be discovered by observation: the amount by which an entity has enhanced its capacity to command resources between specified dates and the amounts of its cash and cash equivalent resources and legally enforceable obligations on a specified date. The sanctioning of choices by present accounting rules thereby contradicts the nature of the accounting task. In some instances these choices are explicit. AASB 1019 permits alternative inventory flow assumptions. AASB 1022 provides that certain exploration and evaluation costs incurred within the extractive industries '*may* be carried forward' (clause .11, emphasis added). AASB 1041 'Revaluation of non-current assets' permits, but does not require, upwards revaluations of non-current assets. AASB 1010 provides that non-current assets are not to be carried at more than their 'recoverable amount', but this may be determined using either discounted or undiscounted cash flows (paragraph 7.2).[7] Other choices are condoned implicitly by accounting standards on account of the vague nature of the criteria that are intended to guide the selection of accounting method. Thus, the method of accounting to be adopted in respect of leases under AASB 1008 'Leases' is dependent on whether 'substantially all of the risks and benefits incident to ownership of the leased asset effectively remain with the lessor' (para. 5.3.1). AASB 1009 prescribes that the recognition of revenues and expenses under a construction contract is contingent on the outcome of the contract being 'estimated reliably' (para. 7.1). However, if it is 'probable' that a loss will result, different procedures are to apply (para. 7.4). Research and development costs may be recognized as an asset under AASB 1011 where such costs 'are expected beyond any reasonable doubt to be recoverable' (clause .31). AASB 1012 'Foreign currency translation' prescribes two methods for translating financial statements denominated foreign currency, with the selection dependent on whether the foreign operation is perceived to be 'self-sustaining' (clause .20) or 'integrated' (clause .21). The differences between the accounting methods sanctioned in these and other circumstances can affect profoundly the form and content of financial reports. Yet, as demonstrated with the preceding examples, the criteria supplied to guide the selection of methods are so littered with contingency terms that diverse interpretations are effectively sanctioned.[8] Discretion in the selection of accounting methods – whether explicit or implicit – contradicts the nature of the tasks that accounting information is said to inform. This is because the financial features of firms are not constituted by choices; they are the actual consequences of past actions. As with other kinds of facts, those of a financial nature are discoverable by observation; they are neither discovered nor made by subjectively adopted procedures of calculation.

The choices in accounting method sanctioned by present accounting rules contradict the widely avowed function of accounting in one further way. Financial reports are intended to serve the needs of a variety of different users, not the idiosyncratic wishes of any one user or class of users in particular. This requires that those reports be free of information that is a function of personal preferences. However, the choices permitted by accounting rules countermand objectivity: non-current assets may or may not be revalued (AASB 1041), first-in-first-out or weighted average assumptions may be adopted to assign inventory costs (AASB 1019), the term and pattern of depreciation and amortization charges are the products of conjectures – variously cautious or optimistic – about the future use of assets. The point is that these choices 'personalize' financial reports in a manner that contradicts their stated purpose of being *generally* useful. The fact that these choices are made by the managers of reporting entities compounds the failing. The accountability function of financial reports is not served by permitting those whose accountability is under evaluation to make opportunistic selections of accounting methods.

Accounting rules and various fields of knowledge

Particular bodies of knowledge are not isolated systems, but marked by inter-dependencies. Thus, what is described as constituting the knowledge of an individual discipline is typically indebted to a variety of other fields:

> For the domain of truth has no fixed boundaries within it. In the one world of ideas there are no barriers to trade or to travel. Each discipline may take from others techniques, concepts, laws, data, models, theories or explanations – in short whatever it finds useful in its own inquiries. And it is a measure of its success in these inquiries that it is asked in turn to give of its riches to other disciplines.
>
> (Kaplan 1973: 4)

Advancing knowledge through this borrowing of ideas is conditional on those ideas being carefully and accurately transported between disciplines. To fail in this regard will not just impede progress, but precipitate regressive outcomes as inferences are drawn on the basis of misunderstanding or ignorance of the findings of those working in other fields.

This matter is of special importance to accounting. Its proximity to other disciplines is such that definitions of accounting are typically constructed around references to those disciplines. The examples provided in Box 4.1 include economics, measurement, communication, and decision making, among others. Recourse to the reliable findings in these fields could make a significant contribution to providing an intellectually rigorous foundation for accounting practice. However, the tendency of present accounting rules to confound rather than respect various specialized bodies of knowledge is widespread. The most fundamental of these transgressions arises in connection with basic arithmetic. There is scarcely an accounting task that does not call upon the processing of numbers: individual assets are summed into class totals, class totals are aggregated to give total assets, liabilities are subtracted from assets to calculate equity, current liabilities are subtracted from current assets to calculate working capital, rates of return are calculated by dividing profit by equity, and so on.

Expressing accounting information in money terms is intended to facilitate these processes: 'Money is the only factor that is common to all business trans-actions, and thus it is the only practical unit of measure that can produce financial data that are alike and comparable' (Wise *et al.* 1998: 14). However, simply adopting a common unit of quantification – such as the Australian dollar – does not necessarily yield data amenable to arithmetic processes. The further conditions to be satisfied have been established by mathematicians and explained, with particular reference to aggregation, by Jourdain (1960: 24):

> In arithmetic we use symbols of number. A symbol is any sign for a quantity, which is not the quantity itself. If a man counted his sheep by

pebbles, the pebbles would be symbols of the sheep. At the present day, when most of us can read and write, we have acquired the convenient habit of using marks on paper, '1, 2, 3, 4,' and so on, instead of such things as pebbles. Our '1 + 1' is abbreviated into '2,' '2 + 1' is abbreviated into '3,' '3 + 1' into '4,' and so on. When '1,' '2,' '3,' & c., are used to abbreviate, rather improperly, '1 mile,' '2 miles,' '3 miles,' & c., for instance, they are called signs for concrete numbers. But when we shake off all idea of '1,' '2,' and c., meaning one, two, & c., of anything in particular, as when we say, 'six and four make ten,' then the numbers are called abstract numbers. To the latter the learner is first introduced on treatises on arithmetic, and does not always learn to distinguish rightly between the two. Of the operations of arithmetic only addition and subtraction can be performed with concrete numbers, and without speaking of more than one type of 1. Miles can be added to miles, or taken from miles.

Quantifications made in accounting are accompanied by verbal descriptions; such as 'inventory', 'plant and equipment', 'accounts payable', 'interest expense' and the like. That is, in the terminology of Jourdain, they are 'signs for concrete numbers' and the caution given of the need to distinguish between abstract numbers and concrete numbers therefore takes on particular significance. The arithmetic functions of addition and subtraction can only be applied to concrete numbers 'without speaking of more than one type'. Concrete numbers, representing common units, are capable of valid addition and subtraction.

Present accounting rules, and the conventional accounting practices upon which they are so often based, appear to treat all amounts expressed in a common currency as being of the same kind. However, such quantifications made in a common unit of currency may be of 'different types'. First, if the purchasing power of the currency is not stable over time then quantifications made at different points in time will be of 'different types' and not capable of valid addition or subtraction. Second, dollar quantifications may be used for a wide variety of attributes of particular items. If these attributes differ then they cannot be validly added to each other nor subtracted from each other.

Ignorance or deliberate violation of these principles is endemic to present accounting rules. Even within single regulatory statements the principles are abandoned. AASB 1019 requires that 'inventories shall be measured at the lower of cost and net realisable value on an item by item basis' (para. 11), thereby permitting costs to be added to net realizable values. AASB 1009 prescribes the disclosure of 'the amount due from customers for contract work', which is to be calculated as 'the aggregate of contract costs incurred and recognised profits; less the aggregate of recognised losses and progress billings' (para. 10.1).[9] The sum is an invalidly derived combination of actual costs, profits recognized on the basis of predicted contract outcomes and amounts invoiced to customers. Only by remote chance could it coincide with any amount legally due from customers.

Gibson and Goyen's (1996) survey of the Australian accounting standard identifies no fewer than seven different methods for valuing assets: cost, allocated cost, current cost, net realizable value, present value, recoverable amount and fair value. In addition, the authors identify nine further 'unclassifiable measures'. It is beyond contemplation that such a diverse array of valuation techniques could act as proxies for a single dated attribute and be capable of sensible aggregation. The result is that amounts for total assets reported in statements of financial position are devoid of empirical meaning.[10] They can be related in no meaningful way to any commercial phenomena or decision.

The propensity of accounting practice – as dictated by applicable regulations – to contradict the established findings of a variety of specialist fields has been explored by Chambers (1991a), noting that 'One object of critical and analytical scrutiny is to guard against the holding of incoherent or incompatible ideas on any matter, for, if one holds incompatible ideas, action cannot be reasonably directed towards any specific goal' (1991a: 9). However, in the case of accounting, the opportunity to benefit from the findings in other fields has been forsaken: 'The practice and teaching of accounting appear to draw very little on the fund of human knowledge that is the foundation of arts and skills similar, or related, to it' (1991a: 1). Instead of present accounting practices corresponding with the 'observations and conclusions of specialists in fields of knowledge and technology . . . that have a demonstrable bearing on elements of accounting thought and practice' (Chambers 1991a: 1), incongruence is more easily discerned.

Accounting rules and the need for coherence

In addition to the tendency of accounting rules to contradict the established findings of a variety of other fields, they show a marked propensity to contradict each other. As mentioned previously, inconsistencies between statements are contrary to the features of a system of knowledge. This is emphasized by Chambers (1955: 22) in an accounting context:

> The system should be logically consistent; no rule or process can be permitted which is contrary to any other rule or process. In particular the symbols used should have a sensibly uniform meaning throughout the system. In accounting this involves that equal things should be represented by equal symbols.

As is already evident from the examples that have been provided, this consistency is absent from the system of accounting defined by accounting rules. To require that different types of assets be valued using widely differing methods is to admit that no coherent specification of assets is operating. For example, application of the lower of cost and net realizable value rule leads to some inventory being represented at its acquisition (or calculated) cost and some at the amount of cash it could be converted to. This can only be explained in terms of the application of fundamentally incompatible ideas about what an asset is. The amount of cash paid for inventory and the amount of cash that would be received from its sale are antonymic qualities, both directionally and temporally. To use both to quantify a single class of assets is to deny that 'equal things should be represented by equal symbols'. The valuation choices offered by accounting standards further evidence this incoherence. Under AASB 1041 non-current assets may be recorded at cost or revalued to fair value. One represents a past cash outflow to purchase an asset, the other is an up-to-date representation of the cash that would be received if the asset was sold. While the accounting standard treats these as substitutable, logic denies that this process can be endorsed as a 'standard'.

Accounting rules and commercial phenomena

To those inconsistencies pertaining to accounting rules that have already been noted, one further may be added. It is an inconsistency of a fundamental kind and it underlies various aspects of the matters already discussed. While the circumstances of the world may change rapidly and be influenced by a multitude of events, accurate descriptions of phenomena existing at a specified time cannot be inconsistent with each other. The implication for accounting is an important one. If the elements in a set of financial reports were temporally consistent descriptions of phenomena, then those reports would automatically acquire a coherent quality. This is so simply because no factual statement can be contrary to any other factual statement. For example, assume that the actual historical cost of a motor vehicle is measured and found to be $14,000. The market value of a second motor vehicle is measured and found to be $10,000. These two statements are factual and not in contradiction of each other. Now suppose that the two amounts are added:

Historical cost of motor vehicle A	$14,000
Market value of motor vehicle B	$10,000
Total	$24,000

The total that has been calculated has no empirical connotation; indeed, it is bereft of meaning. This is the essential clue that logic has been violated: two factual statements have been combined but doing so has yielded a wholly fictitious sum. However, consider if the market value of each car was measured at a common time:

Market value of motor vehicle A	$12,000
Market value of motor vehicle B	$10,000
Total	$22,000

Here the aggregation yields a sum that *does* have empirical content. The sum of $22,000 is the amount that would be received by selling individually each of the two motor vehicles.

The point is that if each and every item in a set of financial reports is empirical – that is, has an actual counterpart in the commercial setting – those reports would automatically replicate the universal consistency that abides among all facts. This does not imply, of course, that accounting can be reduced simply to listing descriptions of phenomena. The questions of which facts should be reported and how they should be summarized and displayed remains. However, restricting the domain of accounting to actual events and circumstances would instil financial reports with the coherence that is innate to those events and circumstances.

Present accounting rules occasionally mandate the reporting of factual information, but more typically prescribe calculations that are dependent on inputs of a conjectural nature. Depreciation is a pertinent example. AASB 1021 'Depreciation' includes the following definitions (para. 14.1):

> depreciation expense means an expense recognised systematically for the purpose of allocating the depreciable amount of a depreciable asset over its useful life.

> depreciable amount means the historical cost of a depreciable asset, or other revalued amount substituted for historical cost, in the financial report, less in either case the net amount expected to be recovered on disposal of the asset at the end of its useful life.

The concepts referred to here are not presently discoverable facts: 'useful life' and 'net amount expected to be recovered' exist only in the imagination as conjectures about the future. In resorting to these imaginary concepts, the prescribed calculation of 'depreciable amount' abandons coherence in favour of the illogical. An imagined future sum ('the net amount expected to be recovered on disposal') is subtracted from an actual past cost (or its substitute) to yield an amount which, when allocated 'systematically', is said to reveal the magnitude of *present* depreciation expense. Encapsulated within this calculation is a portrayal of the strange twilight world which accounting rules inhabit; a world in which the real and unreal are not distinguished. Instead, facts and fancy are intermingled as if they were of one and the same kind. This occurs most obviously in connection with the ubiquitous cost allocations sanctioned by those rules: a process under which actual costs are prised free of their originating transaction and reassigned to become the calculated cost of something else.

Like all systems of instrumentation, the function of accounting is a descriptive one. Financial reports are represented as being *about* an entity. However, by mandating the disclosure of non-empirical quanta accounting rules abandon the entity and pursue a quite distinct subject: the expectations and idiosyncratic preferences of the preparers of the reports. Thus, for example, depreciation expense is a function of the opinions of company managers – their thoughts about an asset's useful life, its residual value at the end of that useful life and the expected pattern of consumption of its unknown future benefits – rather than being descriptive of an actual event that has affected an entity. When the imaginary is favoured over the factual an inherently undisciplined territory is entered. The world of the imagination tolerates all manner of contradictions. However, there are no inconsistencies among the facts of actual events and circumstances. A system of accounting based on factual subject matter would similarly have the capacity to be free of the debilitating inconsistencies that mark present accounting rules and the financial reports resulting from their application.

Summary

A variety of inconsistencies pertaining to accounting rules have been noted; with reference to the function of accounting, other fields of knowledge and between the prescriptions of individual accounting standards. These contradictions derive in substance from the dependence of accounting rules upon imaginary concepts rather than commercial phenomena. This dependence sacrifices the possibility of financial reports replicating the inherent consistency that abides within all factual information. In addition, it means that present accounting rules define a self-referential and closed system. That is, while it may be said that particular financial reports comply with those rules – or at least that breaches of the rules can be denied – no further general qualitative assessment can be made.

Yet, financial statements are universally depicted as descriptive statements. They are represented as portraying the financial position, profit or loss, total assets, total liabilities, and so forth, of particular entities. However, when prepared in accordance with accounting rules, these financial statements are fundamentally lacking in descriptive power. They have no truth-value independent of accounting rules. While it might be said that amounts variously shown for total assets, net profit, or equity have been determined in accordance with those rules, they do not describe any actual feature of an entity.

These circumstances deny that accounting rules constitute, or are derived from, a reliable body of accounting knowledge. The rules, and the financial reports resulting from their application, do not display the fundamental consistency that characterizes knowledge-based statements. On the contrary, compliance with accounting rules can only be achieved by abandoning the domain of reliable knowledge and entering an ethereal world where the basic principles of arithmetic are suspended, where there is no distinction between facts and conjectures, and where illogical calculations are presumed to yield meaningful outputs.

Conceptual frameworks and accounting rules

The inadequacies of present accounting rules have prompted various remedial prescriptions, among which a 'conceptual framework' for financial reporting comprising 'statements of accounting concepts' has been particularly prominent.[11] The AARF and AASB (1995b: paras 5 and 6) describe the nature of their conceptual framework project in the following terms:

> The primary purpose of Statements of Accounting Concepts is as a guide to the Boards when developing and reviewing Accounting Standards and other authoritative documents.
>
> Knowledge of the concepts the Boards use in developing Accounting Standards should assist preparers, auditors and other parties with an interest in Accounting Standards to understand better the general nature and purpose of information reported in general purpose financial reports. The concepts also may provide guidance in analysing new or emerging issues in the absence of applicable Accounting Standards.

Other benefits claimed to be associated with the project include accounting standards being 'more consistent and logical', 'increased international compatibility', standard setters being 'more accountable for their decisions', enhancement of the 'process of communication', and the setting of standards being made 'more economical' (AARF and AASB 1995b: para. 7).

The common theme in these claims is that a conceptual framework will provide the means by which the quality of accounting standards and related rules will be improved.[12] However, such an outcome can only be achieved if the basic failing of present accounting rules – that they are not disciplined by a correspondence with 'real-world' events and circumstances – is addressed.[13] Chambers (1996: 126) describes how a conceptual framework could function as a connecting link between accounting rules and the setting in which accounting is constituted:

> The domain to which accounting refers . . . is the set of financial relationships of an identified party with the rest of the world, and the laws, customs and constraints under which those relationships are managed. A conceptual framework would describe that domain, it would not prescribe. Prescriptions or precepts would emerge by inference from the descriptions, and only in that way.

Conceptual frameworks for financial reporting have not followed these precepts. The concepts statements are prescriptive and appear to be the consequence of an inverted design process that attempts to fit concepts to existing accounting rules.[14] Given the inconsistencies in these rules and their subordination of observed quanta in favour of diversely constituted calculations, the task has been a fruitless one. It has yielded an even more fundamental failing than the inconsistencies of accounting standards. Evaluation of the validity of particular statements can only proceed where the statements are expressed in accordance with the rules of a language. The statements have to be capable of being understood. It is this principle that is violated in present concepts statements.

SAC4 'Definition and recognition of the elements of financial statements' (AARF and AASB 1995a: paras 14 and 38) contains the following definition and recognition criteria for assets:

> 'Assets' are future economic benefits controlled by the entity as a result of past transactions or other past events; and
> 'control of an asset' means the capacity of the entity to benefit from the asset in the pursuit of the entity's objectives and to deny or regulate the access of others to that benefit.

> An asset should be recognised in the statement of financial position when and only when:
> (a) it is probable that the future economic benefits embodied in the asset will eventuate; and
> (b) the asset possesses a cost or other value that can be measured reliably.

Under this definition all assets are reduced to abstractions; when assets are 'future economic benefits' they are only ideas about the future. Thus, it would appear that a motor vehicle (an object) is not an asset, but the future economic benefits that it might generate are (for example, cash inflows from it being sold or used). But this idea is then immediately contradicted in the first of the recognition criteria which purports to *separate* the idea of future economic benefits from the idea of an asset. Recasting the recognition criteria by replacing 'asset' with 'future economic benefits' – as per the definition – creates a nonsense: 'it is probable that the future economic benefits embodied in the future economic benefits will eventuate'. Are future economic benefits an asset? Or are future economic benefits *embodied* in an asset (which presumably must then be something else)?[15]

At the heart of these contradictions is the fundamental confusion of 'a tree with its (expected, hoped for) fruit' (Chambers 1991a: 41). It renders the SAC4 definition of assets largely impotent. The quality of a definition subsists in how precisely it delineates the matter or item in contention. In specialized fields it is often necessary to adopt definitions that display greater precision than those employed in general usage. The word 'random' in common parlance connotes haphazardness or aimlessness. However, in the field of statistics a more precise meaning is invoked. The drawing of a 'random sample' requires that every item in the population under examination has an equal chance of being selected. Similarly, while the word 'evidence' has a broad meaning in common parlance, within a legal context it has a more precise meaning according to what may be admitted as evidence in a court of law. The SAC4 definition of assets – purportedly a specialist definition to be employed to guide the setting of accounting standards and the preparation of financial reports – is condemned by the fact that the ordinary dictionary meaning of the word displays far greater precision. In a financial setting the ordinary meaning of the word asset is unequivocal: 'any property or effects available to meet the debts of a testator, debtor, or company'.[16] The word asset also has a *figurative* meaning: 'a thing or person of use or value'. Remarkably, it is this figurative meaning of the word that bears most resemblance to the definition contained in SAC4. The incapacity of such a definition to assist in delineating the subject matter of financial reporting is described by Schuetze (1993b: 67):[17]

> The definition does not discriminate and help us to decide whether something or anything is an asset. That definition describes an empty box. A large empty box. A large empty box with sideboards. Almost everything or anything can be fit into it.

The confusion manifests further with regard to the requirement that the future economic benefits be 'controlled'. A motor vehicle (as an object) might well be said to be controlled – particularly where it is the subject of legal ownership. However, according to the SAC4 definition, an asset is not constituted by a legally enforceable property right or claim, but by control of the abstraction that is future economic benefits. This is a fanciful notion. First, it is not possible to have control of something that does not presently exist (that is, that resides in the future). Second, to control future economic benefits would suggest an ability to influence their magnitude. On practical grounds this is a remote possibility as it implies a capacity to control the market situations from which such benefits typically derive. It is presumably for these reasons that a highly idiosyncratic definition of control has been adopted that emphasizes only a capacity to benefit from the asset (SAC4: para. 14).[18] Further detracting from the clarity of the definition is the superfluous requirement that 'control' be a consequence of a past transaction or other past event. Control describes a relationship between two 'things' and it is inconceivable that such a relationship could be without an originating event. If there is 'control', there will always have been some past event that will have given rise to that situation.

The definition and recognition criteria for liabilities are similarly incorrigible (AARF and AASB 1995a: paras 48 and 65):

> 'Liabilities' are the future sacrifices of economic benefits that the entity is presently obliged to make to other entities as a result of past transactions or other past events.

> A liability should be recognised in the statement of financial position when and only when:

(a) it is probable that the future sacrifice of economic benefits will be required; and

(b) the amount of the liability can be measured reliably.

The distinguishing feature of the definition is that a liability comprises a present obligation to sacrifice economic benefits. The word 'obligation' describes an absolute concept that cannot be modified by degrees of probability: an entity either has an obligation to sacrifice economic benefits or it does not.[19] However, the first of the SAC4 recognition criteria attempts to attach a notion of probability to this absolute concept. Thus, while a liability is defined as comprising a present *obligation* to sacrifice future economic benefits, it is to be recognized when it is 'probable' that this sacrifice will be required. The juxtaposition of the definition and recognition criteria – necessary if an attempt is to be made to operationalize the SAC4 concept of a liability – give rise to the linguistic absurdity of a modified absolute: an 'obligation' that might only be 'probable'. There can be no such thing and attempts to apply this accounting 'concept' can only be expected to yield confusion. As with assets, the SAC4 definition of liabilities is surpassed in both precision and functionality by the normal dictionary meaning: 'the debts or pecuniary obligations of a person or company'.

The matters just discussed are not instances of mere grammatical infelicities, but of meaning being either absent or obfuscated.[20] Inevitably, the problem extends to the concept of equity. This has been defined in SAC4 as 'the residual interest in the assets of the entity after the deduction of its liabilities' (para. 78). It is, therefore, a concept infected with all of the failings embedded in the definitions and recognition criteria for assets and liabilities. This is accentuated by the revenue and expense components of equity having been defined without any specification of income or profit being adopted.

These observations disclose that recently promulgated statements of accounting concepts do not provide a framework that can be applied to improve the quality of accounting rules. The concepts show evidence of having been derived inductively from those rules and reiterate their primary failing: the generation of accounting numbers that do not correspond with actual features of the firms they purport to describe. Conceptual framework statements have nominated 'future economic benefits' to be the essential subject matter of accounting, with this term central to the SAC4 definitions of each of assets, liabilities, revenues and expenses. This directs attention away from the discoverable and measurable financial features of firms (such as solvency and capacity to command resources) in favour of personalized and unverifiable conjectures about the possible outcomes of economic activity. This emphasis has been adopted without any cogent demonstration of how it can contribute to improving the serviceability of accounting information. Instead, it appears to derive only from 'future economic benefits' being a sufficiently nebulous concept to not contradict the multifarious notions about the function and subject matter of accounting that are embedded in present accounting rules.

Résumé and conclusion

Rules are a ubiquitous feature of human societies and justified generally by a need to impose constraints on behaviour. Speed limits are enforced in order to promote safe driving. University statutes include provisions designed to ensure the integrity of students' academic work. Building codes prohibit certain practices and mandate others within that industry. In any setting, the justification for particular rules is contingent upon those rules serving the particular purpose for which they were established. As with other technologies, the purpose of accounting is a practical one: the provision of information that allows matters of financial significance relating to particular firms – solvency, liquidity and profitability – to be investigated, evaluated and compared. However, present accounting rules are not linked in any robust way to a clearly discernible function. More particularly, these rules are not based on any coherent specification of what is purported to be represented in financial reports, nor a clear quality control objective for those reports.

Underlying these failings is the absence of a design constraint emphasizing the need for accounting data to be derived from the actual events and circumstances – the contemporary selling prices of severable means, changes in the general level of prices, and the magnitudes of legally enforceable obligations – that determine the capacity for commercial action and define the consequences of such action from time to time. Instead, accounting rules place an emphasis on abstractions: future economic benefits, unamortized costs, allocated costs, predicted future cash flows, present values, and the like. As these have no empirical counterpart they cannot be independently authenticated. Moreover, this emphasis disengages accounting from the inherently disciplined task of describing phenomena in favour of personal conjectures about imaginary concepts. Conceptual frameworks for financial reporting have endorsed this situation, having enshrined 'future economic benefits' as the subject matter of accounting.

It is possible to have a 'knowledge of accounting rules'. However, this cannot be assumed to embody an accounting knowledge that yields a functional system of financial instrumentation. The distinction is an important one. The mandate of an accounting profession is not to produce and enforce accounting rules per se. It is to ensure the serviceability of financial information and search for means by which that serviceability might be advanced. Present accounting rules do not provide a means of discharging this mandate. The point was poignantly revealed in the lament of one entrepreneur:

> [Accounting] is becoming less useful as it becomes more regulated. I began to think of this issue as I signed my company's annual returns. For the first time in 30 years I could no longer say that I really understood the returns. And if I could not understand them, who could? I studied accounting at university, I have kept up to date with accounting issues and, more relevantly, I have an intimate knowledge of my

company's affairs. Yet the highly stylised figures in the returns I signed raised no glimmer of recognition. They no longer gave a picture, in any way to which I could relate, of the economic activity of which I am a part.

(Fallshaw 1993: 105)

It is within the context of this evaluation of accounting rules that an explanation for these rules is sought within the following chapter.

5 Explaining the proliferation of accounting rules

> The only way to resolve disputes about fictional concepts . . . is to legislate more and more statutes in more and more detail.
>
> (Sterling 1976: 86)

Introduction

Consistency – comprising internal coherence and correspondence with what is true – is the essential quality of any body of reliable knowledge. The fundamental and pervasive inconsistencies that mark present accounting rules deny any representation that they are the codification of a body of reliable accounting knowledge. Underlying these inconsistencies is a disjunction between the rules and commercial phenomena. Instead of techniques of observation and measurement, accounting rules typically prescribe algorithms for assigning monetary amounts to fictitious constructs. Financial reports are thus deprived of the coherence that would supervene if those reports were isomorphic with the actual financial features of firms. Moreover, the capacity of those reports to serve their widely stated function of informing financial decision making and accountability evaluations is compromised and the operation of any robust process of quality assurance denied. The system of accounting prescribed by present accounting rules is self-referential: it yields calculated outputs that have no truth-value independent of the rules that sanction those calculations.

The purpose of the present chapter is to explain the existence and continued proliferation of these rules. Various explanations for why accounting information needs to be regulated are already available in the accounting literature. Foremost among these is the notion that accounting information is an 'economic good' which is subject to 'market failures'. The corollary of this argument is that, in the absence of regulation, the quantity and quality of accounting disclosures will fall below the optimum defined by marginal cost-benefit parity. Accounting standards and other technical statements are viewed as part of the necessary regulatory response. However, such an explanation is incomplete if it is not accompanied by a demonstration of *how* these regulatory statements overcome the perceived 'market failures'. Technical deficiencies in any good or service are not remedied by regulatory statements per se, but by regulatory statements that redress those technical deficiencies. Paradoxically, formal accounting rules have often endorsed and perpetuated accounting practices that were already in common use, and which have been shown repeatedly to lack serviceability.

An additional – and generally unexplored – issue associated with accounting rules concerns the relationship between those rules and the exigencies of professional authority. The authority vested with professional groups is itself expected to ameliorate 'market failures'. That is, professional practitioners are relied upon to ensure the suitability and quality of the services they provide – not in response to informed consumer choice, but at their own initiative. This emphasis on self-regulation is accorded precedence over the conditions normally required to achieve market efficiency, with the right to supply 'professional' services typically restricted to those deemed qualified by relevant associations of practitioners. Fundamental to these arrangements is the presumption that professionals have exclusive and dependable expertise.

Present accounting rules and their extant justifications abide uneasily alongside these specifications of the nature and responsibilities of professional groups. Specifying that the rules are needed to overcome 'market failures' pertaining to the provision of accounting information appropriates, without replacement, the basic rationale for sanctioning accountants' professional authority. The contention that the rules are the *means* by which accountants administer their professional authority is similarly unconvincing. As discussed in the preceding chapter, accounting rules are not the instruments of cognitive intendance that justifies a professional jurisdiction.

In an effort to transcend these anomalies, this chapter seeks to provide an explanation for accounting rules that is consistent with the nature of those rules. Often, the proliferation of accounting rules and the strengthening of the onus to comply with them have been offered as evidence of accounting advancing as a professional occupation. The common portrayal is of an occupational group that takes its self-regulatory responsibilities seriously and is entitled to draw comfort from the volume of rules governing its technical practices. In challenging this conventional wisdom, present accounting rules are explained in this chapter as being evidential of, and consequential to, the accounting profession's failure to vindicate cognitively its mandate.

Two related propositions converge in support of this understanding. The first is that the proliferation of accounting rules is associated with the lack of a robust theoretical framework to guide the preparation of financial reports. Exactly what is intended to be represented by statements of financial position and performance cannot be discerned from either textbooks, professional pronouncements or, most significantly, the statements themselves. This lack of a coherent design specification has precipitated a reliance on rules: 'input standards' that are needed to direct the accounting task because the expected outcomes of that task are inadequately defined. The second proposition derives from accounting rules having remained subservient to the practices and subject matter of conventional accounting. This has perpetuated a focus on abstract notions, of which 'future economic benefits' is the paragon example. Since these abstractions are not congruent with any actual event or circumstance, only their calculation can be governed, and only by regulatory fiat. That is, the need for accounting rules is not independent of the style of accounting in use. If the contents of financial reports were determinable and verifiable by recourse to commercial evidence then accounting practice would have an innate disciplinary mechanism: establishing correspondence between the reports and the phenomena.

While these two propositions contribute to explaining the proliferation of accounting rules, they both condemn the state of accounting thought and practice. One emphasizes that accounting rules are a response to a lack of clarity in the purpose of the accounting task. The other emphasizes that correspondence with rules has been substituted for correspondence with phenomena. Neither accords with the requirements of an effective system of financial instrumentation. The culmination of these factors is that accounting rules have provided means by which the accounting profession has avoided rather than discharged its responsibility. The volume of rules creates the superficial impression of a rigorous quality control process operating, but it is the wrong kind of quality control. The quality of financial reports is dependent on how accurately those reports depict the financial circumstances of an entity and changes in those circumstances from time to time. Correspondence with commercial phenomena is the proper measure of quality in accounting, not compliance with rules.

The next section of the chapter reviews the historical development of accounting rules. This is followed by a critique of conventional rationales for these rules which draws attention to disparities between the rules and the functions they are said to perform. Proceeding from this critique, an explanation for present accounting rules that is consistent with their nature is developed. This emphasizes that accounting rules have proliferated because of deficiencies in accounting technique that originate from, and expose, the problematic nature of accountants' claims to cognitive authority.

The historical development of accounting rules

While their ascent to dominance is recent, the origins of present regimens of accounting rules can be traced to the first half of the twentieth century. In order to provide a background context for explaining these rules, an overview of their historical development is apposite. Consideration will be made of the historical development of accounting rules within Australia, Canada, the United Kingdom and the United States, along with 'international' accounting standards.[1] This is then followed by a review of the important themes that emerge from this examination.

Australia

The starting point for the development of formally promulgated accounting rules within Australia can be traced to 1946 when the ICAA issued a series of five 'Recommendations of Accounting Principles'. These were based on a set of recommendations that had been issued by the ICAEW and they 'retained the substance and in most respects the detail of the earlier English Recommendations' (Zeff 1973: 3). Two further recommendations were issued by the ICAA (one dealing with depreciation, in 1946 and one dealing with stock valuation, in 1948) before the series 'came to an abrupt halt' (Zeff 1973: 4). The process of issuing recommendations was not revived until 'In late 1963 and early 1964, the Executive Committee [of the ICAA] approved Recommendations on the presentation of the balance sheet and profit and loss account, the treatment of stock-in-trade and work in progress in financial accounts, and accountants' reports for prospectuses' (Zeff 1973: 9). In 1971 the ICAA decreed that the title of its accounting pronouncements would be changed to 'Statements on Accounting Practice'.

Forerunner bodies of CPA Australia also engaged in developing technical statements on accounting practice. In 1940, a committee of the Commonwealth Institute of Accountants 'prepared a pronouncement on cash discounts which was published in *The Australian Accountant*' (Zeff 1973: 40). Commencing in the 1950s, the ASA issued a series of 'practice bulletins' dealing with 'consolidated statements, hire purchase accounting, accounting for leases, and other subjects directly related to the preparation of financial statements' (Zeff 1973: 41). From the late 1960s the ASA and the ICAA began to collaborate on the development of technical statements and this included the joint establishment of the Accountancy Research Foundation in 1965 (reorganized and renamed the Australian Accounting Research Foundation (AARF) in 1974) (ASCPA: 1991).

Two significant developments occurred during the 1970s. First, under the newly adopted title of 'accounting standards', there was a significant increase in the volume of technical statements issued (Rahman 1992: 275). Second, an onus on members to comply with these statements was instigated. The catalyst for change appears to have been growing disenchantment with the performance of the accounting profession, manifesting particularly from a spate of corporate collapses (Birkett and Walker 1971). In May 1971 the ICAA issued *Statement K1* 'Conformity with Institute Technical Statements' which required Institute members to 'support' accounting standards, and the ASA followed with a similar statement in 1973 (Peirson and Ramsay 1983: 289). Initially the emphasis was on ensuring disclosure of material departures from accounting standards. However, the professional accounting bodies subsequently mandated – via their ethical codes and 'Miscellaneous Professional Statements' – that members comply with the standards. Under Statement APS1 'Conformity with Accounting Standards and UIG Consensus Views', issued jointly by the ASCPA and ICAA (1995: para. 10), 'Members are advised that . . . application of the standards set out in Accounting Standards is mandatory.'

Subsequent to the profession imposing its own compliance requirements on members, the authority of certain standards was extended through their formal recognition under the law applying to companies. The effect of this development has been to make non-compliance with the AASB series (previously the ASRB series) of standards in the preparation of the financial reports of certain companies a criminal offence.[2] The accounting profession was an active supporter of this development, as evidenced by the joint submission of the ICAA and ASA to the National Companies and Securities Commission in 1982:

> in the public interest of better financial reporting, accounting standards developed by the profession should be given legislative support in order to promote compliance with such standards, with appropriate provision for disclosure of justifiable non-compliance.
>
> . . . such legislative backing would be most simply and economically achieved by regulations which endorsed standards produced by the accountancy profession through its existing Accounting Standards Board, as augmented appropriately by direct representation of community interests, including government.
>
> ('Australian Accountancy Profession Joint Submission' 1982: 309)

The profession's petition to have its own technical statements granted the status of law without being subject to independent review was initially rejected. Instead, the ASRB was established in 1984 with authority to approve accounting standards submitted to it. However, the accounting profession appeared to achieve its objective of having its own technical statements made legally enforceable. According to Walker (1987: 282) the accounting profession was able to 'capture' the ASRB and 'influence the procedures, the priorities and the output of the Board'. This was reflected in the 'rapid "approval" in 1986 of many existing Australian Accounting Standards [i.e. standards developed by the profession] without any public explanation of the underlying rationale for those decisions' (Walker 1987: 283). While Walker's argument of regulatory capture has been challenged in part by Rahman (1992), the fact remains that *all* of the members of the ASRB were also members of either or both of the ASCPA and ICAA (Parker, Peirson and Ramsay 1987: 239).

The subsequent merger of the ASRB and the Accounting Standards Board of the profession-sponsored AARF to create the AASB appeared to formalize the substantial influence of the accounting profession over the promulgation of accounting rules that have legal backing in respect of incorporated entities. McGregor (1989: 48) described the merger as 'a joint venture between the government and the accountancy profession'. However, particularly in terms of technical input, it would appear that it resulted in the AASB's standard setting process being dominated by accounting professionals. According to Miller (1995: 14):

> the accounting profession could be perceived to be in a privileged position to get across its point of view. The AASB depends on the accounting profession for support staff, who are employees of the AARF which, in turn, is controlled by the ASCPA and the ICAA. Outside accounting circles it may be inferred that there is a cosy relationship between the AASB and the accounting profession.

Further developments in the Australian standard setting process occurred in the late 1990s in connection with the Corporate Law Economic Reform Program (CLERP). This included the establishment of a Financial Reporting Council to oversee the accounting standard setting process. In examining the possible impacts of these changes, Brown and Tarca (2001: 291) note:

> The post-CLERP AASB brings new people to the standard setting table, but some old issues remain. These include the desire to involve people other than accountants in standards setting, while recognizing that the technical expertise needed in standard setting resides predominantly with accountants.

In addition to the now voluminous AAS and AASB pronouncements (around 40 standards in each series, of which some are common), CPA Australia and ICAA members must comply with the 'Abstracts' issued by the Urgent Issues Group (UIG) which was established in early 1995. In the first seven years of its existence the UIG has issued over 40 abstracts. Technical guidance is also provided in the form of Statements of Accounting Concepts and Accounting Guidance Releases.

Canada

In the years following the Second World War, the Accounting and Auditing Research Committee (AARC) of the CICA commenced issuing technical bulletins for the guidance of its members (Zeff 1972: 275). Behind this activity lay 'a fear that one or more bodies outside the profession might begin to prescribe the form and content of financial statements if the profession did not assert itself' (Zeff 1972: 277). The process of issuing recommendations to members continued until 1973, with the various bulletins having been codified into a handbook format from 1968. The AARC was replaced in 1973 by the Accounting Standards Committee, but the new organization remained under the auspices of the CICA. A further reorganization occurred in 2000, with the establishment of an Accounting Standards Board. This operates under the supervision of an Accounting Standards Oversight Council which, in turn, is accountable to the board of directors of the CICA. The handbook of the CICA remains authoritative in connection with company financial reporting, being recognized under Section 44 of Part V the *Business Corporations Act and Regulations*: 'The financial statements shall . . . be prepared in accordance with the standards, as they exist from time to time, of the Canadian Institute of Chartered Accountants set out in the C.I.C.A. Handbook.' The effect of this recognition has been to make technical recommendations, promulgated at the behest of the Canadian accounting profession, legally enforceable with respect to certain classes of business organizations. This is emphasized by Richardson (1997: 644): 'It is noteworthy that the CA Handbook is not subject to any oversight or appeal procedure, thus the creations (and future additions and deletions) of a private document are part of public law.'

As well as containing accounting standards, the CICA Handbook has expanded to include Accounting Guidelines, Emerging Issues Committee Abstracts and Financial Statement Concepts.

United Kingdom

The ICAEW commenced promulgating recommendations on technical accounting matters in 1942. High levels of 'dissatisfaction in the late 1930s and early 1940s with accounting practices' (Zeff 1972: 10) provided the impetus for this action: 'A concern for the inadequacy of published accounts was sufficiently strong that it demanded resolution even in the midst of the war with Germany' (Zeff 1972: 9–10). The issuing of recommendations continued until 1969 but then, in 1970, the ICAEW established the Accounting Standards Steering Committee for the purpose of developing accounting standards with mandatory status. The agent of change had again been public criticism of accounting and accountants, with the ICAEW actions in setting up a standard setting apparatus resulting from it having been 'prodded by increasingly strident criticism in the financial press' (Zeff 1972: 33). Subsequently, five other accounting associations joined with the ICAEW in constituting the committee which was renamed the Accounting Standards Committee (ASC).[3] However, responsibility for the enforcement of standards was left with the individual associations.

The standard setting process in the United Kingdom was revised in 1990 with the establishment of the Accounting Standards Board (ASB). This replaced the ASC but has a semi-independent status. Mathews and Perera (1996: 123) comment that 'Like the FASB, the ASB is institutionally separated from the accounting bodies, and is funded by a number of sources in addition to the accounting bodies.' The ASB initially 'adopted all the extant SSAPs' (Blake 1995: 7), but has also exercised its authority to issue its own statements. The outcome is that the work of professional accountants in the United Kingdom is subject to the stipulations of more than 30 accounting standards, as well as the abstracts issued by the Urgent Issues Task Force and the guidance of other technical statements.

United States

While as early as 1909 a Special Committee on Accounting Terminology had been established by the American Association of Public Accountants (fore-runner to the American Institute of Certified Public Accountants (AICPA)), the beginnings of formally expressed accounting rules emerged most clearly in 1917. This involved the publication of a 'tentative proposal', entitled *Uniform Accounting*, which had been drafted by a committee of the American Institute of Accountants (AIA) and endorsed by the Council of that organiza-tion. It has been described as 'the first such statement in the English-speaking world that carried the approval of a body of public accountants' (Zeff 1972: 115). The statement was reprinted in 1918 as *Approved Methods for the Preparation of Balance Sheet Statements*, and revised and published in *The Journal of Accountancy* in 1929 under the title *Verification of Financial Statements*. During the period of its currency the statement 'became the standard authority for specifying the minimum requirements for balance sheet audits' (Davidson and Anderson 1987: 114).

The next significant development occurred in 1939 when the Committee on Accounting Procedures (CAP) of the AIA commenced publishing a series of bulletins intended to generate greater uniformity in accounting and audit-ing practice. This was a result of the Securities and Exchange Commission (SEC) having 'delegated its authority to establish accounting rules', and the CAP 'became seen as the principal source of "substantial authoritative support" in determining the methods used in preparing financial reports as well as the contents of such reports' (Young 1995: 176). These arrangements formally sanctioned the authority of the accounting profession: 'The jurisdic-tion of the profession included not only the audits of financial statements but also the establishment of "appropriate" measures of corporate performance and financial reporting more generally' (Young 1995: 176). However, this dele-gation of responsibility to the accounting profession did not occur without some unease. In particular, the Chief Accountant of the SEC made a comment about accountants that, for an occupational group claiming the status of a pro-fession, was especially derogatory: 'aside from the simple rules of double entry bookkeeping, there are very few principles of accounting upon which the accountants of this country are in agreement' (Blough 1937: 31).[4]

The bulletins issued by the CAP were essentially advisory in nature, and carried an acknowledgement that their authority derived from the extent to which they were generally accepted. Non-compliance was tolerated subject to the caveat that the burden for justifying such action fell upon those who adopted alternative procedures. A total of 52 bulletins concentrating on 'specific individual problems' (Davidson and Anderson 1987: 116) were issued until the committee was replaced by the Accounting Principles Board (APB) in 1959. Discontent with the performance of the CAP had prompted the change, but its replacement remained firmly under the control of the accounting profession because membership of the APB was 'restricted to members of the AICPA' (Sprouse 1983: 44). The stature of the 'Opinions' that the APB issued was progressively enhanced. Initially AICPA members were required to ensure that departures from Opinions were disclosed, either in footnotes to the financial statements or in the auditor's report. However, the revised *Code of Professional Ethics* issued by the AICPA in 1972 elevated the standing of the APB Opinions. Any departure from an Opinion was to result in a qualified audit opinion unless there were 'unusual circumstances' under which departure was necessary to ensure 'fair presentation'. Description and justification of the departure was required (Davidson and Anderson 1987: 118).

The issue of Opinions by the APB continued from 1959 until 1973 when the FASB was established. Underlying this change was a belief that the APB lacked independence and had failed to provide an adequate conceptual basis for the statements it had issued (Kessler 1972; Larson and Holstrum 1973). The formal instruments of change were two committees appointed by the AICPA (commonly known by the names of their respective chairmen as the Trueblood and Wheat committees). The Wheat committee developed the proposal for the FASB and upon the establishment of this body in 1973 the AICPA formally recognized it as the body to establish accounting principles and imposed on its members an ethical duty to comply with its pronouncements.

Since its inception, the FASB has promulgated a vast number of accounting rules, including more than 140 Statements of Financial Accounting Standards along with guides to their implementation in the form of interpretations and technical bulletins. Six statements of Financial Accounting Concepts have also been issued. Although ostensibly an independent body, the extent of the FASB's independence remains contested. According to the chairman of the committee that recommended the establishment and structure of the FASB, the 'primacy' of the accounting profession in the development of standards was 'assured' (cited in Kessler 1972: 381). Similarly, Tricker (1983: 39) refers to 'accounting standards developed by the accounting profession through the FASB but with the SEC as the final arbiter'. Buckley (1980: 58) states that 'The most distinguishing feature of accounting in America is the profession's *de facto* authority to establish accounting and auditing standards.' According to Lee (1996b: 187), 'the state . . . has tended to permit the accountancy profession to manage the standards process'. However, for Sprouse (1983: 47) the FASB 'is independent of any special interest group'. Puxty *et al.* (1987: 286) attribute to the accounting profession 'some influence' over the FASB, through lobbying and the supply of expertise. Turner and Jensen (1987: 36) acknowledge only a 'present incomplete understanding of the institutional interactions and relationships within the regulatory process'. In spite of the ambiguity surrounding the extent of its independence, the standing of the FASB now appears to be well established: 'there is recognition that the FASB must be the group to perform standard setting if it is to remain in the private sector' (Davidson and Anderson 1987: 122).

After examining the historical development of accounting rules in the United States, Zeff (1984: 466) concluded that 'Perhaps the strongest force was the profession's fear of active involvement by government in the establishment of accounting principles.'

International accounting standards

Accompanying the development of accounting rules within national jurisdictions has been the emergence, growth and influence of 'international' accounting standards. These have been issued by the International Accounting Standards Board (IASB – originally named the International Accounting Standards Committee) which was established in 1973 with a membership comprising national accounting bodies (Blake 1995: 9). The IASB has issued over 40 International Financial Reporting Standards (previously titled International Accounting Standards) which have exerted influence on accounting practice in a variety of ways: being adopted as national requirements without modification, providing the basis for development of national standards, as an international benchmark in countries that develop their own accounting standards, through the endorsement of regulatory authorities and stock exchanges, and by application by individual companies (Kropp and Johnston 1996: 284).

This internationalization of accounting rules has drawn its rationale from a claimed need for accounting practices to be consistent across national boundaries. The AASB, for example, has adopted a policy of 'international harmonization', with the intended outcome that compliance with AASB standards will also ensure compliance with IASB standards. The justifications offered for this policy include that increasing the comparability of financial reports prepared in different countries will improve the quality of investment and credit decisions, remove barriers to international capital flows and reduce financial reporting costs (AASB 2002: para. 7).

Review

The overview of the historical development of formally issued accounting rules that has been provided permits some common themes to be identified. First, the original initiatives for promulgating such rules came from associations of accountants (albeit typically in response to external pressures). This is important, as it reveals that while the extent of influence of these organizations within some standard setting jurisdictions is now a matter of debate, they clearly were the originators of the general style of this form of regulation. The concept of 'accounting standards' as they are known today was devised and legitimated by the accounting profession.

Second, accounting associations have retained various degrees of influence over accounting rule-making. The extent of this influence is not always easily discerned, but it would appear to be strong in Canada and perhaps only slightly less so in Australia. Present standard setting processes in the United

Kingdom and the United States are often said to be independent of the organized accounting profession, but such perceptions are not universal. Also, in both countries accounting standard setting was clearly dominated by the accounting profession in the years prior to the establishment of the ASB and the FASB. In any case, influence over the setting of accounting standards is not confined to just present institutional processes. Having established and legitimated the idea and style of present accounting rules, associations of accounting professionals have exerted an influence that transcends current institutional arrangements. This is evident, for example, in Australia and the United Kingdom. Irrespective of the nature of current standard setting processes, it is clear that within both of these jurisdictions substantial proportions of present accounting standards were created by the accounting profession. Prior to the reorganization precipitated by the CLERP proposals only one of the standards made legally enforceable with respect to companies within Australia – that dealing with foreign currency – came from a source other than the accounting profession (Godfrey, Hodgson and Holmes 1997: 329). One of the first actions of the 'independent' ASB in the United Kingdom was to adopt all of the SSAPs that had been developed by the accounting profession. More generally, no standard setting body – independent or otherwise – has shown a willingness or ability to escape the dominance of the accounting profession's conventional accounting techniques, with their emphasis on diverse valuation bases, cost allocations and the 'matching' of costs and revenues. This has been so in spite of the analytical and empirical evidence revealing the unserviceability of those techniques.

Third, concerns about the quality of financial reporting and the performance of the accounting profession have provided the impetus for the continued issuance of formal accounting rules and changes to the structures of the bodies responsible for their promulgation. The significance of this observation is most apparent when it is considered in conjunction with the preceding point. That is, the era of accounting standard setting has engendered changes of an institutional rather than a technical nature: accounting practices carrying only the imprimatur of convention have been enshrined in formally sanctioned documents, obligations to comply with the provisions of those documents have been imposed, and the bodies responsible for issuing accounting rules have been periodically changed in name, structure and status.

Fourth, accompanying the development of accounting standard setting apparatuses has been a change in how accounting regulation is perceived. Emphasis on the propriety of the *process* by which rules are formulated has been accorded priority over their technical fitness for use of those rules:

> Observation of accounting standard-setting in various countries suggests that accounting standards are rules established as *social conventions*, the authoritative character or validity of which results from the legitimacy of the process whereby they are developed and promulgated.
>
> (Archer 1997: 237, emphasis in original)

Behind this outcome is found only the explanation that technical accounting regulations have 'economic consequences' (Hines 1983, 1987; Solomons 1978, 1983; Watts and Zimmerman 1978; Zeff 1978). That this should have emerged as a revelation of the 1970s is curious given that, as Most (1993: 7) notes, 'if accounting does not have economic consequences, it has no purpose'. Further, as the quotations presented in Box 4.1 reveal, accountants have long defined their discipline precisely in terms of it having repercussions for the allocation of economic resources. However, as summarized by Solomons (1978: 65), these *consequences* have now also been recognized as a legitimate *determinant* of accounting practice:

> to judge from current discussions of the standard-setting process, accounting can no longer be thought of as nonpolitical. The numbers that accountants report have, or at least are widely thought to have, a significant impact on human behavior. Accounting rules therefore affect human behavior. Hence, the process by which they are made is said to be political. It is then only a short step to the assertion that such rules are properly to be made in the political arena.

Australian standard setters no longer even purport that the process of formulating standards should be exclusively guided by a search for representationally faithful accounting. Instead, the 'economic consequences' of standard setting are expressly required to be considered and, quite possibly, privileged in standard setting deliberations (Collett 1995).

Fifth, the number of rules has continued to increase and shows no sign of abating. This is most evident in the output of the FASB, but in other jurisdictions the volume of new regulations also continues to exceed the occasional few that are withdrawn. In the space of only a few decades – and growing from the relatively humble beginnings of technical recommendations – an 'ever-thickening scatter of rules' (Gerboth 1987: 98) has come to occupy a position of dominance in contemporary accounting.

Progress towards this outcome did not occur without controversy. While this has been evident in debates over the content of specific accounting standards and the processes by which they are formulated, there has also been evidence of some underlying discontent with the basic proposition that accounting practitioners should be subject to rules imposed by fiat. Olson (1982: 61) documents that there was initial resistance from members of the AICPA to the promulgations of the APB: 'They believed that the development of detailed rules would reduce auditing to a mechanical function rather than a professional activity.' In Canada, the AARC decided initially not to issue regulations on auditing on the grounds that 'publication of such bulletins has a tendency to detract from the professional nature of the practice of public accounting', noting that 'no other profession lays down rules as to the manner in which work is normally to be performed by its members' (Dominion Association of Chartered Accountants 1950: 10).[5] Similar sentiments prevailed in Scotland:

Through the years, the Scottish Institute's Council has elected not to issue guidance statements to members on technical accounting and auditing questions. . . . The reason most frequently given for the Council's policy of abstaining from the issuance of official guidance on accounting and auditing is that such matters are best left to the integrity and judgement of Institute members, in the light of the quality of their apprenticeship training and subsequent experience.

(Zeff 1972: 51)

In 1961, a committee of the ICAS concluded that 'the more authoritative the recommendation is the more it must tend to rigidity, to the discouragement of future progress and to the embarrassment of members who happen to disagree with it' (ICAS 1961: para. 44). An editorial in *The Australian Accountant* ('Statements on recommended accounting practice' 1971: 245) also recognized some ambivalence concerning the desirability of technical rules:

Opinions on the merits of mandatory or, at least, recommended standard practices are still divided. There are those who contend that such practices tend to force the profession into an intellectual strait-jacket, stifling thought, experimentation and hence progress.

Such reservations, however, appear to have offered only minimal resistance and accounting standards have clearly become 'an established part of the financial reporting scene' (Solomons 1983: 107).

Conventional explanations for accounting rules

Given the prominence of formally promulgated accounting rules, a cogent explanation and justification for their existence and continued proliferation might have been expected. Review of the relevant literature fails to satisfy such anticipation. Instead, it offers only general rationales for regulating accounting information that do not explain accounting standards and related rules in particular. No demonstration has been made of how present accounting rules contribute to fulfilling the regulatory need which is claimed to provide their justification. Failure to articulate clearly the nature of the regulatory responsibilities which are the proper companion of professional authority has added to this confusion. The contribution of 'professional knowledge' to governing the quality of accounting information and how this interacts with accounting rules has not generally been explicated.

The imposition of some form of public regulation over the financial reports of business organizations emerged with the first general laws relating to companies. The *United Kingdom Joint Stock Companies Act of 1844* required, *inter alia*, that a balance sheet be prepared for shareholders and that an auditor be appointed to audit it. These provisions encapsulate the basic issues that have been the focus of subsequent debate over the regulation of accounting information: what, if any, information should companies be required to disclose? What means, if any, should be employed to regulate the quality of that information? A lack of consensus in responding to these questions is evident in the history of the regulation of accounting information and the debates that have shaped that history.[6]

The argument that the regulation of accounting information is unnecessary is developed from an analysis that posits accounting information as an 'economic good' (Leftwich 1980: 193) and the firm as 'the nexus of a set of contracting relationships' (Jensen and Meckling 1976: 311). This perspective depicts shareholders, creditors and other interested parties as having incentives to demand accounting information for the purposes of making investment decisions and accountability evaluations. In turn, company managers are deemed to have incentives to respond to this demand. That is, they are willing to supply accounting information on the grounds that it will assist in attracting and retaining investment funds that will aid the continued existence and future expansion of the company. In addition, company managers may have incentives to report on their stewardship; to seek 'monitoring' contracts which 'often involve accounting and auditing' (Watts and Zimmerman 1986: 184). Those seeking information and those able to supply it are thereby deemed to have a stimulus to contract voluntarily for the provision of specified financial reports. Moreover, according to this analysis, this unregulated interaction will result in the optimal quantity and type of information being provided at the optimal price. Even the issue of audit is claimed to be capable of resolution in this manner. Company managers may benefit from subjecting themselves to 'monitoring' contracts and therefore appoint an auditor voluntarily (Watts and Zimmerman 1986: 184). Alternatively, shareholders may organize and request the appointment of an auditor if they believe that the marginal benefits arising from this action will exceed the marginal costs. Thus, according to this perspective, 'The auditor checks that the numbers used in contractual provisions have been calculated using accepted procedures and whether the contractual provisions have been breached' (Watts and Zimmerman 1986: 312). The need for public regulation of accounting information is thereby questioned. In support of this 'anti-regulation' stance Watts and Zimmerman (1986: 197) point to 'a long history of voluntarily supplied audited corporate accounting reports'. Other opponents of regulation draw on related arguments pertaining to a lack of demonstrated positive effects (for example, Stigler 1964a, 1964b) or the costs exceeding any benefits that are generated (for example, Benston 1980, 1982a, 1982b; Leftwich 1980).

The counter-argument – that there is a need for some form of public regulation of accounting information – is derived typically from the same form of analysis adopted by those who oppose regulation. That is, accounting information is again depicted as an economic good and at issue is whether the socially optimal information set will be produced in the absence of any external regulatory force. Prescriptions for regulatory activity are constructed around propositions that there are 'failures' in the 'market' for accounting information. The following summary of 'market failures' said to exist in connection with accounting information is derived from Leftwich (1980):

- Accounting information displays the features of a public good. That is, 'consumption of the good by one individual does not diminish the quantity available for others' (Leftwich 1980: 198). This manifests in a disincentive to supply accounting information as suppliers are not fairly compensated for their efforts.
- Management have a monopoly control over information and, in the absence of regulatory intervention, will exploit this circumstance in the usual manner attributed to monopolists: restricting supply and selling at a high price.
- Investors are 'naive' and may be exploited on account of their inability to comprehend and deal with the complexities of accounting information.
- Investors are subject to 'functional fixation' and unable to appreciate the importance and effects of different accounting policies.
- Conventional historical cost-based accounting reports contain 'meaningless numbers' which need to be corrected by regulatory intervention.
- Conventional accounting practice is characterized by a diversity of procedures (for example, the variety of techniques available for calculating depreciation) and this makes it difficult for the users of financial reports to make necessary comparisons. It also offers scope for managers to conceal relevant information through the selective adoption of accounting techniques.
- Accounting policy choices are not made on objective grounds.

The accounting literature contains significant discussion – both explicit or implicit – of these alleged failures in the 'market' for accounting information (Briloff 1972, 1981; Chambers 1973b; Chambers, Ramanathan and Rappaport 1978; Leftwich 1980; May and Sundem 1976; Okcabol and Tinker 1993; Solomons 1983; Watts and Zimmerman 1986; Whittington 1993). With reference to this debate Laughlin and Puxty (1983: 453) conclude that 'The great majority of writers on regulation assume that it is necessary, justifying the need on the basis of economic disequilibrium arguments.'[7] A substantial body of empirical evidence supports these arguments: 'Accounting history is littered with examples of financial information used as a means of deception' (Edwards 1989: 143). Further, it was these deceptions that provided the impetus for regulatory action (Edwards 1989: chs 12–16). Thus, the 'long history of voluntarily supplied audited accounting reports' (Watts and Zimmerman 1986: 197) is not also a history of the provision of serviceable financial information. As in many other contexts, the mere fact that commodities are supplied does not negate arguments that their quality should be regulated.

In more practical terms, there is no doubt that the protagonists of regulation have won the debate in the sense that accounting information is regulated. Whittington (1993: 316) interprets this as providing further evidence of the *need* for regulation: 'Empirically, we may call upon the supporting evidence that accounting and auditing are, in fact, regulated in some form in all advanced free market economies, and that this system seems to have widespread support from accountants, auditors and users of accounting information.'

Mandatory technical rules, such as accounting standards, are viewed as an integral component of this regulation:

> Advocates of a regulatory approach to accounting seem to believe that market failures or anomalies and perceived asymmetry in regard to the quantity and quality of financial information available to various interested parties, which lead to a decline in investor confidence, can be rectified through regulation. Furthermore, researchers have indicated that regulation, particularly through accounting standards, may be useful to preparers, auditors and regulatory agencies as it provides clear guidelines for reporting, verification and overseeing purposes, respectively.
>
> (Mathews and Perera 1996: 115)

It is at this point that the debate over accounting regulation has lost clarity and impetus. The need to protect the users of accounting information has been offered as the rationale for accounting rules. However, this provides a rationale only for rules which serve that purpose; rules that endow financial reports with a functional fitness for use which would otherwise be lacking. The nature of accounting rules and the processes by which they are formulated contradict this expectation. There is no robust link between the posited need for accounting rules and the rules themselves, and this discrepancy is evident in a variety of contexts.

Rather than being guided by an explicit design framework that would ensure their capacity to serve as a consumer protection device, accounting rules are often justified only by the inferior criterion of promoting 'consistency'. Thus, for example, Solomons (1983: 107) argues in favour of accounting standards on the ground that 'there can be no return to a state where, from a multiplicity of accounting methods, the managers of each business enterprise can be left entirely free to choose whichever one suits them'. Whittington (1993: 318) pursues a similar proposition: 'The need for regulation arises from the need for a standard form of financial reporting' (see also Henderson 1985: 51, 1988: 6; Kessler 1972: 379; Langfield-Smith 1990: 6–7; Peirson and Ramsay 1983: 289). The premise is that the quality of accounting information is primarily a function of commonality; that a method of accounting is made serviceable by being prescribed for all entities. Notwithstanding the fact that present accounting rules do not in any case eliminate choices in accounting method, consistency is an inadequate criterion of quality for accounting rules. There is nothing to be gained – and much to be lost – from consistently applying defective methods of accounting. In other regulatory processes intended to protect consumers, consistency is not the criterion that is to the fore. The purpose of specifying safety standards for motor vehicles is not the manufacture of identical units of output. It is to ensure that all motor vehicles have basic safety features that protect consumers who lack the expertise to make their own judgements on such matters. Yet, in connection with accounting rules, the criterion of uniformity has often been substituted for serviceability. A further example of this emphasis concerns the 'international convergence and harmonization' policy of the AASB, which is intended 'to assist in the development of a single set of accounting standards for world-wide use' (AASB 2002: para. 2). It is a search for sameness that remains unmatched by a search for improved technical quality.

The processes by which accounting rules are developed also contradict the notion that they can be justified as instruments of consumer protection. Accounting rules can only function to protect the users of accounting information when their development proceeds as a technical task overseen by those with relevant expertise:

> Only those who know well the impact and the technicalities of profes-
> sional work can have a legitimate right to determine its style. Medical,
> legal, engineering principles are not established by democratic vote or
> deliberation of the technically uninformed. Neither should accounting
> principles be so established.
>
> (Chambers 1972: 161)

In defiance of this, concerns over the processes by which accounting rules are developed have been accorded precedence over their technical quality. That is, accounting rules are justified by the 'due process' of their development rather than their technical attributes.[8] The users of financial reports, however, are not protected by pluralism in rule-making processes; they are protected by the application of accounting methods which yield a reliable system of financial instrumentation. Paradoxically, while 'market failures' are said to cause technical deficiencies in accounting information, accounting rule-making purports to remediate those deficiencies by procedural rather than technical propriety.

However, the most significant contradiction between accounting rules and the arguments advanced in their defence is found in the nature of those rules. As discussed in the previous chapter, present accounting rules lack functional coherence. The notion that these rules can be justified by their capacity to overcome 'failures' in the 'market' for accounting information is unsubstantiated. Their application does not yield a reliable, serviceable, or even understandable, commodity. Justifying accounting rules as a necessary consumer protection device requires that the rules be responsive to consumer needs. But, in what way does the asymmetry of valuing inventory at the lower of cost and net realizable value protect the users of financial reports? The same question, of course, might be asked in connection with tax-effect accounting, the diverse array of asset valuation practices, the representation of costs as assets and the prescriptions for the apportionment of costs between assets and expenses.

No answers to these questions are to be found in the accounting standards themselves. Instead, these documents are generally devoid of explanation for how the rules they prescribe aid the decision-making processes and account-ability evaluations of the users of financial reports. Consider, for example, the 'purpose' of AASB 1019 (para. 4.1):

> The purpose of this Standard is to:
> (a) specify the method of measuring inventories, including the manner in which costs are to be assigned to inventories
> (b) specify the recognition of expenses relating to inventories
> (c) require specific disclosures to be made in relation to inventories.

No justification is offered beyond the implication that the imposition of particular practices by fiat is beneficial. Other standards offer only an asser-tion of usefulness, typified by that contained in the original version of AASB 1028 'Accounting for employee entitlements' (as issued 1994: para. iii):

> general purpose financial reports shall provide information useful to users for making and evaluating decisions about the allocation of scarce resources. Such decision making is likely to involve users in assessing the performance, financial position and financing and investing activities of the company or economic entity. The establishment of an accounting stan-dard for employee entitlements will assist users in making these assess-ments by providing relevant and reliable information about employee entitlements in the accounts and consolidated accounts and by ensuring that employee entitlements are accounted for on a consistent basis.

The utility of accounting standards is thus represented as being innate: 'The establishment of an accounting standard ... *will* assist users by providing relevant and reliable information' (emphasis added). Logically, the assertion needs to be of a different form: an accounting standard will assist users *if* its application results in the provision of relevant and reliable infor-mation. This, of course, then demands demonstration of how and why the prescriptions made will achieve this end. Instead, technical accounting rules are represented as having an a priori capacity to advance the serviceability of accounting information. That is, rule-making is presumed to have a func-tional role that is independent of the quality of the rules.

The counter to the criticisms that have been presented is likely to be of the form that even though present accounting rules contain technical defi-ciencies, their application makes the quality of financial reports better than would otherwise be the case. That is, while accounting rules do not overcome the effects of 'market failures' they make some worthwhile contribution towards that end. However, such an assertion overlooks three important matters. First, given that present accounting rules *mandate* deficient proce-dures there is no assurance that in the absence of those rules improved methods of accounting would not come to the fore. This is particularly so if an overall quality standard remained operational:

> Consumers and consumer protection agencies concentrate on products, not the processes from which they emerge. Possibly the specification of serviceability evokes a natural selection mechanism by which a common production process emerges. If it does – then so be it. If not – does it matter? If there were a number of different ways of achieving the same thing, it would not matter if one producer used one method and a second chose another. Accounting regulation might well benefit from adopting a similar approach.
>
> (Clarke, Dean and Oliver 1997: 244)

Second, the argument that present accounting rules are 'better than nothing' overlooks the adverse consequences associated with enshrining those rules in mandatory and officially endorsed statements. The risk is that this will insti-tutionalize those practices – indeed, may have already done so – and thereby deflect attention from a search for means of improving upon those practices. Third, a 'better than nothing' rationale suggests a tolerance of mediocrity that is fundamentally incompatible with the onus of professional responsi-bility. It is this 'professional' perspective on accounting rules that is explored in the following section.

Professionalism, accounting rules and commercial phenomena

The elevated occupational authority that characterizes professional groups is a particular kind of regulatory device which is relied upon to overcome market failures arising from asymmetries in the knowledge and skill of the suppliers and consumers of specified services. While consumers may confidently make their own selection of everyday grocery items, the purchase of dental services, for example, has an entirely different context. Here it is the provider of those services who has greatest influence in specifying the needs of the consumer and how they are to be satisfied. This inversion of the supplier–consumer relationship has its most extreme expression in the traditional, and still respected, concept of 'doctor's orders', under which the consumer submits to the direction of the supplier. To act professionally is to discharge properly this elevated occupational authority; to accept responsibility for the services that are provided and ensure their propriety. Achievement of this outcome is contingent upon the authority of the providers of professional services being underwritten by specialized expertise.

An intention to rely on professional authority as the primary means of disciplining the quality of accounting information is evident in the law relating to companies. Traditionally such legislation has specified the general nature of financial reports that must be prepared but not the detailed technical accounting procedures to be applied in their preparation. Instead, general qualitative standards have been provided. The first companies legislation, the *United Kingdom Joint Stock Companies Act of 1844*, required the preparation of a 'full and fair' balance sheet (section 35). The term 'true and correct' appeared in the regulations of the *Joint Stock Companies Act of 1856*. The *Railways Companies Act of 1867* provided for the appointment of an auditor whose duty was 'to ascertain that the balance sheet of the company contained a *full and true* statement of the financial condition of the company' (Lee 1979: 154, emphasis in original). In the United States, the general qualitative standard of 'present fairly' emerged in the audit reporting requirements of the New York Stock Exchange in 1933 (Lee 1994: 35). The term 'true and fair' was adopted in the *United Kingdom Companies Act of 1948* (section 149), along with the requirement that company auditors be professional accountants (Lee 1994: 34). This United Kingdom legislation also provided 'the basis of modern Australian companies legislation' (McGregor 1992: 68).

The effectiveness of general qualitative standards of the kind referred to was, and remains, predicated on there being a body of accounting knowledge that would give effect to those standards. The accounting profession has been relied upon to provide that knowledge, as explained by Peirson and Ramsay (1983: 287 and 288, emphasis in original) with specific reference to the Australian situation:

> *The Companies Act* does *not* legislate accounting measurement standards and cases decided by the courts have *not* established any general accounting measurement standards which must be applied in order to produce a true and fair view. . . . [T]he accounting methods underlying the reports remained the responsibility of the accounting profession.

It is difficult to envisage a profession being favoured with a more congenial general quality standard for its work than 'true and fair'. The term contains felicitous allusions to scientific rationality ('true') and moral fortitude ('fair') that seem ready made for capturing public confidence. A coherent specification of the technical qualities of 'true and fair' financial statements would have justified the regulatory faith placed with the accounting profession: 'if accountants could demonstrate their possession of systematic knowledge and hold that knowledge with conviction, no other authority could interpose in matters of professional (accounting) knowledge and judgement' (Wolnizer 1987: 178).

However, with its authority derived principally from social rather than epistemic factors and armed with technical practices carrying only the imprimatur of convention, the accounting profession has struggled to discharge its mandate. Financial reporting failures were the inevitable result and precipitated calls for formally stated accounting rules, commencing in the United Kingdom and United States:

> In the United Kingdom in the early 1930s, the Royal Mail case was followed by considerable questioning by accountants about the desirability of explicit, common professional standards; by the establishment of committees of various accounting Institutes to consider the question; and in 1942 by the publication of *Recommendations on Accounting Principles* by the Institute of Chartered Accountants in England and Wales. In the United States, the financial failures of the 1930s and the scandal associated with the Kreuger, McKesson and Robbins, and other cases, were followed by substantial restatement by the American Institute of Accountants of earlier promulgations on the verification of financial statements; by a statement of the broad principles of financial statement preparation and presentation; and in 1939 by the establishment of a full-time research staff. . . . By the early 1940s accountants in both countries were organizing themselves to answer public criticism as a body and, if possible, to anticipate and avoid such criticism by developing and promulgating common standards.
>
> (Birkett and Walker 1971: 97–8)

The pattern was repeated in Australia:

> The impetus for change was largely provided by both political and economic factors. The 1960s saw a significant number of company failures, even after auditors had certified accounts as 'true and fair'. Public concern, media pressure and the threat of government intervention prompted closer cooperation between the ICAA and the ASCPA, with the joint formation, in 1965, of the Australian Accounting Research Foundation (AARF) to carry out research and issue accounting standards.
>
> (Godfrey, Hodgson and Holmes 1997: 328)

These observations are significant for revealing that the programme of issuing accounting standards was born of a crisis in accounting practice and marked the response of the accounting profession to circumstances that threatened its status. Birkett and Walker (1971: 136) describe the alternative response that the deficiencies in accounting technique made obvious by company collapses might have engendered: 'What was required was a new type of response – critical research into the profession's standards, into all that accountants had traditionally done, into the "tenets of professional faith".' However, 'the profession's response in this regard was negligible' (1971: 136).

Instead, rules have been promulgated and offered as evidence of technical progress that strengthens accountants' professional claim. In 1971, when the move to reliance on formal rules began in earnest in Australia, an editorial in *The Australian Accountant* dealing with statements on recommended accounting practice announced: 'such statements are aimed at attaining a higher level of professional competence and accomplishment' ('Statements on recommended accounting practice' 1971: 245). Such an outcome could only be achieved if the statements were vehicles of technical reform; that is, they contributed to overcoming the deficiencies and anomalies of conventional practice. Instead, accounting rule-making has taken conventional accounting practices – emphasizing the use of actual and reallocated historic costs – and enshrined them in statements with mandatory application. The belief, apparently, has been that deficient accounting practices could somehow be made serviceable if they were expressed as formal edicts.

Thus, accounting rules have perpetuated the notion that assets are conjectures about the future that can be expressed meaningfully in terms of deferred historical costs. Similarly, profit determination has remained beset by the convention of 'matching': 'The ideal is to match costs incurred with the effects attributable to or significantly related to such costs' (Paton and Littleton 1940: 15). It is, however, an unworkable ideal as it typically involves a fundamental *mismatch*: trying to associate *known* past costs with *unknown* future revenues. The proliferation of accounting rules is not independent of this continued reliance on conventional accounting ideas, which are not disciplined by a need for financial reports to be descriptive of the presently existing circumstances of firms and changes that have occurred in those circumstances from time to time.

Were financial reports to describe actual features of firms then the process of preparing those reports would provide its own disciplinary mechanism: the degree of correspondence between the reports and the phenomena they purport to represent. If the reported profit figure of an entity was required to correspond with the actual change in that entity's capacity to command resources (that is, its real spending power increment) over a specified period of time, then particular events would either have, or not have, implications for that change. In addition, those events having implications would be of particular magnitudes. In this way a clear specification of the actual feature of a firm that a profit figure was intended to describe – that is, a single rule – could deliver a discipline to the determination of periodic profit far exceeding that offered by the multiplicity of rules that apply currently.

The same argument applies in connection with the statement of financial position. Defining assets in terms of cash, or resources with a current equivalence to cash, provides an unequivocal test for establishing what is, and what is not, an asset.[9] It has a potency for regulating this aspect of accounting practice that goes well beyond that of present accounting rules with their variety of recognition criteria and valuation practices. Specifying that liabilities are the legally enforceable obligations of an entity existing at balance date would, similarly, provide a more objective criterion for recognizing and valuing this financial statement element than the inconsistent prescriptions of present rules which mandate speculations on the likelihood and magnitude of future dispositions of economic benefits.

Present accounting rules do not, as has often been represented, have their genesis in 'failures' in the 'market' for accounting information. They do not provide robust means for overcoming those failures and, in any case, a framework for regulating accounting information preceded these rules and remains current. This has involved a general specification of the accounting information required to be reported by companies and a general qualitative standard to be applied to that information. Responsibility for operationalizing this general qualitative standard came to be vested with the accounting profession which in many jurisdictions has maintained a monopoly right to attest to whether the general qualitative standard is achieved in particular circumstances. The accounting profession's continued failure to enforce effectively that general qualitative standard – and instead persist with its conventional technical practices – lies behind the present proliferation of accounting rules. These conventional practices defy the requirements of a serviceable system of financial instrumentation. Data crucial to the determinant of the financial position and progress of firms – in particular, the price changes that affect an entity's capacity to participate in exchange transactions – are largely ignored. Instead, the magnitudes of historical transactions are persisted with long after their relevance to informed financial action has passed. The process of allocating and reallocating these magnitudes does not, and cannot, restore their relevance.

Rather than evidence the legitimacy of the accounting profession's claim to professional status, present accounting rules are a manifestation of its adherence to conventional practice and the inadequacy of that practice. This 'system' of accounting has no coherent output specification: the purpose and significance of the statements of financial position and performance it yields remain unspecified. Guided by only such vagaries as 'matching', an idiosyncratic rule for valuing inventories, a general preference for historical rather than up-to-date values and uncertain criteria for recognizing transactions, conventional accounting practice is a disordered activity. Present accounting rules have not provided an alternative to that practice. Instead, with few exceptions, they are concerned with perpetuating it. Historical cost valuations have been sanctioned (with some idiosyncratic modifications) and prescriptions that seek to standardize the matching of costs and revenues predominate. The number of rules committed to sustaining these conventions is an index of their underlying inadequacy.

While it remains anchored to convention, accounting rule-making is on an impossible mission. The abundance of rules already issued has not succeeded in rigorously disciplining and standardizing accounting practice. More rules of the same kind must similarly fail. This is so because conventional accounting practice is centred on a purely abstract process: the apportioning of costs (or substituted amounts) in an attempt to quantify deferred and consumed benefits. The output yielded by this process is not descriptive of any actual circumstance existing within an entity. No firm 'has' a deferred cost. While accounting is concerned with such abstractions it is dependent on rules that specify algorithms for their calculation. However, such rules can discipline only those calculations. They cannot discipline the output of those calculations because the outputs are not relatable to any phenomena that would permit their truth-value to be independently evaluated.[10] As stated by Sterling (1988: 4, emphasis in original), 'with rare exceptions accounting numerals do not represent phenomena, *any* phenomena, and . . . making numerals represent or not represent phenomena is a matter of choice'. Present accounting rules are largely the consequence of that choice being resolved in favour of persisting with conventional accounting practices that do not yield representations of phenomena. This is so in spite of the intent of regulatory provisions in legislation being to the contrary (Chambers and Wolnizer 1991).

Yet, perversely, accounting rule-making has functioned to mask the failings from which it has been born. In an environment often uncritical of professions and their expertise, superficially agreeable aspects of these regulations have caused them to be, not just tolerated, but welcomed – both within and outside of the accounting profession. The label of 'accounting standards', with its connotations of quality and uniformity, has distracted from the reality that these rules have failed to engender either of these qualities within financial statements. The volume of regulations promulgated, coupled with the churning caused by frequent and inconsequential amendments, has created the impression of a profession that is active in responding to new challenges and changed circumstances. This has masked the absurd nature of the ritual of self-regulation being practised: 'Inexplicably, the most common financial nonsense arising from complying with an endorsed accounting practice is implied to be acceptable, whereas the common sense arising from deviating from many of the endorsed practices is not' (Clarke, Dean and Oliver 1997: 19).

Present accounting rules are the consequence of underlying failures in accounting technique rather than failures in the 'market' for accounting information. Socially contracted to provide a knowledge-based mediation within the accounting domain, the accounting profession has, instead, offered rules that have no firm cognitive foundation and the Sisyphean expertise of comprehending and applying those rules. Moreover, there is evidence that the accounting profession has been deceived by its own rhetoric about the worth of this ritual. Removal of the general qualitative standard of 'true and fair' has been petitioned for on the ground that its role has been supplanted by accounting rules: 'While the concept of "true and fair" may have been justified in an environment lacking an explicit framework of accounting standards and statements of accounting concepts, in today's environment it is an accounting anachronism' (McGregor 1992: 71). This claim that 'true and fair' – an output standard intended to ensure that financial reports possess demonstrable fitness for use – is anachronistic signals an abdication of the notion of professional quality assurance within accounting. It points to the perfunctory task of achieving compliance with rules not only supplanting the purposive task of ensuring that financial reports correspond with financial phenomena, but a contentment with that outcome.

Résumé and conclusion

This chapter has been concerned with explaining the proliferation of technical rules within the field of accounting. In some instances the organizations overseeing the development of these rules have been attributed with a degree of independence from the accounting profession. However, it is clear from a review of the history of accounting rule-making that the idea of promulgating formal technical statements that accounting practitioners would have an onus to comply with was devised and legitimated by professional accounting associations. This process of legitimation persists in the accounting profession's continued endorsement of present accounting rules and sanctioning of the development of more rules of a similar kind.

The justification commonly provided for accounting rules is that they are necessary to redress 'failures' in the 'market' for accounting information. However, this justification is incomplete if it is not accompanied by a demonstration of how the application of those rules protects the users of financial reports. The literature on accounting regulation *has* provided justifications for regulating accounting information. However, it has not justified the accounting rules that are now the dominant form of regulation. No demonstration has been made of how present accounting rules overcome the 'market failures' that are said to necessitate those rules. Instead, a need for regulation has been offered simply as the justification for the regulatory apparatus that is in place.

Present accounting rules perpetuate – indeed, institutionalize – the very deficiencies in the quality of accounting information that they are relied upon to remediate. Temporally heterogeneous data are required to be combined in a single dated summary. Choices in accounting method are, either explicitly or implicitly, condoned. Invalid aggregations are prescribed. Arbitrarily selected procedures are imposed. The fundamental paradox presented by accounting rules is that compliance with those rules actually provides entitlement to withhold information that *is* relevant to financial decision making. Thus, while thousands of pages of accounting rules have made financial reports among the most regulated of commodities, they remain peculiarly sequestered from the demonstrable fitness for use that would provide the only justification for existing regulatory arrangements. That the preparation and audit of financial reports is overseen by an occupational group that claims professional status and enjoys the usual privileges associated with that status compounds the perplexity of this situation. The practices of a profession are presumed to be derived from a body of reliable knowledge, creating an expectation that the quality of professional services will exceed standards that apply more generally. Yet, in spite of the intendance of a professional group *and* a vast array of technical rules, financial reports remain beset by defects of a fundamental kind which consumers of other commodities are not expected to endure.

These observations disclose the inadequacy of conventional explanations for accounting rules. In addition, they repudiate the notion that the proliferation of accounting rules is a testimony to the legitimacy of the accounting profession's mandate and the vigour with which it has sought to discharge its responsibilities. On the contrary, the testimony is to the extent of cognitive discord within the accounting profession and its continued preoccupation with abstractions rather than commercial phenomena. Here is a profession charged with measuring profits which has adopted no specification of what a profit is. A profession charged with reporting on the financial position of firms that has no coherent definition of assets, nor a standard practice for their measurement. A profession that has sought to make a purely abstract concept – 'future economic benefits' – its main subject matter. Present accounting rules are a manifestation of these circumstances. Lacking a robust theoretical framework that would define the expected outcomes of accounting tasks, directives have been substituted. Continued recourse to convention in establishing these directives has accentuated their need. The task of describing phenomena provides its own disciplinary mechanism: establishing correspondence between the description and the phenomena. However, the abstractions that dominate present accounting techniques cannot be disciplined in this way. Instead, processes for the calculation of non-empirical data can only be regulated by decree.

These circumstances indicate that the accounting profession is yet to provide a knowledge-based substantiation of its authority. However, they also reveal how the accounting profession has manoeuvred to protect its privileged status. Process has supplanted purpose: achieving compliance with accounting rules has been made an end rather than a means. Accounting 'expertise' now largely subsists in interpreting and applying accounting rules. The numerosity and complexity of the rules do not render these simple tasks. But the mandate of an accounting profession is to ensure the serviceability of financial reports. An assurance that particular processing rules have been complied with cannot, of itself, discharge this mandate.

The consequences of this emphasis on correspondence with rules – in substitution rather than in aid of the functionally proper task of ensuring that financial reports correspond with commercial phenomena – extend beyond accounting technique. As well as having failed to provide a mechanism for advancing the serviceability of financial reports, these rules have contributed to an intellectual malaise within a discipline that already carries a reputation for being 'obsessively technical' (Tinker 1985: viii). It is this issue that is explored in subsequent chapters, commencing with accounting discourse in Chapter 6.

6 Professionalism, accounting rules and accounting discourse

> There are critical differences between proper research and the recommendations or pronouncements of authorities.
>
> (Chambers 1970b: 9)

Introduction

In spite of its posited regulatory role and extensive output, accounting rule-making has not effected substantive changes in accounting practice. Instead, it has endorsed the substance of accounting methods that were already in use. Those changes that have been provided for tend to be incremental and idiosyncratic: valuation techniques peculiar to specific assets and liabilities, and prescriptions that are to be applied within only certain industries.[1] Derived from convention and modified by ad hoc changes, present accounting rules provide neither a serviceable system of accounting nor an epistemological validation of the accounting profession's authority. The continued proliferation of rules is reflective of these circumstances and bound to the inadequacies of conventional accounting technique and the accounting profession's persistent reliance on that technique. An enduring emphasis on reporting accounting numbers that are not descriptive of actual commercial events and situations has thwarted the operation of a system of empirical discipline. Faith has been placed in formal rules to overcome this lack, and compliance with these rules substituted for correspondence with commercial phenomena as the primary measure of quality in financial reporting.

While accounting rule-making has not yet been an effective instrument of technical reform, it has not been without implications. The number of rules issued and the superficially agreeable connotations of 'mandatory standards' have provided a public relations shield for the accounting profession, disguising the imbalance between its elevated occupational authority and discordant epistemic circumstances. Moreover, it appears that the accounting profession has now been deceived by its own rhetoric and contented itself with the ritualized task of applying accounting standards. While accounting is defined functionally (in terms of the provision of useful financial information), it is administered procedurally (in terms of rule-compliance). The technical inadequacies of the rules impose a disjunction between function and procedure that is evident in a variety of settings. Accounting education is centred on learning rules (to be discussed in Chapter 7), and accounting practice on applying rules (to be discussed in Chapter 8). Neither of these tasks accords with the function of accounting as a professional occupation. The disabling consequences of this formalism are also evident in the discourse of accounting researchers and this forms the subject of this chapter.

There are persuasive grounds for believing that a properly operating system of professional authority – based on the application and ongoing refinement of socially beneficent and reliable accounting knowledge – could make a substantial contribution to the effective regulation of the accounting domain. The commercial environment is complex and volatile, being constituted by variables such as prices, specific and general price changes, legislative influences, consumer preferences, changes in technology and the strategic actions of competitors. In these circumstances a cognitive form of governance has a potency and enduring relevance that specific rules will always lack. In particular, it has the capacity to be responsive to the dynamic nature of commercial interaction and the new kinds of transactions evolving within it.[2]

In the period since the ascent to dominance of formal rules, accounting discourse – and particularly that of accounting researchers – has turned away from the practical concern of improving the serviceability of financial reports. In some instances the choice has been explicit, and defended on the ground that accounting is an inherently unscientific discipline that cannot be advanced by scholarly inquiry. Others have based their abdication on an endorsement of the notion that accounting methods should be determined by 'democratic' rather than intellectual processes. Still others seem only to have had their curiosity assuaged by the number of rules that have been promulgated, with each accounting standard construed as a resolution terminating the need for further investigation. Against this background, the discourse of accounting researchers has come to focus on the behaviour of those involved with accounting, and sophistication in method has taken precedence over the significance of discovery. These circumstances contradict the exigencies of professional authority. Professions are relied upon to supply knowledge relevant to the conduct of human affairs and which can be applied to mediate the administration of those affairs. The capacity of an accounting profession to discharge this responsibility derives from robust discourse on the principles, means and details of a reliable and functional system of financial instrumentation.

The next section of the chapter provides an overview of the nature of scholarly discourse and knowledge accretion in professional fields generally. This is followed by an analysis of the state of accounting discourse which is developed from a specification of the responsibilities of researchers within professional jurisdictions. A call is then made for a reorientation in the discourse of accounting researchers to make it better serve the public interest and so be more in accord with the responsibilities of professional authority.

Scholarly discourse in professional fields generally

As noted in Chapter 2, statements proclaiming the epistemic foundation of professions abound in the sociology of professions literature. However, exactly how bodies of professional knowledge come into being and subsequently evolve has been less confidently articulated. The observation of Cooper and Zeff is telling:

> we had occasion to examine some of the literature on the history and the sociology of the professions. We had hoped to learn something about how a profession and its scientific research component were held together. We could not find any discussion of this topic.
>
> (cited in Bricker and Previts 1990: 1)

This finding is supported by the observation of Eraut (1994: 40) that there is 'a remarkable ignorance about professional learning' and his call for 'more information about how professionals use and develop knowledge' (1994: 57).

Some views on how professional knowledge comes into being and is diffused among practitioners are scattered through the relevant literature. According to Whitehead (1933: 76):

> the advance of scholarship, and of natural science, transformed the professions. It intellectualized them far beyond their stage of advance in earlier times. Professions first appear as customary activities largely modified by detached strains of theory. Theories are often wrong; and some of the earlier professional doctrines erred grievously and were maintained tenaciously. Doctrines emerged as plausible deductions, and survived as the wisdom of ancestors. Thus the older professional practice was rooted upon custom, though it was turning toward the intellectual sunlight.

This 'turning toward the intellectual sunlight', and in particular the development of scientific inquiry, is emphasized by Carr-Saunders and Wilson (1933: 295–7):

> for several centuries some half-dozen professions provided all those skilled intellectual services upon which the day-to-day functioning of society depended. By 1700 the architects had come in, and the eighteenth century witnessed some further changes. Then the flood-gates opened. New vocations arose and filled the ears of the public with demands for places alongside the ancient professions. What was it that released the flood?
>
> From about the middle of the sixteenth century there had been a movement at work which was destined to bring new professions to birth. . . . The spirit of free and original inquiry gained a firm hold in the seventeenth century and led to systematic research. . . .

The rise of new professions based upon intellectual techniques is due to the revolution brought about by the work of the engineers and thus indirectly the coming of science.

This journey from scientific forms of inquiry to professional knowledge was not made without delay: 'for some 200 years the scientific movement made so few additions to the arts that it exerted little influence upon the existing professions and brought no new professions into being' (Carr-Saunders and Wilson 1933: 296).

The importance of scientific inquiry in the development of professions is qualified by Halliday (1987: 29): 'the success of contemporary professions cannot be attributed primarily to science *per se* because two of the three longest-standing professions – law and the clergy – are not scientific in any narrow sense of the term'. Consistent with this view, some writers have emphasized the importance of *institutions*, rather than particular *methods*, in facilitating the creation and dissemination of professional knowledge. In particular, attention has been drawn to the role of universities in this process. Barber (1963: 674), for example, stresses 'the university professional school's responsibility for the creation of new and better knowledge on which professional practice can be based'. In a similar manner, Wilensky (1964: 144) emphasizes 'the strategic innovative role of universities and the early teachers in linking knowledge to practice and creating a rationale for exclusive jurisdiction'. This theme is found also in Freidson (1986: 83):

> Though there are important variations among the professions in their dependence on academics as their knowledge class, it can be asserted that by creating a shelter for full-time teaching and research in professional schools . . . professions create one important mechanism by means of which they can maintain control over innovations to the body of knowledge they claim as their own by keeping it within the professional family.

The contribution of educational institutions is, according to Abbott (1988: 57), a prerequisite for the preservation of professional authority: 'The academic knowledge system . . . provides new treatments, diagnoses and inferences for working professionals; if it fails in this function, professional jurisdictions gradually weaken.' However, recognition of the importance of a knowledge-creating academic élite within professions is not universal, as evidenced in the views of Eraut (1994: 54):

> A much broader framework is needed for studying the creation of professional knowledge; and the situation looks very different if we move the academic researcher from the centre of the universe. . . . [W]e notice that new knowledge is created also by professionals in practice, though this is often of a different kind from that created by researchers. Moreover, in some professions nearly all new practice is both invented and developed

in the field, with the role of academics being confined to that of dissemination, evaluation and *post hoc* construction of theoretical rationales. In others, knowledge is developed by practitioners 'solving' individual cases and problems, contributing to their personal store of experience and possibly that of their colleagues but not being codified, published or widely disseminated.

The general dissonance that this study has noted to be a feature of the sociology of professions literature is thus further evident in perspectives on the origin and development of professional knowledge. Customary activities, scientific inquiry, institutions of higher education and the experiences of individual practitioners are all deemed to have played important roles. As suggested by Eraut (1994: 54), this circumstance might be explained by the dynamics of knowledge discovery varying across professional groups. More generally, it may accord with the thesis of Feyerabend (1988: 1) that knowledge accretion is not guided by a single and universal method: 'not every discovery can be accounted for in the same manner, and procedures that paid off in the past may create havoc when imposed on the future'.

In spite of apparent uncertainties concerning the origins of professional knowledge, one important theme is affirmed. Whatever their precise form, knowledge-enhancing processes within professional fields give rise to findings that are applied in practice. This is cognate with the observation that the term 'profession' is usually associated only with occupational groups that deal with matters of frequent and practical significance in the conduct of human affairs. Profound developments have occurred in the knowledge base of each of astronomy, physics and medicine. Yet, of these three disciplines medicine alone enjoys instant recognition as a highly professionalized occupation. What differentiates medicine is the universality of demand for the life-enhancing and life-saving properties it delivers. This gives rise to the economic circumstances that allow medical practitioners to operate in public practice, and such familiar concepts as the 'family doctor'. While sharing with medicine a rapidity of knowledge development, astronomy and physics are not usually conducted in public practice, and certainly the idea of a 'family astronomer' or 'family physicist' is unfamiliar. The explanation is that the knowledge base of these sciences, while profound, is of less direct relevance to the conduct of ordinary day to day affairs.[3] Copernicus' description of a heliocentric universe revolutionized astronomy, but held few implications for everyday human behaviour. Similarly, while the laws of physics govern many human activities – riding a bicycle, climbing a flight of stairs – these can usually be undertaken in the absence of any knowledge of these laws. The majority of the population, however, have regular need to seek access to medical knowledge via consultations with qualified practitioners, and commonly draw on the funds of knowledge of legal experts, dentists and optometrists among others.

Two crucial points evident in this discussion complement the apprehension of 'profession' outlined earlier in this study. The first is the need for professional knowledge to be of practical significance in the conduct of human affairs. Professions are relied upon as mediating forces within domains of social significance. Bodies of knowledge that are without significant, recurring and practical relevance to social organization and well-being may command the respect and even awe of the general public. However, by their very nature they are unlikely to substantiate an occupation-based authority that can be relied upon to promote social order. The second point, following closely from the first, is that it is the role of professional knowledge to generate prescriptions or normative propositions pertaining to human conduct. This is inherent to the word 'profession'. It is derived from the Latin *profiteri*, meaning 'to declare aloud or publicly', and the Latin *professio*, implying a 'public declaration'.[4] This normative imperative is evident especially in medicine, where the word 'prescription' has become part of the profession's nomenclature.

These observations provide a framework for examining and evaluating the nature of accounting discourse. The principal concern is whether knowledge-enhancing processes – whatever their exact nature and form – yield findings that are applied to advance the technical quality of professional practice. The authority of a technically stagnant profession will be deserving of challenge on two grounds. First, in line with rising community expectations generally, there is entitlement to demand continuing improvement in the quality of professional services.[5] Second, the dynamic nature of the environments in which professions operate necessitates the constant development and adaptation of expertise. Medical practitioners are confronted by new diseases, lawyers by new laws and accountants by new forms of commercial transactions. As a result, the details of bodies of professional knowledge are not immune to obsolescence. Ongoing professional capacity is contingent upon new knowledge which yields prescriptions that enhance the technical quality of the services provided by practitioners. In connection with accounting, this necessitates a continuing search for means by which the capacity of financial reports to function as reliable financial instruments can be advanced.

Accounting discourse

In the preceding section, the grounds for expecting there to be a strong nexus between scholarly discourse and practice within professional fields were explained. Professions are charged with providing and applying knowledge to mediate the administration of human affairs in specified domains. Research findings emerging from scholarly discourse are the means for effecting and refining this role: 'The object of research is to promote knowledge' (Chambers 1960: 33). For a profession's scholarly discourse to be disconnected from its practice would be anomalous and disabling. It would condemn either the significance of research findings (for the lack of utility of the knowledge produced), or professional practice (for not being based on knowledge or being unresponsive to the new knowledge emerging from scholarly discourse). Or it would condemn both.[6]

With regard to accounting, research questions (what is to be found out?) and research methods (how is it to be found out?) are diverse. In 1977, the AAA Committee on Concepts and Standards for External Financial Reports noted 'many differences in problems addressed, assumptions made, and analytic methods employed', and that the differences were 'fundamental and starkly visible' (1977: 25). There are grounds for suggesting that these differences have subsequently compounded rather than diminished. The discourse of accounting researchers 'is developing in diverse ways' (Cooper and Hopper 1987: 407), and according to Chua (1986a: 602) 'dissension is rife'. The outcome of this 'proliferation of alternatives' and their associated 'public battles' has, in the view of Laughlin (1995: 64), been to 'leave those starting out on the road to research, and even those well-grounded in one perspective, perplexed and confused as to the significance or otherwise . . . of undertaking research'. However, behind this dissension and confusion, a single strong and unifying theme can be discerned in perspectives on scholarly discourse in accounting: its lack of impact on accounting practice.

The inconsequence of accounting discourse

That accounting discourse and the research findings discussed within it are largely without consequence for accounting practice, is the united view of a wide variety of contributors to the accounting literature who embrace a diverse range of ideas about accounting. The statements presented in Box 6.1 bear testimony to this.

As well as stressing that the discourse of accounting researchers is disconnected from accounting practice, the statements in Box 6.1 contain expressions of regret concerning this circumstance. The disconnection is 'a general malady', 'lamented' and a source of 'disenchantment'. Accentuating the intolerable nature of the divide is the fact that 'Academic accountancy ultimately depends on practice and would scarcely be likely to exist without it' (Stamp 1985: 111). The blame is attributed, variously, to confusion about the nature of research activities, the immaturity of the discipline, the isolation of accounting academics from the real-world problems confronting practitioners, the pursuit of inquiries that lack relevance to practice and the use of research methods that are incomprehensible to practitioners.

Underlying these views is a more fundamental explanation that accords with the basic contention of this study and provides further evidence to support it. It is that accounting practice is not guided by the application of systematic knowledge, but by the mandatory application of rules that have been endorsed only as 'social conventions' (Archer 1997: 237). These rules do not provide a bridge between scholarly discourse and practice, but create a formidable barrier which invokes the force of regulatory fiat in defence of the status quo. In turn, the implications of this ceding of cognitive governance in favour of institutional sanction have extended beyond practice to influence accounting discourse.

Box 6.1

Statements affirming that scholarly discourse and research findings in accounting are disconnected from accounting practice:

There is, at present, in my opinion, a much bigger gap between academic researchers and the practising members of the accounting profession than in any other profession that I know – including law, medicine and engineering.

(Bevis 1966: 39)

Since the 1930s, associations of professional accountants in Australia have been interested in promoting research into accounting. Over the years, the professional associations have individually or jointly fostered a variety of ventures labelled 'research'. Different organizational devices have been tried, different processes of inquiry have been followed. But . . . the product of these investments of time and money have been minimal. This failure . . . [is] ascribed to confused ideas about the nature of research.

(Birkett and Walker 1972: 35)

The ineffectual nature of accounting research is a more general malady. It apparently reflects the discipline's immaturity; it may also follow from the indeterminate state of opinion on financial accounting objectives.

(Larson and Holstrum 1973: 10)

Any practitioner or teacher in the field of accounting would find it difficult to assert that there is a congruence between research in his field and actual education and practice.

(Sterling 1973b: 44)

I can't help asking 'For goodness sake, what has happened to *The Accounting Review?*' Most of us, and here I include academic types as well as practitioners, find this foreign language magazine almost impossible to read. . . . I cite this as an illustration of just how far apart academic and applied accounting have become.

(Mautz 1974: 356)

A study of the U.S. experience suggests that the academic literature has had remarkably little impact on the writings of practitioners and upon the accounting policies of the American Institute and the SEC. Too often, accounting theory is invoked more as a tactic to buttress one's preconceived notions, rather than as a genuine arbiter of contending views. This circumstance, which is hardly unique to the United States, is much to be lamented. It surely places accounting, as a professional calling, below both law and medicine.

(Zeff 1974: 177)

The problem with research in accounting is that it appears to be an isolated activity. The results of research have very little impact on teaching or practice.

(Sterling 1975a: 58)

The impact of behavioural research on accounting practice has been almost nonexistent.

(Dyckman, Gibbins and Swieringa 1978: 87)

I am . . . pessimistic about the ability of empirical research to give us many insights into many varied and important questions now confronting the accounting profession.

(Kaplan 1978: 168)

. . . a survey of the accounting literature over the past ten years . . . provides little evidence to believe a priori research causes changes in accounting practice.

(Bedford 1978: 2)

Therefore, in answer to the question: Does accounting research matter? Our response is: Yes – but not very much.

(Henderson and Peirson 1978: 32)

. . . it is generally concluded that financial accounting theory has had little substantive, direct impact on accounting practice or policy formulation despite half a century of research.

(Watts and Zimmerman 1979: 273–4)

Academic and practising accountants are distinct genera with different *weltanschauungs*, *modus operandi* and motivation.

(Buckley 1980: 60)

. . . preoccupation with complex modes of analysis is almost certainly at the root of the disenchantment of the practising arm of the profession with the academic arm: one hand does not know what the other is doing. That too is disruptive of the role of accounting in society at large. If a larger part of the research effort were directed to inquiries having obvious relationship to the usefulness of information, carried out in a manner more generally comprehensible, I feel confident that rapport between academics and practitioners could be vastly better. So too would the capacity of accounting to serve as a dependable basis of commercial and financial understandings and negotiations.

(Chambers 1980: 175)

. . . quite simply, much of what is wrong with accounting research is that it has accomplished very little in improving accounting.

(Jensen and Arrington 1983: 6)

There is presently an urgent need to bridge the constantly widening gap between accounting research and professional accountants (including accounting students).

(Mattessich 1984: 1, emphasis omitted)

. . . most practitioners find most academic writing so obscure and difficult to read that material published by academics seldom has first-hand impact on practice.

(Stamp 1985: 121)

. . . academic accountants in recent years have tended to retreat from the traditional normative literature and have had less to say about desirable improvements in policy making and practice.

(Zeff 1986: 131)

. . . accounting research [has] often tended to move further from the accounting problems of the profession. The more theoretical approach resulted in more isolation of research-oriented faculty members from real-world problems and less contact with professional accountants.

(Langenderfer 1987: 312)

. . . the large majority of accounting research activities do not appear to have had a major part to play in shaping the content of professional education programmes or the conduct of accounting practice, despite continuous concern that the opposite is the case. A considerable proportion of research appears to exist in increasing isolation from education and practice.

(Lee 1989: 237)

. . . too many academic researchers seem to have relatively little interest in policy issues and seem content with their interests in

modeling and number-crunching on a grand scale. For the last
quarter century academics have pursued research activities that
practitioners have generally found irrelevant to their needs.

(Wyatt 1991: 103)

. . . since the 1960s, there has been a wholesale abandonment (by
academic accountants) of the traditional concerns of accounting
and a corresponding wholesale acceptance of other disciplines
(especially economics) which are considered to be scientific.

(Mouck 1993: 35)

. . . accounting research should lead practice. Instead, it often
follows. Unlike doctors and lawyers, accountants typically do not
look to researchers, or research journals, for solutions to their problems.

(Sunder 1991: 134)

By and large, practitioners do not and cannot understand much of
academic research. Their inability to understand no doubt has frus-
trated them. And those frustrations are reflected in their negative
reactions to all academic research and in their claims of a lack of
relevance.

(Leisenring and Johnson 1994: 75–6)

The descriptive-explanatory nature of much academic research
means that a person wishing to use such research to settle a normative issue must supply a normative criterion, since the research in
general does not.

(Schipper 1994: 63)

. . . academic research has contributed to a widening of the schism
between practitioners and academics. Academic accounting
research often seems to demonstrate the obvious or to deal with
issues irrelevant to practitioners.

(Bloom *et al.* 1994: 25)

. . . much academic research does not find its way off the pages of
scholarly journals and into the field.

(Howieson 1996: 30)

The development of accounting discourse

While perspectives on *how* professional knowledge is discovered and translated into practice have been shown to differ, there are repeated representations in the sociology of professions literature that such a process does occur. Medical research gives rise to new methods of diagnosis and treatment. In law, the decisions of the judiciary are examined for precedents that will affect how legal practitioners subsequently advise and represent their clients. Engineers make use of knowledge pertaining to the qualities of newly derived materials. However, audited financial statements not only fail to display evidence of being based on a body of knowledge, but remain isolated from the reforms necessary to change this circumstance.

Historical analyses of the development of accounting discourse highlight that endeavours aimed at improving the technical quality of financial reports have comprised only a small portion of researchers' efforts. Henderson and Peirson (1978: 28–9) provide the following classification of stages in the evolution of this discourse:

> 1801–1955: Explanatory period during which researchers 'devoted their efforts to testing hypotheses which described, explained and justified the existing system'.
> 1956–1970: Normative period, marked by a search 'for a better accounting system'.
> 1970–the present: Descriptive period, 'concerned with testing descriptive hypotheses'.

According to this framework, for only a scant 15-year period have accounting researchers had improving the quality of accounting information as their main objective. The emphasis has, instead, been on describing, explaining or justifying what accountants actually do. In this manner, accounting discourse has departed from the pattern expected in a professional field. The brevity of the time spent searching for 'a better accounting system' is particularly evident when compared, for example, to medicine where efforts to devise suitable treatments for specific medical conditions may span decades.

One explanation for this circumstance may be the relative immaturity of accounting as a scholarly discipline (Larson and Holstrum 1973: 10), and an associated perception that because 'accounting had developed to meet a practical need, it was considered to be atheoretical' (Sterling 1977: 238). However, the explanation for the apparent lack of technical progress in accounting goes beyond just the discipline's relative immaturity. It embraces factors that perpetuate this immaturity and which derive from the social rather than cognitive foundation of the accounting profession's authority. Conventional accounting technique, as explained by Sterling (1977: 234–5), was not the product of systematic inquiry:

> Our history shows little indication that the bookkeeper ever left his high stool to directly examine the objects of wealth or to observe the exchanges; instead, he made his entries and calculations on the basis of instructions from the owner-manager. The entries – inputs to the accounts – were supposed to reflect exchanges, but the bookkeeper did not observe exchanges; instead, he observed written documents from the owner-manager. The balances of the accounts were supposed to represent objects of wealth. But the bookkeeper did not observe these objects of wealth and make comparisons of his balances to those observations. Instead, he calculated those balances on the basis of instructions received from the owner-manager. . . . [I]t was the responsibility of the owner-manager to supply the method of calculation – it was the responsibility of the bookkeeper to make the entries and do the calculations. Hence, the bookkeeper was a human calculator, not an empiricist.

Accounting thus emerged as a calculative rather than empirical discipline, and the seeds of accounting technicalism – with accountants directed by instructions and rules rather than independent knowledge – were sown. In spite of this intellectual subordination, accountants were successful in marshalling sufficient resources of a social dimension to elevate the standing of their occupation. However, the resultant mismatch between accountants' occupational and cognitive authority laid the foundation for a pattern of discourse that would perpetuate, rather than remedy, this mismatch. In circumstances where a robust theoretical framework for a profession's work is in place, scholarly discourse can properly focus on refinement; gradual accretions and improvements that accord with the general principles already established. Perhaps gratified by the rise in status of their occupation, accountants have clung to a presumption that the technical practices delivered to them by convention are both theoretically and practically sound. Thus, much accounting discourse has proceeded as if a reliable general framework for accounting was in place when it was, in fact, absent. The outcome has been a concentration of effort in seeking to explain and justify inherently deficient accounting practices rather than seek their replacement.

Of early writers on accounting, Henderson and Peirson (1978: 27) state:

> Beginning in about 1800 writers on accounting attempted to explain the reasons underlying the detailed bookkeeping rules and procedures. Although this period began about 1800, it was not until the beginning of the 20th century that this phase in the development of accounting research began to flourish. The incentive to explain and justify accounting practice was provided by a desire to improve the quality of instruction in accounting.

With regard to historical cost accounting in particular, Chambers (1994: 87) attributes its persistence to the efforts of accounting writers and educators:

Of the cost doctrine it might be said that it is the illegitimate offspring of a counterfactual teaching device and the propensity to preserve and defend valiantly, in defiance of commonsense, what one has learned at the hands of one's mentors.

The 1940 Paton and Littleton monograph, *An Introduction to Corporate Accounting Standards*, provides a salient illustration of accounting writing functioning to rationalize conventional practice. The authors proclaim that 'Accounting standards should be systematic and coherent, impartial and impersonal, and in harmony with observable, objective conditions' (Paton and Littleton 1940: 1). These noble sentiments, however, were effectively abandoned in favour of a defence of extant techniques. Financial statements are affirmed as being 'provisional in character' (1940: 10). On the ground that the accountant 'deals primarily with the administration of the affairs of the continuing business institution', it is said that he or she 'accordingly emphasizes the flow of costs and the interpretation of assets as balances of unamortized costs' (1940: 10–11). However, no nexus of relevance between cost and continuing business activity is demonstrated.[7] Cost itself is reinvented euphemistically as 'measured consideration' and a 'price aggregate' (1940: 11–12). But while derived from 'exchange activities', costs are said to be capable of being reassigned in the absence of an exchange and 'marshaled into new groups that possess real significance' (1940: 13). The basis for this is a presumption that costs have an ability to 'attach' (1940: 13), and can therefore be viewed as 'clinging to definite items of goods sold or service rendered' (1940: 15) as part of a process of quantifying 'effort' for 'matching' against 'accomplishment' (1940: 14–15). The necessarily subjective, and often arbitrary, cost allocations endogenous to this process depart fundamentally from the authors' stated criteria that accounting standards should be 'impartial and impersonal, and in harmony with observable, objective conditions'. These contradictions, however, are camouflaged by an eloquence of language that embellishes the discord of conventional practice with a contrived veneer of rationality.

Early efforts to improve accounting practice through prescriptions that sought to change rather than justify conventional practices include those of Canning (1978/1929), Sweeney (1964/1936) and MacNeal (1970/1939). However, as Henderson and Peirson (1978) indicate, changing accounting practice was not a firm priority of accounting researchers until the mid-1950s; spurred by the observations of Chambers (1955: 17):

There are undoubtably several systems of thought about the practice of accounting: systems which attempt to categorize the kinds of things accountants do in practice. These systems are almost all the subject can boast of in the way of theory, and for this reason accounting lacks the sharpness, the progressiveness and the vitality of other technologies. Other technologies are based on systems of ideas which serve as references or criteria of performance. Their systems of ideas are not simply descriptions of practice; they transcend applications as, indeed, any theory should. Only if a theory can deal with the ideal can it serve as a guide to developments and improvements in the practice of the related technology. The conditions under which the practitioner works will inevitably cause his work or his results to fall short of the ideal, for the conditions are never ideal. But if the points at which the conditions fall short are discerned, or if the deficiencies in the technique are known (by reference to the theory), there is hope that the practice will be gradually improved.

Subsequent expositions of theory-based accounting systems (AAA Committee to Prepare a Statement of Basic Accounting Theory 1966; Chambers 1966b; Edwards and Bell 1961; Sterling 1970) that prescribe departures from customary practices did in fact generate significant debate, as well as raise the general standard of accounting inquiry (Gaffikin 1988). In addition, there is evidence that the proposals resulted in some change in accounting practice, although not necessarily of a permanent nature.[8] However, in recent decades the academic accounting community has, again, largely abandoned concern with what Sterling (1990a: 97, emphasis in original) has described as 'the fundamental question of accounting': '*What* ought accounting practices be? More fully, *which objects and events*, and *which attribute(s) of them*, should be represented in accounts and on financial statements?'

The nature of contemporary accounting discourse

Contemporary accounting discourse has returned to the descriptive mode that was to the fore during the first half of the twentieth century. However, that choice has now been made explicit and resolute. According to Watts and Zimmerman (1986: 2, emphasis in original), 'The objective of accounting theory is to *explain* and *predict* accounting practice.' Additionally, the accounting theory sought by these authors is wholly isolated from prescriptions aimed at influencing accounting practice (1986: 7):

> By itself, theory, as we describe it, yields no prescriptions for accounting practice. It is concerned with explaining practice. It is designed to explain and predict which firms will and which firms will not use a particular method of valuing assets, but it says nothing as to which method a firm should use.

The main justification offered for this focus on prediction and explanation is the claim that it is 'the scientific concept of theory' (Watts and Zimmerman 1986: 13). This and related propositions have been examined and found wanting by a number of writers (Boland and Gordon 1992; Chambers 1993; Christenson 1983; Demski 1988; Hopper *et al.* 1995; Lowe, Puxty and Laughlin 1983; Mouck 1992; Okcabol and Tinker 1990; Peasnell and

Williams 1986; Sterling 1990a; Tinker, Merino and Neimark 1982; Tinker and Puxty 1995; Whitley 1988; Whittington 1987; Williams 1989). What remains, however, is to critique the usefulness of a theory that 'yields no prescriptions' within a professional field.

The authority vested with a profession is a particular kind of regulatory mechanism and its effective operation is predicated on the existence of special knowledge and skills. The operation of this form of regulation – as with all other regulatory arrangements – necessarily involves prescriptions that guide or modify human behaviour. In professional fields these prescriptions are commonly made at two levels. First, individual practitioners act on behalf of clients or advise them concerning the appropriate action to be taken in specific circumstances: the desirability of pursuing a legal action on the basis of the likely outcome, the treatment to cure an illness. Second, practitioners may collectively, as a profession, issue more general proclamations: advice to government concerning changes in the law, or announcements related to matters of public health. A research programme that 'yields no prescriptions' is antithetical to these responsibilities, as alluded to by Bricker and Previts (1990: 11): 'It is as anomalous for accountancy researchers to be uninterested in the concerns and issues of practitioners as it would be for medical researchers to hold such an attitude about research related to cancer, or Acquired Immune Deficiency Syndrome (AIDS).'

Yet the pursuit of 'positive accounting theory', as called for by Watts and Zimmerman (1978, 1979, 1986, 1990; Watts 1992; Zimmerman 1987/ 1980), has been a dominating feature of contemporary accounting research. In the words of Chambers (1993: 21):

> Of the present dominance of the work and *modus operandi* of the PA [posi-tive accounting] cult there can be no doubt. Its doctrines have, from the outset, been propagated with proselytizing zeal and beguiling rhetoric. Its products have attracted prestigious awards, engaging the emulation of others. It has spawned new journals only too willing to publish work of its kind. Its devotees, rising to editorial and referential posts, have shifted publication opportunities in its favour; it is the avowed policy of some journals and the implicit policy of others to disregard submissions not of its genre. Its products have captured the allegiance of whole schools in teaching across the breadth of English-speaking communities, and perhaps elsewhere.

The dominance of a research programme that defines itself by its absten-tion from prescription is anomalous in a professional field. The origin of this anomaly derives in part from the fact that the progenitors of positive accounting theory sourced their theoretical framework from economics, more specifically Friedman's (1953) *Essays in Positive Economics* (Watts and Zimmerman 1986: 8, 1990: 147–8; Zimmerman 1987/1980: 175). The distraction caused by this choice derives from economics being expressly and necessarily concerned with *policies*. For example, decisions relating to levels of government taxation and expenditure, interest rates, tariff protection and subsidies will be dependent on, and reflect, a government's particular social and economic priorities. A positive knowledge of the relationships between variables may well influence decisions but, in the end, a government will have a macro-economic *policy* that will be shaped by social preferences. Almost inevitably, alternative policies will be favoured by others on account of 'fundamental differences in basic values, differences about which men can only fight' (Friedman 1953: 5). The prescriptions of a profession, however, are to be founded on objective professional knowledge. A solicitor engaged to prepare legal documents or represent a client is expected to do so on the basis of knowledge of the law. Similarly, a surgeon's procedures are not determined by policy choices but by what has been established as sound surgical practice. And few would be inclined to trust a bridge if, during its construction, matters of policy were respected rather than engineering principles.

What is perplexing about the research programme advocated by Watts and Zimmerman is not just that it has a framework contrary to the essence of professional responsibility. It is that such a research programme could come to dominate the scholarly discourse of a profession. This perplexity is compounded by the modesty of the programme's findings relative to the volume of publications from which they are drawn. As summarized by Watts and Zimmerman (1986: 354), positive accounting theory has identified 'three general regularities in accounting procedure choice':

> (1) managers of firms with earnings-based compensation plans are more likely to choose procedures that increase current earnings (bonus hypothesis); (2) the larger a firm's debt/equity ratio the more likely the firm's manager is to select procedures that increase current earnings (debt/equity hypothesis); and (3) the larger the firm, the more likely the manager selects procedures that decrease current earnings (size hypothesis).

These findings can be further summarized into a single proposition: when accounting is a matter of policy and various policy choices are available, company managers will select those most in accord with their private interests. But almost half a century earlier, MacNeal (1970/1939: vii) offered precisely the same proposition: 'For more than four hundred years, since the publication of Pacioli's book on double entry bookkeeping in 1494, accounting methods, and hence accounting reports, have been based on expediency rather than on truth.' Chambers (1966b: 344) identifies the same outcome and, with respect to asset revaluations, even articulates what subsequent researchers adopting a claimed positivist approach have affirmed as their own finding:[9]

> Revaluations of assets upwards and downwards, for example, appear to have been treated as *ad hoc* tactical moves, made to be realistic only under severe pressure, but otherwise made to be attractive or distractive. Again,

if, in fact, conventional processes failed to reveal pertinent and contemporary facts, on the ground of their own self-interests merchants and managers would be content to leave them alone; for financial statements which are not indeed representative of the facts . . . will serve to shield them from the criticisms of others.

Despite the elaborate nature of its methods, the findings of positive accounting theory are not profound and, in connection with the issue of accounting policy choice, not new.[10] A variety of explanations have been offered for why contemporary accounting discourse has been dominated by this style of inquiry. Whitley's (1988) interpretation is that even though superficial and misdirected, the scientification claimed by positive accounting theorists facilitated the pursuit of academic respectability and autonomy (see also Hopper *et al.* 1995: 522). Lee (1989: 250) suggests positive accounting theory may have been welcome precisely because it 'is not a threat to the status quo'. Sterling's (1990a: 132) explanation is the tendency of accounting researchers to be too easily seduced by 'the fickle winds of fashion'. Chambers (1993: 2) cites the appeal of 'a seemingly respectable verbiage, an apparently sophisticated research apparatus, a nodding familiarity with the concerns of scientists and economists' at a time when accounting was 'passing through a period of external and internal criticism and self-doubt'. Mouck's (1992: 55) explanation differs in that as well as emphasizing the adoption of a 'rhetoric of science', he claims that the acceptance of this rhetoric was accentuated by a conservative political environment sympathetic to anti-regulation stances implicit in the contracting theory utilized by positive accounting researchers (see also Tinker and Puxty 1995).

This study has no cause to doubt that these explanations contribute to explaining the direction that accounting discourse has taken in recent decades. However, it identifies an additional explanation that derives from the observation that positive accounting theory rose to prominence at a time when the resolution of issues related to the technical practice of accounting had been made firmly the responsibility of accounting standard setting bodies.[11] That is, it coincided with academic researchers being relieved of responsibility for dealing with the 'how to account' issues that confront practitioners. In this sense, positive research helped to fill the lacuna faced by academic accountants witnessing their discipline transform into one dominated by the application of formal pronouncements. If, following the usual pattern in professional fields, accounting researchers were relied upon to offer solutions to practical accounting problems, it is difficult to envisage how a discourse divorced from those issues could achieve prominence. Where such a reliance is in place – for example, in medical research – it is precisely the generation of solutions to real-world problems, such as improved methods for diagnosing and treating disease, that dominates research activity. In accounting, however, the 'resolution' of issues has come to be perceived as a function of rule-making rather than scholarly inquiry.

Positive accounting researchers have adopted research questions that coincide with the marginalized role that regulatory developments have consigned them. But they have also sought to legitimate that role and assert its importance. In so doing they have implicitly condoned present accounting technique. Watts and Zimmerman (1986: 14), for example, make the following proclamation: 'Positive accounting theory is important because it can provide those who must make decisions on accounting policy (corporate managers, public accountants, loan officers, investors, financial analysts and regulators) with predictions of, and explanations for, the consequences of their decisions.' Accounting is thus defined – without justification – as a matter of *policy*. Underlying this specification is a denial of the possibility of a cognitive grounding for accounting practice. Instead, the production of accounting theory has been characterized as a 'market for excuses' (Watts and Zimmerman 1979). Licence was thereby granted to the accounting profession – and the academic community in particular – to abandon efforts to seek a coherent theoretical grounding for accounting practice on the grounds that any such efforts would be futile.

Significant doubt now attaches to the worth of Watts and Zimmerman's 'excuses' theory: 'Its onetime exponents now shuffle their theoretical feet with embarrassment when excuses theory is mentioned' (Tinker and Puxty 1995: 9). But, at the time of its publication, the paper triumphed and was honoured with the AICPA Notable Contribution to the Accounting Literature award. This is suggestive not just of the sometimes transitory nature of academic accomplishment, but of scholarly evaluation being made subordinate to the convenience of protecting occupational status. Watts and Zimmerman's 'excuses' paper itself provided a series of excuses that granted the accounting profession relief from a variety of concerns. It excused the profession's failure to provide the reliable knowledge necessary to substantiate its privileged status, and also denied that accountants should have any concern over this failure. The chaotic nature of accounting practice was excused on the grounds that accounting practice could not be disciplined by a coherent theory. The profession's reliance on an increasing array of inconsistent rules was excused similarly on the grounds that accounting could not be comprised of anything else. And the academic community was excused from responsibility for seeking order within their discipline on the grounds that none could possibly be found.

In this manner, accounting discourse has returned to the perfunctory role it performed during the first half of the twentieth century. Accounting researchers act as followers (justifying and explaining what is) rather than innovators (offering prescriptions for improving the technical quality of accounting information). In defending positive accounting theory Watts and Zimmerman (1990: 149) claim that 'criticisms have failed the market test because they have had little influence on accounting research'. Researchers, they note, 'have not changed their approach' and 'Referees and editors of journals have not asked researchers to alter their methodology' (1990: 149). This appeal to a 'market test', however, summarily nominates publication as the terminal outcome of accounting research. If a 'market test' is to be applied to accounting research it must extend beyond publication to include the significance and practical implications of the research findings. The 'market test' for medical research does not subsist in the volume of publications, but in its capacity for improving the quality of human health. When evaluated by criteria that extend beyond just publication, the contribution of positive accounting theory is less evident: 'The accomplishments of PAT [positive accounting theory] are nonexistent. Instead of bringing forth interesting or unexpected or edifying results, PAT has presented us with findings that are empty and commonplace' (Sterling 1990a: 131). Further, the 'market' success claimed by Watts and Zimmerman may owe much to sympathetic and self-perpetuating academic cliques (Chua 1996: 137; Lee 1995a, 1997; Panozzo 1997; Williams and Rodgers 1995).

Emerging themes in accounting discourse

In spite of its self-replicating forces, the dominance of positive accounting theory has now been described as waning (Tinker and Puxty 1995). In its place, or at least in parallel, new themes in accounting discourse have achieved some prominence, including those labelled as 'critical' (Cooper and Hopper 1987, 1990) and 'new accounting research' (Morgan and Willmott 1993). Cooper and Hopper (1987: 407) define the purview of the critical research programme in accounting as follows:

> There is a growing body of research that seeks to explore the silences and lacunae – the unseen – of conventional accounting theory. This research – often critical of the theoretical orthodoxy – is frequently informed by sociology and political theory. Many of those who are critical of conventional research are also concerned to develop new accounting systems, accounting institutions and even systems of social organisation. Yet a commitment to critical research perspectives and a concern to develop new social and accounting designs do not necessarily go hand in hand.

What Morgan and Willmott (1993: 4, citations omitted) have described as 'the new accounting research' (NAR) bears similar themes:

> NAR . . . is distinguishable by its (fuller) recognition of accounting as constitutive of, as well as constituted by, the social and organizational relations through which it travels, and with which it engages. Although the embeddedness of accounting practices in the social and organizational contexts of their development and application is readily acknowledged by practitioners who, when pressed, are obliged to make accounting contextually relevant, it is widely overlooked by many accounting academics and (other) idealogues of the accountancy 'profession'.

NAR directly, or implicitly, problematizes the way that a seductive, positivistic rhetoric of objectivity has been mobilized to shape and represent accounting practice, and has thereby acted to empower its authority and force. By refusing to recognize and respect its authority to demarcate a neutral, objective domain, NAR contrives to render visible, and amplifies, accounting's wider social and historical constitution and significance as a technology of social and organizational control. Accounting is seen as a technology that actively (and politically) constitutes the world rather than passively (and neutrally) regulates and/or reports it.

These frameworks are suggestive of a *pre-professional* discipline, with the emphasis on seeking understanding of what accounting 'is' (Arrington and Francis 1989, 1993; Arrington and Schweiker 1992; Broadbent 1995; Burchell, Clubb and Hopwood 1985; Burchell *et al.* 1980; Cherns 1978; Chua 1986a, 1986b, 1988, 1996; Cooper and Sherer 1984; Davis, Menon and Morgan 1982; Day 1995; Dillard 1991; Gambling 1977; Hammond and Oakes 1992; Hines 1992; Hopper, Storey and Willmott 1987; Johnson 1995; Lavoie 1987; Lehman and Tinker 1987; Morgan 1988; Richardson 1987a; Shearer and Arrington 1993). That is, it continues a pattern of inquiry that Sterling (1972: 1–2) describes as research 'about' accounting ('efforts to explain how accounting fits into the total scheme of things'), and which differs from research 'in' accounting ('efforts to establish what the subject matter of accounting ought to be and to discover the attributes of that subject matter').

It is, perhaps, still too early to judge the utility of these new directions in accounting discourse. By their own admission, much of the work of critical accounting theorists 'has had a marginal and eccentric status attributed to it by conventional scholars, brought up in the traditions of positivism and economic understandings of accounting' (Cooper and Hopper 1990: 2). According to Panozzo (1997: 464), 'European accounting research' has yet to proceed beyond a 'fragmented adhocracy'. In common with the positivist style of research, critical researchers have yet to engage in systematic debate over 'how to account' issues, although this has not been precluded: 'we trust that critical accounting research will develop a maturity which may lead to a better set of accounts' (Cooper and Hopper 1990: 10). To date, however, in common with the majority of accounting research activity in recent decades, progress towards achieving this 'better set of accounts' is not yet easily discerned.[12]

Reorienting accounting discourse

Contrary to established perspectives on the important role of scholarly discourse within professional fields, the discourse of accounting researchers has been largely without consequence for accounting practice. Conventions, rather than research findings, continue to dictate accounting practice and accounting rule-making has fortified this pattern. These observations reinforce that accounting is presently a rule-based rather than knowledge-based discipline and that 'professionalism' in accounting is therefore of an anomalous form. In addition to illustrating this anomaly, the disconnection between accounting discourse and accounting practice also perpetuates it by influencing the nature of accounting discourse. Chambers (1970a: 2) explains how the technical practices of a profession are advanced:

> There are conservatives in every profession, but there are also progressives, who try out the ideas which emerge from the laboratories of the researchers, and adopt those which seem to be fruitful. A profession advances in this way, the superior knowledge and skill of the progressives gradually replacing the old-style practice of the conservatives. The rate of progress depends on the rate at which new ideas which can be tested are put forward by research workers.

At present, in accounting, neither of these two conditions for progress – the development of ideas and the testing of ideas – are operational. Practitioners are forbidden to 'try out the ideas that emerge from the laboratories of the researchers' by the hegemony of mandatory technical rules. In response, accounting researchers have, with few exceptions, chosen not to pursue research inquiries intended to yield ideas relevant to the practice of accounting.

Progress towards validating accountants' professional authority requires that this debilitating disjunction between scholarly discourse and practice be broken. In accordance with the patterns established in other professional fields, knowledge-enhancing processes within accounting should be expected to yield serviceable prescriptions that are applied to improve the technical quality of accounting practice. Accounting discourse should not be subordinate to, and marginalized by, the present proliferation of accounting rules. Exactly the reverse should prevail: it is the role of scholarly discourse to overcome the unserviceable and inconsistent prescriptions of those rules and so contribute to the development of a body of reliable accounting knowledge.

A significant impediment to the development of this discourse is the persistence of a belief, particularly within the academic accounting community, which has the effect of denying the possibility of professional accounting knowledge. This denial originates from two propositions. The first is that it is not possible to describe the financial features of firms in an objective and systematic manner because such features do not possess an independent and discoverable reality (for example, Hines 1988a, 1991; Ingram and Rayburn 1989; McSweeney 1997; Morgan 1988). The second concerns the unlikelihood or impossibility of achieving agreement concerning how the financial features of firms are to be described (for example, Demski 1973, 1976; Gerboth 1973; Kinney 1989; May and Sundem 1976; Watts and Zimmerman 1979). A third proposition that also enjoys some currency is that irrespective of whether or not the serviceability of accounting practices can be advanced, those practices should be determined by an ostensibly democratic and participative process. That is, preservation of the right of affected parties to influence accounting practice should be privileged above matters of technical propriety (Gerboth 1973; Hines 1983, 1987). Each of these propositions will be considered in turn.

The proposition that there is no reality independent of an observer – and that therefore descriptions of the financial features of firms must necessarily be personal rather than objective – is articulated by Morgan (1988: 484, emphasis in original):

> Accountants are enmeshed in a process of reality construction. They grasp and articulate complex realities in partial ways, and these graspings and articulations help to sustain the realities *as perceived*.
>
> One of the major challenges facing the accounting profession is to come to grips with these essential limitations. Rather than cling to an outdated concept of objectivity, they should confront the basic subjectivity of their craft and develop means of dealing with these limitations. In my view, this will lead them to adopt a much more interpretive style of accounting, building on the principles that: (a) accounting is an interpretive art and always perspective-based; and (b) that the challenge facing accountants is to develop forms of practice that emphasize how accounting statements and insights should be regarded and used as elements of a *conversation* or *dialogue*, rather than as foundational claims asserting a particular kind of objectivity or 'truth'.

These propositions founder on a fundamental contradiction. If, as Morgan (1988: 482) states, to present the reality of a situation in a 'true' manner is 'an impossible ideal', then this proposition itself must be disregarded as merely one of perspective. Scruton (1996: 6) makes this plain: 'A writer who says that there are no truths, or that all truth is merely relative is asking you not to believe him. So don't.' Moreover, those investors and other users of financial statements who have suffered losses on account of misleading accounting are unlikely to be persuaded that those losses are merely matters of perception. As Wolnizer (1995: 51) states: 'solvency is a real world condition, discoverable at any time only from real world data – from the amount of money commanded and owed, and the (money) prices assets would fetch in an orderly market'. So it is with other important financial features of firms. The process of reliably discovering and reporting these features does not require their construction, it requires only that the features (for example, assets, liabilities and profit) be defined in empirical terms: 'socially constructed phenomena are just as real as physical phenomena' (Shapiro 1997: 174). In this sense accounting has the potential to proceed in the same way as the physical sciences where the ability of scientists to study and report on phenomena (chemical reactions, the behaviour of particular species of animals, the common symptoms of an illness) commences from an acceptance of these phenomena existing and having been clearly defined. This orientation is a necessary condition for developing a body of professional accounting knowledge: 'Pursuing the science of accounting is the only cement that can bind together the factions within the profession, for science represents neutral ground' (Buckley 1980: 62; see also Sterling 1975b, 1979).

The second proposition that denies the possibility of a coherent body of accounting knowledge is the belief that accounting issues must necessarily and perpetually be in dispute. Under this perspective, accounting is said to be condemned to eternal disorder because it is unable to escape the influence of human preferences. Demski (1973: 720), for example, states that 'in general, no set of standards exists that will single out the most preferred accounting alternative without specifically incorporating the individual's beliefs and preferences'. May and Sundem (1976: 762) conclude in a similar manner, offering that 'the social choice dimension of accounting policy making' renders unlikely the possibility of identifying 'the most desirable accounting policy alternative'. Underlying these perspectives is the view that the 'ideal' of accounting practice is universal acceptance. If this is the condition sought, then, undoubtedly, it is unattainable. But the condition is an impertinent one. The construction of any robust body of knowledge is a painstaking process, but it is not dependent on universal acceptance. In the case of a profession, what the members consensually validate is what counts as professional knowledge; there is no expectation that the whole population must subscribe to the propositions. Almost invariably there will be those outside a profession (and possibly some within) whose private interests may be adversely affected by its prescriptions and who will voice their opposition. Professional authority is a regulatory device and regulatory activity commonly aggrieves particular parties. Witness, for example, how cigarette manufacturers persisted in denying the medical profession's assertion that smoking has adverse health consequences. The medical profession, however, did not respond to this opposition by modifying its pronouncements on public health in order to make them more widely accepted. On the contrary, it pursued them with even greater conviction. As is the case with other professions, external pressures and opposition should be expected within the accounting domain, particularly from those accustomed to exploiting the laxity of conventional practice. Professional practitioners are expected to suspend personal interests or preferences in favour of objective evaluation. On these grounds there is no basis for absolute denial of the possibility that accounting professionals might achieve agreement on fundamental concepts within their discipline.

Nothing radical is implied by this perspective as accountants already have shown evidence of a capacity for having shared ideas. Wells (1976: 473–4) states that historical cost accounting achieved, following the framework of Kuhn (1970), the status of a paradigm or disciplinary matrix during the course of the first 75 years of the twentieth century. That is, it came to 'dominate the literature and practices of accounting', and engendered 'shared commitments', such as 'the so-called realization and matching principles, the notion of going concern and the cost basis of asset valuation'. These principles were not imposed by fiat but enjoyed widespread acceptance within the accounting profession.[13] The point is that if the concepts of historical cost accounting – now shown to be deficient in significant and prevalent ways – were able to achieve widespread acceptance within the accounting profession, then it is erroneous to deny that a possibly superior set of concepts might also achieve such status. At the minimum, it suggests that efforts aimed towards developing a general, theory-based and prescriptive body of accounting knowledge should not, as some writers have stated, be condemned as futile.

The third commonly posited impediment to the development and application of a coherent body of accounting knowledge is the belief that the technical quality of accounting information should be made subordinate to the preferences of those with an interest in such information. The proposition is that the bounds of accounting practice should be determined by 'democratic' rather than intellectual processes. Gerboth (1973: 479 and 481) espouses this perspective:

> the fundamental concern of accounting inquiry can no longer be with the verity of the accounting rules that result from a decision making process; it must rather be with the acceptability of the process itself. . . .
>
> Said another way, the fundamental question of accounting inquiry is not 'What is income and wealth?' or even 'How shall we compute income and wealth?' Instead, the fundamental question is 'How shall we go about deciding rules for computing income and wealth?'

Hines (1983: 24) offers the following rationale for making accounting 'democratic':

> Why is there a need for participation by parties outside the accounting profession in the accounting standard-setting process? Probably the major reason for the need for representation, is that accounting standards have 'economic consequences'. Financial accounting standards can affect behaviour in the economy and therefore wealth distribution. . . .
>
> Since standards can affect resource allocation and income distribution, many people believe that the standard-setting process should be a representative, democratic process. After all, few people would accept say monetary or fiscal policy, should be determined by a private, non-representative group.

Indeed, but would anybody accept that medical practices should be determined by plebiscite? After all, the decisions of medical practitioners also clearly have economic consequences: decisions concerning what drugs to prescribe, how long a patient should stay in hospital, the certification of a period of incapacity, all have economic implications. However, if the decisions made by medical practitioners are based on their expert knowledge the resulting economic implications do not establish a case for denying professional authority. Similarly, if the accounting profession could demonstrate that its practices were based on a serviceable and coherent set of ideas then its authority would be rightfully elevated rather than diminished by the responsible application of those ideas.

This study has found no justification for accounting researchers not diligently pursuing inquiries that have some prospect of yielding contributions to improving the technical quality of financial statements. Further, no grounds have been identified for denying the possibility that such inquiries and associated debate might ultimately provide the accounting profession with a theory-based body of knowledge capable of supplanting the inconstancy of present rules. The achievement of such an outcome may be unlikely to occur in the short term, but this is not unexpected. The path that leads to reliable knowledge is travelled only slowly and has repeatedly been shown to have many dead-ends and few short-cuts. According to Kuhn (1970: 152): 'Conversions will occur a few at a time until, after the last holdouts have died, the whole profession will again be practicing under a single, but now different, paradigm.' With respect to accounting in particular, Chambers (1980: 167–8) records that 'the emergence of an agreed, serviceable form of accounting, from a "trial and error" stage, through speculation, experimentation and confirmation, to execution, cannot be expected to occur speedily'. The only means of expediting progress towards a serviceable form of accounting is diligent scholarly discourse undertaken with this objective firmly in mind. This requires a reorientation from present patterns of discourse and a recognition that research findings, particularly in a professional field, can contribute to the enhancement of human well-being:

> all knowledge is valuable only within the context of the public interest
> . . . The public interest is the only responsible guidance we have to the
> conduct of research. We are responsible for the consequences of that
> research.
>
> (Arrington 1990: 14)

The views of those who persist with the belief that there cannot be a theory-based, prescriptive body of accounting knowledge that is generally accepted by accounting professionals must, for the present time, be respected. The conclusive evidence to deny this belief would comprise such a body of knowledge and, at present, its existence cannot be affirmed. However, control of a coherent body of knowledge must provide the core justification for the elevated occupational authority and associated privileges enjoyed by accountants. These privileges extend to the academic community, not least because recognized professional status is an important determinant of which disciplines occupy space within university teaching and research programmes. It is incumbent upon those who deny the possibility of professional accounting knowledge to offer some alternative justification for the position they occupy within the university system.

Résumé and conclusion

Consistent with its affirmations that professions are characterized by cognitive authority, the sociology of professions literature has emphasized the importance of scholarly discourse within professional fields. Such discourse is relied upon to yield new knowledge and refinements of existing knowledge for application by practitioners. The emphasis, therefore, is necessarily on propositions of a prescriptive nature that contribute to maintaining the cognitive authority of practitioners within the dynamic and complex environments in which they operate.

The profession of accounting departs, fundamentally, from this pattern. The single unifying theme in commentaries on scholarly discourse in accounting is that it has generally been without consequence for accounting practice. This observation is consistent with, and reaffirms, the basic theme of this study: that accounting is presently a rule-based rather than knowledge-based discipline. However, the thesis of the present chapter extends beyond further evidencing that the professional authority of accountants still awaits cognitive vindication. It is that the accounting profession's contentment with present rules and its self-assigned task of interpreting and applying those rules has stymied the development of discourse oriented to seeking improvements in accounting practice. The offering of prescriptions for improving the technical qualities of financial reports has been disavowed by many researchers, and inquiries having little relevance to the 'how to account' issues that confront practitioners have been dominant.

The discourse of accounting researchers is thus characterized by a disengagement that derives from an obsequious acceptance of current regulatory processes. It has returned the academic accounting community to the role it occupied during the first half of the twentieth century: justifying and excusing extant practices rather than pressing for their reform. Accounting researchers should be discontented with this role and the fact that accounting knowledge – the product of academic accounting labour – is marginalized by present institutional arrangements. Redress of these circumstances requires a reorientation in accounting discourse. In particular, there is need to recognize that it is the proper function of scholarly discourse in a professional field to yield prescriptions that improve the ability of the profession to discharge its regulatory duty. With respect to accounting, this necessitates a robust and ongoing discourse focused on improving the capacity of financial reports to serve as reliable financial instruments. Only by contributing to such discourse can accounting scholars reverse the dishonour associated with participating in professional privileges while failing to contribute to validating the authority that endows them.

Sterling (1973b: 51) emphasizes the importance of 'connecting' accounting research: 'If we choose to continue research, then we must connect it to education and practice. To find the solution to a problem and then fail to teach it or practice it is to fail to solve the problem.' Present accounting rules have not facilitated connections but, instead, established and perpetuated divisions. This chapter has sought to demonstrate how these divisions have contributed to a disabling of accounting discourse. This theme of cognitive disconnectedness is pursued further in the next chapter in the context of accounting education.

7 Professionalism, accounting rules and accounting education

> A profession is more than a trade or a business; and professional education is more than mastery of facts and rules.
>
> (Vatter 1964: 429)

Introduction

The prolific accounting rule-making of recent decades has mandated techni-cally deficient practices and invoked an emphasis on rule-compliance rather than serviceability as the criterion of quality in financial reporting. The theme introduced in the preceding chapter is that these circumstances have also pre-cipitated a weakening of the intellectual fabric of the accounting profession. Exploration of this theme commenced with an examination of the nature of scholarly discourse within accounting. This was shown to be characterized by a diverse range of inquiries generally disconnected from the practical matter of 'how to account'. Seemingly content with – and often endorsing – account-ing practice being dictated by the vagaries of present rules, accounting researchers have largely abdicated responsibility for improving the technical quality of accounting information. This divide between practice and scholarly discourse has disabled a basic means by which the technical standards of a profession are advanced. The purpose of this chapter is to pursue this theme further, but now within the setting of accounting education. Particular emphasis is to be placed on processes that are relied upon to pass on to a new audience comprehension of established ideas and practices as well as develop more generic competencies. Within the professional accounting context it encompasses university and professional qualification programmes.[1]

Learning is among the most satisfying and rewarding of all human endeav-ours, yielding in its elevated forms a comprehension of causes and effects that leads to enlightened patterns of behaviour and an enriched sense of purpose.[2] However, not all learning is accompanied by a detailed understanding of what is observed or experienced. A young child may learn not to touch a radiator purely on the basis of misadventure. Similarly, particular facts may be incul-cated by instruction or rote processes. These shallower forms of learning –

where descriptive or prescriptive statements are accepted without explanation or justification of their validity – are appropriate in particular situations. A bicyclist need not know why a bicycle is stable vertically in motion but falls to the horizontal when stationary. A person involved in the preparation and sale of foodstuffs can be instructed in appropriate hygiene procedures without a detailed knowledge of bacteriology having been imparted. In circumstances such as these, responsibility for detailed understanding and explanation of observed phenomena and prescriptions that guide human action is left to others.

In professional fields, however, responsibility for understanding and justifying what is practised cannot be transferred elsewhere. As stated by Moore (1970: 15–16), a professional, as a specialist, 'must be supreme, for who other than another similarly qualified specialist, can challenge him?'. For this reason, education in professional fields cannot properly be reduced to just technical instruction. Only when the exercise of skill is transcended by understanding is a valid rationale for professional authority established: 'We may acquire skills by learning the rules, but skills without understanding are potentially dangerous' (Chambers 1966b: 2). The ideals of professional education, therefore, must extend beyond the development of technical proficiency to emphasize the acquisition of knowledge. This requires that what is taught be supported by logical argument or other persuasive evidence. Such an emphasis engenders a strong sense of purpose in both the educated and the educator and provides the foundation for the inherently satisfying qualities commonly associated with professional work (Goode 1960: 903; Mumford 1983: 250). In addition, it promotes an affinity for that work and a dissatisfaction with any matters related to professional practice being inadequately justified or understood. An expectation that the knowledge imparted will have practical and socially beneficent applications accentuates these outcomes and entices practitioners to seek the continuous improvement in their work that makes for the betterment of their profession.

Against these measures, accounting education – increasingly immersed in the mundane and chaotic mire of rules detached from commercial realities – departs fundamentally from the expected role of education in professional fields. Instead of the authority of knowledge, it is the authority of regulatory fiat that holds sway. In addition, the shaping of accounting education by the prescriptions of official pronouncements has turned what should be an intellectually invigorating process into one marked by antonymous qualities: 'going by printed rules is not very interesting or stimulating' (Paton 1967: 11). Thus, the argument developed in this chapter is that present accounting rules and the accounting profession's satisfaction with them have diminished the intellectual vitality of accounting education.

The following section of the chapter canvasses perspectives on the nature and role of education in professional fields generally and this is followed by an analysis of views on the state of accounting education. The adverse impacts of a reliance on regulatory pronouncements within accounting education are then examined. The chapter then proceeds to offer proposals for the reform of accounting education, emphasizing the need for students to learn about accounting rather than just accounting rules.

Professional education generally

That the right to practise in a professional field is preceded by an extensive education process, which imparts specialized knowledge and establishes practitioner competence, is routinely mentioned in trait-based characterizations of professions (Barber 1963: 673–6; Goode 1960: 903; Greenwood 1966/1957: 11; Millerson 1964: 4; Moore 1970: 10–13; Pavalko 1971: 26; Wilensky 1964: 144). The general tenor of this literature is exemplified by the comments of Barber (1963: 674):

> The university professional school has as one of its basic functions the transmission to its students of the generalized and systematic knowledge that is the basis of professional performance. Not only the substantive knowledge itself, but knowledge of how to keep up with continuing advances in professional knowledge is what the university school seeks to give its students.

This notion that prerequisite education programmes directly serve to prepare intending practitioners appears to be a tributary that flowed into the professional doctrine rather than being firmly present at its source. Elliott (1972: 30), recounting the educational requirements for entry to the medical profession in eighteenth-century England, illustrates how the connection between education and preparation for professional practice was originally somewhat tenuous:

> Examinations for the Licentiate and the Fellowship of the Royal College of Physicians were brief, oral, conducted in Latin and covered the classical languages and a few fields of medicine. The important qualification was a degree from Oxford or Cambridge. This was even preferred to a degree from a Continental or Scottish university, though by the end of the eighteenth century these were giving vocational medical education in the newly developed areas of medical science. Graduates of these universities were unable to become more than licentiates of the Royal College unless they also held an English qualification. There was little or no instruction in any subject at this time at Oxford or Cambridge, and especially none in medicine.

In this manner, educational requirements served primarily as a means of screening for social rather than intellectual standards: 'no matter how vague the educational requirements or how much of a formality the recruitment procedures, the leaders of all the professions justified their systems on the grounds that they ensured that only men of the necessary social standing gained access to the professions' (Elliott 1972: 30). Carr-Saunders (1966/ 1928: 5) expresses a similar view, suggesting – with particular reference to professional associations that emerged during the first half of the nineteenth century – that would-be members were sometimes excluded 'for reasons not strictly relevant to professional competence'. However, in the course of the second half of the nineteenth century the focus of prescribed educational qualifications began to align more closely with the particular knowledge and competencies that would equip professionals for their work environment. This transformation occurred with such rapidity that by the early twentieth century Carr-Saunders (1966/1928: 5) was prepared to proclaim that 'With a few unimportant exceptions, professional associations can now be said to be exclusive only in the sense that they exclude the unqualified.'

Accompanying the emergence of education programmes that placed an emphasis on preparation for professional practice was 'the beginning of various experiments with different systems of occupational selection and training and of debate about their vocational and social consequences' (Elliott 1972: 43). Many of these 'experiments' established features of professional education that have persisted, including the development of 'professional schools' that attempt 'to define and pass on a central core of professional knowledge and skill' (Elliott 1972: 44). Examinations were introduced as a means of testing competence, supplanting the 'various systems of patronage' that had operated previously (Elliott 1972: 44; see also Carr-Saunders and Wilson 1933: 317; Eraut 1994: 7; Hoskin and Macve 1986, 1994; Millerson 1964: 121–9).

As a consequence of these developments the link between 'education' and 'professions' became firmly established, as Freidson (1986: 26) explains:

> Since the nineteenth century . . . some kind of formal higher education marks professionals off from other workers, distinguishing both the nature of their training and the nature of their skill. Such education is a basic credential for professionals; it delineates the foundation of their expertise. The distinction has lain at the root of thinking about professions as a special class or category of occupations.

Gradually, and particularly during the twentieth century, universities assumed increased responsibility for the formal education that provides the entrée to professional fields. This has supplanted in large part previous systems of apprenticeships, articled clerkships and pupillage, and also privately administered schools (Slayton 1978: 131; Wilensky 1964: 144; Wright 1978: 125–6).

This change did not proceed without dissent, particularly over perceived conflict between 'university education' and 'professional education', and the related struggle for ascendancy between academics and practitioners. The origins of this divide and its surrounding debate can be traced back to Francis Bacon, who opined:

Among so many great foundations of colleges in Europe I find it strange that they are dedicated to professions and none left free to arts and sciences at large. This I take to be a great cause that hath hindered the progression of learning because these fundamental knowledges have been studied but in passage.

(cited in Carr-Saunders and Wilson 1933: 308)

The conflict alluded to by Bacon has, according to Eraut (1994: 8), persisted in the form of a 'tension between university and professional-oriented perspectives on knowledge'. However, the resolution of this tension has not been exclusively in favour of the perspective of professions:

Professional organizations . . . increasingly need university validation to confirm the status, worth and complexity of their knowledge base. However, they also lose a significant degree of control over part of the professional preparation process. They can still influence university courses, some with more impact than others, but they cannot fend off university influences on staff and students. Universities will seek to broaden and academicize the knowledge base, and to challenge some cherished, long-established, professional practices.

(Eraut 1994: 7–8)

Carr-Saunders and Wilson (1933: 316) held out the hope that reconciliation of the perceived conflict between 'professional' and 'university' education would flow from a common recognition of the need for 'theoretical instruction'. It would appear that this optimism has not yet been vindicated, on account of different emphases: 'The norms of higher education tend to favour scientific knowledge rather than professional knowledge' (Eraut 1994: 9).

Two fundamental criticisms of professional education have their origin in this perceived conflict. The first is that 'in virtually every profession there have been complaints that professional education is too academic, theoretical, or unrealistic, that it fails to prepare novices for practice' (Freidson 1986: 212).[3] The second has been advanced by contributors to the sociology of professions literature labelled as adopting 'critical' or 'monopolist' perspectives. While there are variations in the precise arguments pursued by these writers, the common theme is of unnecessary elaboration in professional education that functions to maintain market scarcity by artificially restricting the supply of practitioners. That university-based professional education programmes are typically subsidized by the state, compounds the concerns of these writers (Mustard 1978: 147). Larson (1977: 70, emphasis in original), for example, stresses the importance of formal education in the development of the privileged economic and social status of professions:

control of the market ultimately required the institutionalization and the control of a system for the standardized production of producers. The professions' potential for *both* market control and superior ranking largely depended, therefore, on the organization of an educational system along modern lines.

It is the state that enables this occupational empowerment: 'the creation of professional exchange value ultimately depends upon the state – or, more precisely, upon the state's monopolistic appropriation of a social system of education and credentialing' (Larson 1977: 211; see also Turner 1995: 139).

Within these critical commentaries the pedagogic worth of professional education programmes has been viewed with some scepticism. Duman's (1979: 132) criticism is subtle, with 'a system of training and testing of candidates' described as part of the 'formula' of professionalization. However, Collins (1979: 146), with particular reference to medicine, is forthright: 'the elaborate educational requirements leading up to and including medical school have served primarily for screening, indoctrination into the group, and for an idealized facade'. Similarly, Rueschemeyer (1983: 53) alleges that 'over-education with the aim of public respectability' has been 'more or less common', while Collins (1990: 37) characterizes professional education as constituting 'a particular kind of ritual' rather than a necessary preparation for practice.

These perspectives have not passed unchallenged, with Freidson (1986: 73–4) among the most vigorous respondents:

> The formalization of professional education in the early part of this century was based on much more than the desire to raise the professions' prestige and restrict the supply of practitioners, as the crude conspiracy theories of recent revisionist histories of the Progressive Era imply. The reorganization of professional education was also an attempt to satisfy a very real need to create a more reliable system of market signals than that which existed earlier.

Following from this reassessment, Freidson (1986: 82) returns to the functional role of professional education articulated by the trait theorists: 'Credentialed graduates are expected to absorb the knowledge and skill of their professions and then go out into the world to practice them.'

This résumé of perspectives on professional education further illustrates the often discordant nature of the sociology of professions literature. Seeking escape from this limitation, this study returns again to a more pragmatic understanding which emphasizes that professions are characterized by an elevated occupational authority which must have exclusive and cognitively-grounded expertise as its fundamental justification. As a particular kind of regulatory system, professional jurisdictions are neither favoured nor condemned on a priori grounds, but to be evaluated empirically in terms of their contribution to enhancing social order. The pertinent issue within the context of professional education concerns preparation for the effective administration of these jurisdictions: 'Professional expertise is above all a function of professional education' (Slayton 1978: 137).

As a consequence of their elevated occupational authority, professionals construct their work context rather than just operate within it. That is, the technical aspects of professional practice are not usually determined by the directives of clients or external regulatory agencies but by professionals themselves. To accord with this independent status, professional education must embrace more than just the teaching of skills which equip practitioners with a capacity to perform certain tasks. Instead, the onus of professional education is preparation for the administration of an authority that is not subject to close external invigilation.

The bounds of professional education must therefore extend beyond those of other educational experiences. The training and testing necessary for the acquisition of a driving licence are intended to ensure that drivers comprehend road safety and have achieved at least a base level of driving skill. There is no intention that licensed drivers will be qualified to administer the road transport system. However, professional qualifications provide admission to membership of occupational groups that are vested with responsibility for overseeing particular domains of social importance. This requires the development of a sense of duty to the discipline itself, as explained by Flexner in connection with medicine:

> A medical school cannot expect to produce fully trained doctors, it can at most hope to equip students with a limited amount of knowledge, to train them in the method and spirit of scientific medicine, and to launch them with a momentum that will make them active learners, observers, readers, thinkers, and experimenters for years to come.
>
> (cited in Mustard 1978: 143)

Consistent with this perspective, the establishment of effective professional education programmes involves striking a balance between equipping students with the expertise that provides immediate technical competence and providing a more general understanding of the discipline. Krever (1978: 157) outlines the nature of this problem within the context of professional legal education:

> As in the case of all other 'true' professions, professional legal education is characterized by the inherent and perpetual problem of combining judiciously the sound theoretical base of the intellectual body of knowledge that is the hallmark of what I have called the true professions with a training in the practical application of the principles found in that intellectual body of knowledge, before the new practitioners are certified as competent to a public incapable of judging competence without assistance.

Saul (1997: 74) warns of the consequences of failing to resolve this problem within education generally: 'A student who graduates with mechanistic skills and none of the habits of thought has not been educated. Such people will have difficulty playing their role as citizens.' The burden carried by professional education is even greater on account of the authority ceded to professionals. Preparation for the administration of this authority is the imperative of professional education. This mandates, above all, a need for professional practitioners to be knowledgeable about matters that pertain to their jurisdiction.

Accounting education

Evidence of discontent with the state of accounting education is abundant, and also shown to be longstanding by Carr-Saunders and Wilson's (1933: 220–1) comment: 'we must ask if the accountant's . . . education is such as to fit him for the varied and highly skilled duties which he is called upon to perform'. The authors concluded that 'the volume of dissatisfaction that has been expressed suggests forcibly that reform of the syllabus could be carried further with advantage' (1933: 224). Part of the explanation offered for this circumstance was the relatively late arrival of accounting within the university system (Bloom *et al.* 1994: 7; Carr-Saunders and Wilson 1933: 318; Millerson 1964: 141–2; Paisey and Paisey 1996: 108; Van Whye 1994: ch. 1; Wright 1978: 126). However, the consolidation of accounting as a university discipline has not eliminated criticism:

> accounting education began to swing to the universities at the end of the nineteenth century. That created opportunities for enrichment and refinement, by recourse to the established and fruitful methods of analysis and inquiry of other disciplines. But the opportunities have been passed by.
>
> (Chambers 1987: 100)

Dissatisfaction with the state of accounting education has not been the preserve of any single group. Official inquiries, academics and practitioners have all expressed concerns about accounting education in universities, and programmes leading to professional qualifications have also been criticized. Each of these areas will be considered in turn.

Official inquiries

Inquiries into the state of accounting education that can be labelled as 'official' – on account of having been commissioned by recognized institutions – include the following:

- *Survey of Accountancy Education in Australia*, conducted by W.J. Vatter ('Vatter Report' 1964) and sponsored by the Australian professional accounting bodies.

- *Future Accounting Education: Preparing for the Expanding Profession*, prepared by The AAA Committee on the Future Structure, Content, and Scope of Accounting Education (1986) under the chairmanship of N. Bedford ('Bedford Report').
- The Accounting Education Change Commission (AECC), established in 1989 by the AAA and which commenced promulgating 'Issues Statements' and 'Position Statements' in 1990.
- *Accounting in Higher Education: Report of the Review of the Accounting Discipline in Higher Education*, under the chairmanship of R. Mathews ('Mathews Report' 1990) and commissioned by the Australian Government.
- *Accounting Education: Charting the Course Through a Perilous Future*, a report authored by Albrecht and Sack (2000) and sponsored by the AAA and various professional associations and accounting firms.

Each of these inquiries has found much to criticize.[4] The author of the Vatter Report described Australian accounting education as being in need of 'drastic revision' (1964: 445) and this provided the impetus for the introduction of graduate entry to Australian professional accounting associations. This firmly established accounting as a university discipline within Australia, but disquiet over the quality of tertiary education in accounting has been ongoing. The Mathews Report, in particular, identified a number of concerns. It describes accounting education in Australian universities as being 'in great need of support and revitalisation' (1990, vol. 1: xix), and providing 'insufficient opportunity for graduates to gain the skills and knowledge they require to participate as educated citizens and professionals in the social, political and ethical environments in which they will live and work' (vol. 1: 86). With respect to accounting staff in institutions of higher education, 'many' were said to 'lack any sense of intellectual curiosity' (vol. 1: xxii).

In the United States, the conclusion of the Bedford Report was that 'future accountants are not receiving the preparation they need to meet the increased demands of the expansive, more complex profession that is emerging' (1986: 178). The report notes that 'textbooks and faculty have required students to learn more factual rules and procedures to be applied in a rather rigid fashion', and identified the existence of a 'primary focus in many cases . . . on the acquisition of knowledge needed to pass professional examinations' (1986: 177). Concerns were expressed that such approaches 'are not conducive to creative thinking and do not motivate students to self-development' (1986: 177). In response to these criticisms the AECC (1990, emphasis in original) proposed that university programmes in accounting 'should prepare students to *become* professional accountants, not to *be* professional accountants'. A focus 'on developing analytical and conceptual thinking, not on memorizing professional standards' was favoured.

The extent of the impact of these proposed reforms remains problematic (Davis and Sherman 1996: 159; Fogarty 1997; Van Whye 1994: 221), and in the more recent study by Albrecht and Sack (2000) accounting education is portrayed as being in crisis. The authors express their 'belief that accounting education today is plagued with many serious problems' and their 'concern that if those problems are not seriously addressed and overcome, they will lead to the demise of accounting education' (2000: 1). According to Albrecht and Sack (2000: 1), 'things cannot get much worse', with declining numbers of students seeking to study accounting, and widespread dissatisfaction among accounting graduates and their employers with accounting education.

Academic commentators

Perhaps somewhat curiously, in view of ostensibly being in a position to most directly influence accounting education, accounting academics have been among its most fervent critics. The statements of accounting academics from the United States, United Kingdom and Australia presented in Box 7.1 support this assertion.

Box 7.1

Statements critical of accounting education made by accounting academics:

> In many universities throughout the country accounting training has lost sight of the purposes of a university education and has attempted to teach much too much technical detail and other minute bits of knowledge, thereby failing to produce the best professional accountants universities are capable of producing.
>
> (Weiser 1966: 518)

> We have not done as good a job of educating our students as we should.
>
> (Sterling 1975a: 52)

> . . . the trend in accounting education must make one pessimistic. For many years, academic critics viewed accounting – wrongly, to my mind – as unworthy of a place in higher studies. It got in at last. Now that we are substituting rule-of-thumb for reason, one must sadly admit that our critics were right.
>
> (Baxter 1994/1979: 20)

> Historically ankle-shackled to three-legged stools in backrooms divorced from decision-making, accountants have moved to the forefront of economic decision-making. But have the universities positioned themselves responsively to the accountant's emerging role? In many ways, we think not.
>
> (Jensen and Arrington 1983: 5–6)

Today's students and tomorrow's practitioners are saturated with a litany of rules and procedures that are supported by little other than expedient reasoning, ad hoc explanations, and piecemeal rationalizations. Professional accounting education is certainly not a talkshop for exploring the meaning of social existence: rather it resembles a rote learning process in which students are inculcated with the profession's party line by pedantic and legalistic methods. . . . The ultimate trivialization and degradation of accounting is the near obsession with rules and bookkeeping procedures.

(Tinker 1985: xx–xxi)

. . . the standard textbook and curriculum foist on their consumers a peculiar and in-bred dogma, rather than invite them to explore what is considered as reliable knowledge in other fields.

(Chambers 1987: 101)

The undergraduate accounting major of today is narrowly educated. . . . in order to function effectively in the complex business environment of the 21st century . . . the future professional accountant will need a broader educational base than is provided under the current educational pattern for a degree in accounting.

(Langenderfer 1987: 330)

Beginning with the textbooks for the first financial accounting course and continuing through the intermediate and advanced accounting textbooks, the subject is offered as if a tedious catalogue of practice were being inputted into computer memory. Accounting is not presented as an *interesting* subject that figures importantly in the calculations of managers, investors and creditors, and government policy makers but instead as a collection of rules that are to be memorized in an uncritical, almost unthinking way.

(Zeff 1989a: 203–4, emphasis in original)

. . . financial accounting is taught as if it were in a strait-jacket. Students are indoctrinated in the rules of extant practice and are seldom exposed to the historical background or institutional framework that has shaped current practice.

(Zeff 1989b: 167)

The thorough reform of accounting requires an appreciation of the purpose and nature of accounting. But such an intellectual investment has not been made by the profession. Aspiring accountants are still encouraged to learn the litany through legalistic and pedantic rules.

(Mitchell *et al.* 1991: 20)

... there is a significant resistance to change on the part of accounting educators. Concentrating myopically on the authoritative interpretations of generally accepted accounting principles (GAAP), many instructors persist in explaining the role of accounting in terms of objective and functional rules.

(Bloom et al. 1994: 5)

... the emphasis on rote learning, shallow education, following the orthodoxy, applying the rules and algorithms and treating accounting as a sort of advanced plumbing [are] the terminally tedious characteristics which typify accounting education and training [and] leave the accountant, however well-intentioned, without the wherewithal to reflect upon their own experience.

(Gray 1995: 254)

Much teaching observed by us consisted of a 'drumming of facts' into students and an emphasis upon technical and numerical exercises. Indeed, so widespread was this norm that students – and even staff – vigorously resisted efforts to depart therefrom. . . . The 'givens' of standard practice were emphasised, particularly in financial accounting courses. 'Truth' was found in quantification and in abstract and mathematical regularity, with students being encouraged to learn 'certain' rules.

(Gallhofer and Haslam 1996: 23)

... despite the large investment, it is frequently asserted that entry-level accountants are neither well educated nor adequately prepared to enter the profession, and, even where their technical preparation is adequate, other aspects such as communication skills and ethical aspects are not sufficiently developed.

(Mathews 2001: 380)

The common themes in these perspectives are that accounting education is superficial, excessively technical, mundane and often based on algorithmic or rote processes.

Practitioners

Criticisms of accounting education made by practitioners centre on allegations that novices are inadequately prepared for the work environment. In this manner the criticisms of practitioners have often been at variance with those levied by their academic colleagues. Mautz (1974: 356), for example, has asked:

Isn't it just possible that we have gone a little far in stressing concepts at the expense of techniques, that we have been carried away with teaching accounting as a subject like one might teach history, that we've forgotten that most of our students will be expected to become performers, not critics, shortly after they graduate?

Similar concerns were identified in the Mathews Report (1990, vol. 1: 83):

Students, graduates and employers were often critical of course structures and content. Students' and graduates' overwhelming criticism was that courses were not 'practical' enough in the sense of not being related to the world of business. Some employers, especially those from small chartered firms and public practices, agreed, complaining that many graduates 'do not know a debit from a credit'.

These reservations over the technical proficiency of accounting graduates have also been accompanied by concerns over deficiencies in more general qualities, such as communication skills, the ability to work cooperatively, organizational skills, self-learning and capacity for analytical thinking (Albrecht 1997; Dow and Feldman 1997; Saudagaran 1996; Taylor and Fisher 1990; Williams 1991).

Professional qualifications

The completion of a university level course is usually only the first step towards qualifying as an accounting practitioner. The status of 'professional accountant' is generally associated with the successful completion of an education programme administered by an accounting association and undertaken subsequent to university studies.[5] At this level, criticism is, again, significant. Indeed, while these programmes constitute the 'higher' component of professional accounting education, criticism of their educational worth is often of the most fundamental kind. In the context of the United Kingdom, Roslender (1992: 37) alleges that:

As far as the professional examinations are concerned it is normal to see the worst features of learning almost universally practised. Reliance on study manuals and question and answer books rather than conventional textbooks is extensive. . . . In the same way as this word processor stores these paragraphs in its memory for as long as it is switched on (unless they are purposefully saved) so the various knowledges needed to pass particular examinations are learned quickly and forgotten.

Within this milieu it is suggested that 'only the profession's recommendations count as knowledge' (Puxty, Sikka and Willmott 1994: 88). In professional auditing examinations, 'theory is the standards and guidelines' and

'Some questions require answers which amount to little more than a precis of the main points of a guideline' (Roslender 1992: 184–5). As a consequence:

> There is no place . . . for critical thinking, for reflecting on doing audits. You either know the prescriptions or you are a waffler (who might just get through on the discussion questions). . . . In this way auditing is represented as a mainly technical activity. It is rarely viewed as an activity which has social, organisational and behavioural dimensions and for this reason it is dangerously myopic.
>
> (Roslender 1992: 185)

The textbooks recommended for use by students reinforce this restrictive understanding:

> Most of the authors generally seemed to regard auditing standards and guidelines as oracles of wisdom . . . failing to recognise that auditing standards and guidelines, like most regulations are the result, not of wisdom, but of power and authority. . . . The students, in the opinion of this writer, need to be made aware that such pronouncements are mere opinions and not facts. These neophytes, upon seeing the same things repeated again and again (for example, auditing standards and guidelines) without much of a challenge and the professional examinations' insistence on testing the students' ability to recall and apply 'official knowledge', will no doubt be persuaded to believe that the books are describing facts.
>
> (Sikka 1987: 301)

In the United States, the main professional qualification has been subject to a similar style of criticism: 'The Uniform CPA Examination . . . emphasizes detailed, objective information over general, subjective knowledge' and 'much of the Examination tests the candidates' knowledge of "generally accepted accounting principles" (including the latest pronouncements) and their application to concrete cases' (Zeff 1989b: 167–8). However, it is Power's (1991) autobiographical reflections on qualifying as a chartered accountant with the ICAEW that offer, perhaps, the most poignant critique of the nature of educational programmes that lead to professional accounting qualifications. He relates that 'The dominant instructional idea is not to develop understanding but to score marks in the most efficient manner possible' (1991: 340–1). Any deeper interrogation of accounting is censured: 'The ultimate sanction is the demand "not to think . . . that's the road to failure. Why waste energy contemplating issues that lie beyond the syllabus?" ' (1991: 343). According to Power (1991: 346), 'the system as a whole is perceived as an elaborate hurdle' that is surmounted by variables other than competence: 'many factors intervene in examination success but intellectual ability is rarely one of them' (1991: 345). Instead of offering a rewarding and enlightening experience, accounting education is described as 'a limiting context' (1991: 351).

Accounting rules and accounting education

The concerns over the quality of accounting education that have been noted are so comprehensive and pervasive as to suggest that they are unlikely to be wholly attributable to purely pedagogic factors. Indeed, there would not appear to be any obvious reason for suspecting that participants in accounting education – teachers, textbook writers, students and others – are inherently inferior to their counterparts in other disciplines. Rather, the most promising clue for explaining the malaise in accounting education is found in the observation of Eraut (1994: 56): 'The quality of initial professional education depends to a considerable degree on the quality of practice.' That is, the most fundamental problem with accounting education is accounting. This study has argued that claims that the accounting profession's authority has a firm cognitive grounding are unsubstantiated. It is this anomaly that begets many of the failings in accounting education. In particular, it gives rise to the basic contradiction of expecting professional outcomes from accounting education when the primary means for enabling such outcomes – a robust body of knowledge that provides a framework for guiding practice – is lacking.

That formal accounting rules now play a dominating role in accounting education – in university and professional qualification programmes – is beyond doubt. It is repeatedly alluded to in the quotations presented in Box 7.1 and made evident from even a cursory examination of accounting textbooks and syllabuses. Indeed, it would be a surprise if such a scenario did not prevail given the sovereignty of these rules within the contemporary accounting setting. However, no coherent theoretical framework underlies the rules; their prescriptions are beholden only to the convenience of convention and the expediency of institutional endorsement. Inevitably, an educational experience anchored to these rules cannot escape their limitations. More particularly, the pedagogic impact of present accounting rules has been to fragment accounting curricula, establish barriers to comprehending the nature of the commercial environment, mandate the teaching of accounting practices that cannot be substantiated by argument or evidence, and foster superficiality in both learning and teaching. Each of these issues will be considered in turn.

Fragmentation of accounting curricula

Accounting rules contain prescriptions pertaining to particular accounting 'inputs'. They do not deal with the aggregative 'outputs' – financial statements – that are the 'finished products' of accounting. Hence, the focus is typically on the individual line items in financial statements, or even individual forms of transactions, rather than provisions of a more general qualitative nature. Accounting standards contain prescriptions, for example, on accounting for inventories, leases, taxation, research and development costs, construction contracts, depreciation, employee entitlements and the like. This study has already noted that these 'inputs' are not guided by any sense of a coherent whole. That is, accounting standards are 'building blocks', but they have not been designed with recourse to the requirements of a 'whole product'. One consequence of this, in an accounting education context, is that accounting curricula become fragmented. Textbook writers have come to treat individual accounting standards as distinct realms: each is assigned a separate chapter and rarely is any attempt made to evaluate the result of their combined application. On the contrary, achieving compliance with individual rules is customarily treated as a terminal outcome.

Two deleterious consequences arise from this circumstance. The first is that accounting education is significantly bereft of the 'patterns' that enable learning by understanding: the identification of basic concepts that can be reapplied in like circumstances. The second is that this absence necessarily imbues accounting education with qualities of technicalism (treating prescribed procedures as ends in themselves). Paradoxically, what is 'learned' from one accounting standard is not only unlikely to be able to be reapplied in connection with other accounting issues, but likely to impede understanding of such issues. The valuation rules, for example, applying to different classes of assets and encompassing present values, costs, realizable values and recoverable amounts cannot be linked in spite of the fact that they are concerned with a common aspect (valuation) of a common input (assets) to the preparation of a statement of financial position. That research and development costs can be recognized as assets when they are expected 'beyond any reasonable doubt' to be recoverable (AASB 1011, clause .31), sheds no light on how to account for pre-production costs in the extractive industries (AASB 1022), even though the accounting issues would appear to be the same. Upwards revaluations of non-current assets under AASB 1041 (para. 5.5) are generally required to be credited to a reserve, but for insurance companies (only) a revaluation that relates to an investment is required to be recognized in the statement of financial performance (AASB 1023, para. 10).

Unable to locate with confidence any patterns or consistent principles in the accounting standards they are required to master, accounting students are forced to adopt the most mundane of learning methods: rote processes. The idiosyncrasies of individual standards are justified only by the authority that accompanies official pronouncement and the educational process is reduced to one of direction rather than understanding. The outcome is that the 'parts' of accounting are inculcated in the same manner in which factory workers might be trained in particular production line processes; that is, without having any coherent understanding of the overall activity in which they are participating, or the nature of the completed products they are contributing to producing.

Separation from the commercial environment

A professional's conception of his or her task is, according to Chambers (1969/1965: 658), 'tempered by an understanding of and a sympathy with the environment of that task'. For the practising accountant, that environment comprises commercial activity. Present accounting rules, however, impose an artificial, yet formidable, divide between the accounting student and the complex and uncertain nature of the commercial environment. Nowhere is this more evident than in transactions of the following kind which accounting students, commencing from introductory courses, are routinely required to 'account for': 'Purchased for $20,000 a motor vehicle which is to be used equally in each of the 10 years of its useful life after which it will be sold for $1,000.' How was the 'useful life' established? How was the future market value derived? And on what grounds was the pattern of future use determined? These are fundamental issues that are concealed from the student in order to contrive a standard outcome; the 'right answer'. There is, of course, a place for simplifying assumptions in education. Reducing complexity – for example, by minimizing the volume of data under consideration – may foster desirable educational outcomes by helping to ensure that attention is focused on important concepts or issues. But, carried too far, simplifying assumptions give rise to a deceit that is the antithesis of education.

Accounting rules disconnected from the realities of commercial action foster such deceits: 'accounting teachers seduce the students by making them believe that accounting problems are well structured, well defined, and have an easily recognizable solution' (Sterling 1975a: 55). The ubiquitous cost allocations required by accounting standards are an obvious example. Were students required to find – rather than simply be given – the inputs necessary to determine calculation-based depreciation charges, the extraordinarily subjective nature of these calculations would be made evident. Instead, accounting education conspires to shield this understanding via a neat and simplistic textbook world where questions are designed to 'fit the rules' rather than invite inquiries that promote understanding of the commercial environment and the role of accounting within it. The useful lives of assets, cost allocation methods, the expected residual values of assets, the likelihood of expenditures giving rise to 'future benefits', the possibility of income tax assets being realized, the recoverable amounts of assets, and so on, are invariably treated as 'givens' in accounting education. But they are not given in the real-world commercial environment in which the accounting professional must operate, they must be estimated. Further, there is often no reliable data on which to base such estimations with the result that arbitrary conjectures must be substituted. To hide this fact from accounting students is a deceit that has no place in any university or professional education programme. The outcome is mis-education: students are endowed with a misplaced faith in accounting procedures that are made to appear workable by the contrived data of textbook problems.[6]

A further illustration of how accounting rules impose an artificial divide between students and the commercial environment concerns the selection of topics for inclusion in textbooks and curricula. The promulgation of an accounting standard is treated as signalling that a topic should be included (and, of course, it provides a framework for dealing with the topic). Within Australian textbooks, for example, accounting for employee entitlements was rarely mentioned until after a standard dealing with this matter was issued (AASB 1028). Since then it has been made the subject of whole chapters (for example, Henderson and Peirson 1998: ch. 14; Whittred, Zimmer and Taylor 1996: ch. 9). However, other apparently important accounting topics remain omitted from textbooks and curricula as they are yet to be honoured by an accounting standard. In this way, accounting education is really 'education in accounting rules', both in terms of what topics are included and how they are treated. The agendas of standard setting bodies are determined by the interaction of a complex set of forces, including the extent of perceived 'problems' in the absence of a standard, the likelihood of obtaining adequate consensus, the complexity of proposed topics, the lobbying of interested parties, and the standards already issued in other jurisdictions. As a result, the subject matter of accounting education also ends up being driven significantly by these factors rather than an objective assessment of which particular aspects of commercial activity warrant attention.

Financial reports are expected to correspond (Chambers 1966b; Sterling 1989, 1990b) or be isomorphic (Wolnizer 1987: 56) with the commercial realities that define a firm's financial position and progress. Only this quality can make these reports reliable guides for human action. Accounting education programmes that fail to promote understanding of the complex, changing and uncertain nature of the commercial environment must inevitably compromise the capacity of those who are required to operate within that environment.

Treating what is wrong as right

The tendency of accounting rules to contradict the established findings in various fields of knowledge relevant to accounting practice has been noted earlier in this study (Chapter 4). This gives rise to a basic conflict within accounting education. It is 'wrong' to aggregate costs and net realizable values in order to determine an overall value for inventory, since such a process breaches a fundamental principle of arithmetic. However, it is 'right' to apply such a process in order to achieve compliance with present accounting standards. In a similar manner, it is 'right' under such rules to subtract a future value from a past cost in order to determine a present quantification of depreciation expense, in spite of the nonsensical nature of the calculation. It is 'right' to attempt to apportion 'taxation effects' to individual transactions and balances in spite of the fact that it is the aggregation of total assessable income and allowable deductions that determines a taxation liability. It is 'right' when accounting for construction contracts under AASB 1009 to add progressively recognized profits to costs incurred and then deduct progress billings. The result of this bookkeeping algorithm is then represented in the balance sheet as an asset or a liability (the amount due to, or from, customers for contract work), according to the happenstance of whether a debit or credit balance results.

While such practices are 'right' according to accounting rules, they are 'wrong' when criteria based on legitimate aggregation, legal principles and informed commercial action are applied. Accounting textbook writers and educators are thus confronted by a dilemma that is typically resolved in favour of giving priority to what is mandated by the rules. The outcome is indoctrination rather than education: 'Novices have neither the experience nor the wisdom, nor even the fortitude, to question their mentors. They suppose that what is taught with authority, and what is said to be established practice, is taught and practised for good reason' (Chambers 1994: 76).

This treatment of what is 'wrong' as what is 'right' in accounting education highlights the fundamental contradiction encountered by a profession that has turned to regulatory fiat, rather than reason, to govern its technical practices. No simplifying assumption or any other pretence can be offered to justify the systematic teaching of accounting ideas and practices that depart in significant and recurrent ways from what constitutes reliable knowledge. The authority of official decree has supplanted disciplined observation and thought. Particularly in the university system, where commitment to free and open inquiry and a rejection of dogma are axioms, it is a circumstance that should abide uneasily.

Superficial education

The cumulation of the foregoing factors is a superficial and inadequate educational experience. Mediocrity in teaching is tolerated: 'Standards are a godsend to the feebler type of writer and teacher who finds it easier to recite a creed than to analyse facts and to engage in argument' (Baxter 1994/1979: 20). It is the students who bear the brunt of this mediocrity. A listing of the general qualities desired to be found in graduates of any professional education programme might include a capacity for logical thought, analytical skills, an ability to identify and make use of connections between related subject matters, independent resourcefulness and, most importantly, a conceptual understanding of the specialist subject matter within the profession's purview. These qualities cannot expect to be acquired from a survey of regulatory statements in which evidence of the application of such qualities is itself rarely to be found. Instead, as accounting education is increasingly immersed in the technical process of applying rules – typically to data contrived to fit those rules – it imparts the antithetical quality of a dependence on those rules. Such a dependence – and the superficial understanding of accounting that it implies – does not accord with the responsibilities that are the proper companions of professional authority.

Reforming accounting education

All learning must take place around a subject matter. This is obviously so when the learning objectives relate to technical outcomes, such as the ability to prepare double entry accounting records or comprehend an accounting standard. However, it also applies where the learning objectives are of a more abstract kind, such as the development of capacities for logical thought, critical analysis, self-learning, problem-solving, acting resourcefully and establishing connections between related ideas. Although these outcomes are abstract, there must be a subject matter that provides the means for their pursuit: there must be something to think about, to analyse, problems to solve and so on. This leads to the heart of the crisis in accounting education. The most common criticism is that present educational experiences fail to develop the general competencies reasonably expected of aspiring professionals. A primary explanation for this is that the accounting subject matter that presently fills education programmes – based significantly on regulatory pronouncements – is not sufficiently robust to be an effective vehicle for achieving the outcomes expected of professional education.

This environment places accounting educators within an uneasy bind. Part of their responsibility lies in equipping students with at least a basic level of technical competence in preparation for the work environment, and this necessitates that existing practices be taught. But those practices are chaotic and not an effective instrument for achieving the more general outcomes expected of professional education. In addition, teaching such practices reinforces them: 'Students tend to identify theoretically correct with accepted practice' (Sterling 1973b: 49; see also Chambers 1994; Puxty, Sikka and Willmott 1994: 88; Sterling 1989: 82). Accounting education is thus fundamentally implicated in shaping the future development of accounting, according to Sterling (1989: 82) perhaps to a greater extent than any other factor:

> Today's students are tomorrow's practitioners and the ideas we impart to them will determine, in significant measure, the future course of accounting practice. Also a small fraction of today's students are tomorrow's faculty and the ideas we impart to them will influence the future course of accounting education and accounting research. The impact of teachers is certainly much greater than usually recognized, and in regard to long-term impact I would venture that it is greater than that of researchers, administrators and, yes, even standard setters.

These observations mark out the challenge for accounting education but also its potentiality. Accounting education can only advance if it provides the means for enabling wider progress and reform. Achieving these ends requires a reorientation of accounting syllabuses. The conventional structure, within the context of a three-year university programme, is described by Mathews (1994: 91–2):

> First-year Accounting Principles courses tend to be black/white, right/wrong procedural affairs, with not much discussion of alternative views of accounting (social) objectives. Second year subjects such as Corporate

Accounting and Cost and Management Accounting continue the procedural emphasis but at a higher level. Corporate Accounting often concentrates on accounting standards (perhaps without covering conceptual frameworks) while Cost and Management Accounting may introduce alternatives, but reinforces form and structure through the use of computer modules or accounting information systems, supplemented in some cases by the study of Business Finance. In many cases it is only in the final year that perhaps some discussion of theoretical or philosophical perspectives takes place as part of Accounting Theory, Advanced Financial Accounting or elective units.

This framework is inconsistent with the notion that cognitively-based expertise is the heart of what constitutes a profession. Only at the final year level is an emphasis on accounting theory introduced, and then only in subjects disconnected from the accounting procedures that students learn in the absence of any significant theoretical guidance. Thus, accounting procedures are taught while the means for evaluating them are withheld until the procedures have been thoroughly inculcated. The observation of Chambers (1969/1967: 675) remains current: 'The student is confronted by a *fait accompli*, and he has been so indoctrinated by concentration on how to do it that he does not stop to ask why do it at all.'

There is no need for accounting education to proceed in this manner. Consider the definition of accounting offered by the AAA Committee to Prepare a Statement of Basic Accounting Theory (1966: 1): 'the process of identifying, measuring, and communicating economic information to permit informed judgements and decisions by users of the information'. This definition appears routinely in the introductory chapters of accounting textbooks and it lists a compendium of significant subject matters: measurement, communication, economics, decision making. As Chambers (1991a) shows, subjects of this kind are a fount overflowing with ideas for understanding the nature of accounting and its possibilities. But, it seems, they are rarely pursued. The AAA committee itself reveals the consequences of this failure, particularly with reference to measurement: 'The term "measurement" includes the *choice* of an accounting method' (1966: 1, emphasis added). Choice in measuring processes is restricted to the unit of measurement (for example, miles or kilometres, pounds or kilograms). To contend, as the AAA committee did, that the measurement of inventory involves the choice of an inventory flow assumption (1966: 1) is to demonstrate a fundamental misunderstanding of the nature of measurement (see Sterling 1970, Chapters 5 and 6). Inventory flow assumptions relate to processes of calculation – assigning costs – rather than measurement. As stated by Sterling (1988: 12), 'it is impossible to measure the expired cost of goods sold or the unexpired cost of inventory'. This basic misunderstanding has persisted, with Albrecht and Sack (2000: 59–60) – in spite of their many concerns about accounting education – contending that 'We understand measurement and we teach it well.'

Rather than proceeding from a theoretical framework, accounting education typically begins with processing transactions, guided only by convention and rules. Transactions are recorded at historical cost without any consideration being given to how such quanta can be a useful input to decision-making processes. The reality of price changes and their consequences for informed commercial action are ignored. The basic principles of arithmetic are casually abandoned without explanation or apology as monetary units of different purchasing power and representing different attributes are aggregated. The purpose of accounting is said to subsist in aiding decision making, but the nature and structure of decision-making processes are not investigated. Accounting information is said to be communicated to interested parties, but the principles of effective communication are left unexamined. Instead, idiosyncratic definitions are attached to common words and a private language invented. The point is that effective education – and honest education – requires that students be provided with the means of understanding the discipline they are studying. In professional contexts it is an imperative.

This requires that at least a preliminary survey of various fields of knowledge having implications for accounting (see Chambers 1969/1965, 1991a) be undertaken *before* accounting processes are examined. In the context of what is usual in professional education this is far from radical. Aspiring medical practitioners do not just learn 'medicine'. They learn chemistry, physiology, biology, anatomy, pharmaceutics and other foundational subjects. These subjects provide the means for understanding the intricacies of the human body and the treatment of illness. Similarly, law students are educated in the structure of the legal system, theories of justice, statutory interpretation, the doctrine of precedence and other subjects that provide the means for understanding law. Accounting education must also strive to provide such means. Its present failure to do so is disabling and distinct: 'Except for some theologies, I don't know of any other discipline that perceives its duty to be the passing along of accepted practices' (Sterling 1973b: 49).

Résumé and conclusion

Development of the special competence that is the core justification for professional authority commences in prerequisite education programmes that confer eligibility to practise. As well as imparting knowledge and fostering skills that are of direct relevance to the work environment, such programmes are expected to contribute to the development of more general qualities that are essential for the effective discharge of a professional mandate. These include judgement, self-evaluation, adaptation, a preparedness to scrutinize conventional practice and challenge it when the evidence so demands, and a thorough comprehension of the role and consequences of professional work. A purely technical education cannot deliver these qualities.

What is taught and what is treated as 'right' or 'wrong' in accounting education is increasingly determined by institutional pronouncements. These have been grasped as providing a pedagogic framework; shaping curricula, dominating textbook contents and providing an unchallenged doctrine in the mediation of student assessment. As a result, accounting education programmes are imbued with the same fractious qualities as the official statements upon which they are based. Understanding of the nature of the commercial environment is compromised as it is viewed through the distorting lens of accounting standards that generate monetary quantifications without empirical connotations. Practices that cannot be vindicated cognitively are honoured simply because they enjoy official sanction. The cumulation of these factors is the degeneration of accounting education into the mundane and formalistic process of interpreting and applying a rule-book.

Within this environment, accounting educators are caught in an unenviable bind. They face pressures to prepare students for a work environment that is heavily dependent on the application of formal rules. Breaches of the rules may lead to disciplinary proceedings and judgements of a lack of competence. Preparation for this work environment thereby traps accounting education into perpetuating the mediocrities of current technique. Consequently, as the number of accounting standards and related pronouncements increases so does the tendency for accounting education to be characterized by indoctrination rather than pursuit of an enlightened understanding of accounting and its possibilities. Ultimately, the only means of escaping this unconscionable bind is the reform of accounting itself. In this manner, accounting education must be its own saviour. It must provide students not just with a knowledge of current practice, but with the knowledge to evaluate critically that practice and seek its reform.

In conventional syllabuses, accounting theory is typically treated as a terminal and distinct subject. It is the technique of 'how to account' that is treated as the foundation of accounting education, guided by convention and official pronouncements. However, the foundation of any professional education should not be technique. Introductory accounting courses need to commence with a survey of the various fields of knowledge that have fundamental implications for accounting. Only with at least a basic understanding of such matters as the principles of measurement, valid aggregation, effective communication and decision making – within the context of a comprehension of the commercial environment and the behaviour of firms – are students endowed with a capacity to understand and critically evaluate the subject matter they are expected to master. To fail to provide students with this capacity is to depart fundamentally from the exigencies of professional education and foreclose the possibility of developing a valid professional authority within accounting. The consequences of this failure are presently visible within accounting practice and it is this matter which is pursued in the following chapter.

8 Professionalism, accounting rules and accounting practice

> Accountants have to practise with a system that places them at great risk –
> damned by the consumers of accounting in many cases if they comply with
> approved Standards and damned by their governing bodies if they do not.
>
> (Clarke, Dean and Oliver 1997: xv)

Introduction

The professional person 'has one foot in the academic world and the other in the world of affairs' (Carr-Saunders and Wilson 1933: 485). It is an important premise, signifying the epistemic, yet practical, imperative of professional work. The rationale for sanctioning the occupational authority that characterizes professions derives from their claimed knowledge, but it must be knowledge of a particular kind. Professional mandates are not warranted by expertise in matters that have only trivial or uncertain implications for human affairs. There must be engagement with, and mediation of, situations holding practical significance for human actors. In the words of Cogan (1953: 49), the understanding and abilities of professionals are 'applied to the vital practical affairs of man'. The professional arena, therefore, cannot be confined to research laboratories, libraries and academic exchange. Instead, it must extend to – and indeed find its *raison d'être* in – more practical contexts such as consulting rooms, surgical theatres, courtrooms, construction sites, public offices and the like. It is this realm of practice – focusing on the application of professional knowledge – that is the subject of inquiry in this chapter. This builds upon and complements the examination of the epistemic infrastructure of the accounting occupation that commenced with scholarly discourse (knowledge discovery) in Chapter 6 and proceeded to education (knowledge dissemination) in Chapter 7.

Ideals said to underpin professional practice have been specified in the sociology of professions literature and can also be inferred from the conception of profession adopted in this study. The essential companion of the elevated occupational authority of professions is elevated occupational responsibility. To endow authority without responsibility is to tolerate a power structure that is dictatorial and contrary to orderly social functioning. This responsibility, in turn, demands its own companion. Practitioners who are expected to bear responsibility for their practice have need and entitlement to operate with a measure of independence. This is not a freedom to act indiscriminately, but recognizes that practitioner accountability for work performed follows from autonomy in the conduct of that work. This necessitates, for example, having the right to decline engagements that are considered unethical or for which the required expertise is not held. Within the setting of professional practice the ideals of responsibility and independence are the concomitants of professional authority.

This trinity of authority, responsibility and independence is adopted in this chapter to provide a framework for guiding inquiry into the nature of accounting practice. In particular, there is concern to elucidate the impacts of accounting rule-making on the nature of professional accounting work and the sociology of accounting practitioners. In common with the theme of the preceding chapters, the imposition of rules that embody rather than surmount dissonance in accounting thought is shown to compromise professional ideals. These rules diminish the authority of practitioners by forcing compliance with procedures that lack serviceability and cognitive justification. Professional independence is similarly compromised as practitioners must apply accounting methods that neither utilize nor yield independently verifiable data. By expanding the risks of accounting practice in this manner, present accounting rules have also precipitated a flight from professional responsibility. Blame for accounting failures is deflected, variously, to the misjudgements of company managers, the ignorance of the users of financial reports, and claimed 'inherent limitations' in accounting information. Campaigns to circumscribe the audit function and petitions for artificial restrictions on the extent of auditors' liability have also emerged. In short, accounting rule-making has so far failed to provide an accounting technique capable of supporting the burden of professional responsibility and actuating the protocol of professional independence.

The next section of the chapter expounds on the nature of professional practice generally, drawing upon perspectives contained in the sociology of professions literature. This is followed by an examination of accounting practice and how it departs from the generic ideals of professional practice. The chapter then explores how present accounting rules have contributed to causing and perpetuating these departures.

Professional practice generally

Advances in knowledge are vehicles for social progress, but also deliver problems of social control. This is particularly evident, for example, in medicine. As the means available for enhancing the duration and quality of human life have advanced, so too has the likelihood that the successful treatment of medical conditions will be a consequence of science and technology that is not understood by patients. The consumer sovereignty described by Adam

Smith is thus inverted: ends are decided for the consumer rather than by the consumer. This inversion delivers tensions to the relationship between suppliers and consumers that do not arise in connection with the provision of less complex services. In particular contexts, professionals are relied upon to mediate these tensions:

> The professional can be seen as a mediator between an abstract corpus of accumulated knowledge and the concrete and specific problems presented by particular clients. The task of the professional according to this under-standing, consists of the application of abstract professional knowledge to specific cases in everyday life.
>
> (Burkett and Knafl 1974: 82–3)

Following from this conception, the ideals of professional practice have often been expressed in terms that exactly contrapose the usual depictions of market interactions. In particular, it has been said that the profit motive is supplanted by an altruistic intent: 'The professional performs his services primarily for the psychic satisfactions and secondarily for the monetary compensations' (Greenwood (1966/1957: 17). A congruent specification is offered by Cogan (1953: 49): 'The profession, serving the vital needs of man, considers its first ethical imperative to be altruistic service to the client.' Consistent with these views, it has also been suggested that the suppliers of professional services do not seek competitive advantages. Ethical codes are often explicit in endorsing this notion, with Freidson (1986: 113–14) observing within well-established professions that 'such economic activity as competitive price bidding is forbid-den, as are competitive advertising in general and advertising prices for specific services in particular'. Advertising, especially, has traditionally been looked upon with disfavour: 'If a profession were to advertise, it would, in effect, impute to the potential client the discriminating capacity to select from com-peting forms of service' (Greenwood, 1966/1957: 12). These anti-competitive sentiments also extend to a prohibition of trade secrets: 'The proprietary and quasi-secretive attitudes towards discovery and invention prevalent in the industrial and commercial world are out of place in the professional' (Greenwood 1966/1957: 15). Instead, professionals are presumed to develop their expertise collectively in a process unfettered and unchallenged by exter-nal agencies:

> One of the essential attributes of the professional role . . . is autonomy, or self-control by the professionals themselves with regard to the devel-opment and application of the body of generalized knowledge in which they alone are expert.
>
> (Barber 1963: 679)

Consistent with the general theme that has been outlined, Elliott (1972: 94) nominates 'belief in professional freedom and autonomy in the work situation' as a fundamental professional ideal. Similarly, Benson (1981: 240) prescribes that 'The professional person should be in a position to give service or advice free from the direction or influence of others.' The need for the exercise of judgement in the provision of professional services is said to accentuate this need for professional independence: 'The members must be, and be seen to be, in a position to be independent: independent in mind and outlook and not under the dominance of persons or circumstances which would interfere with their judgement' (Benson 1981: 240).

The cumulation of the foregoing is a depiction of the relationship between the suppliers and the consumers of professional services being controlled by the suppliers, but in the interests of the consumers. Thus, a benevolent autonomy is said to characterize the work environment of professional practitioners. They are not subject to directives from the recipients of their services and are liberated from normal commercial pressures. These ideals have traditionally been rationalized in terms of a need to alleviate the exploitive potential of the relationship between practitioner and client. The usual forces operating in market exchanges are said to be countered, with altruistic motivations supplanting the pursuit of profit and competitive advantage. Within this tractable environment the practitioner's status is privileged: 'The ideology of professionalism has always held that the practitioner should have independence and authority when dealing with a client' (Elliott 1972: 104). However, it is the client who is represented as the beneficiary of these arrangements.

This idealized portrayal of the nature and outcomes of professional practice has not passed unchallenged.[1] In one of the most conspicuous contradictions in the sociology of professions literature, the ideals of professional practice that have been claimed to protect the interests of consumers have also been alleged to serve precisely the opposite function of protecting and enhancing the interests of practitioners. Thus, Abbott (1988: 132), for example, suggests that 'Professionalism arose to make individuals' careers invulnerable to the instabilities of capitalist employment.' In a similar vein, Duman (1979: 114) describes professionalism as 'a unique ideology based on the concept of service as a moral imperative'. But this was not for the protection of the recipients of professional services: 'The professions served as a means to an end – to the gentlemanly life, to the *right* social milieu and to acceptance as a member of the nation's social elite' (Duman 1979: 115, emphasis in original). The ideal of altruistic service is claimed to be exposed as a rhetorical ploy:

> Anti-market and anti-capitalist principles were incorporated in the professions' task of organizing for a market because they were elements which supported social credit and the public's belief in professional ethicality. Thus, at the core of the professional project, we find the fusion of antithetical ideological structures and a potential for permanent tension between 'civilizing function' and market orientation, between the 'protection of society' and the securing of a market, between intrinsic and extrinsic values of work.
>
> (Larson 1977: 63)

As well as providing leverage for the development of the 'social credit' that would facilitate professionalization, it has also been argued that anti-competitive ideals serve the avaricious intents of established practitioners. Restrictions on advertising, for example, have been said to impair the prospects of novices wishing to establish their own practice (Freidson 1986: 188). Likewise, it is suggested that entry requirements for professions are sometimes determined less by an objective assessment of necessary competence than by a desire to restrict the supply of qualified practitioners (Collins 1979: 146; Preston *et al.* 1995: 516; Slayton 1978: 135; Young 1988). Rather than serving clients, the conventions shaping the milieu of professional practice are thus interpreted as functioning to protect practitioners by reducing competition and providing a means for escaping the vagaries of the market-place.

As is often the case, perhaps, with the sociology of professions, the truth seems likely to be found somewhere between the counterpoints of conventional professional rhetoric and ideologically motivated critiques. Moreover, there is hope of progress towards uncovering this truth if attention is re-directed from non-empirical assertions about the motives of professionals in favour of a more reasoned exploration of the consequences of professionalization. The apodictic outcome of professionalization is elevated occupational authority, comprising in its most developed form an exclusive right to define and provide specified services. It is synonymous with what Child and Fulk (1982: 155) have described as the concept of 'occupational control': 'the collective capability of members of an occupation to preserve unique authority in the definition, conduct, and evaluation of their work and also to determine the conditions of entry to, and exit from, practice within occupational parameters'.

This 'unique authority' has an essential corollary. Where the definition, conduct and evaluation of some service are controlled by those who provide it, then no other party can be blamed for any deficiencies in that service. Therefore, the essential companion of professional authority is professional responsibility: acknowledgement and acceptance of the fact that the outcomes of professional work are governed and determined by occupation-specific knowledge and the judgements practitioners make in applying that knowledge. It is as stated by Elliott (1972: 147): 'The profession claims unique responsibility for some aspect of the public good. It also claims to know how that good should be achieved.'

This returns professional expertise to the centre of attention in efforts to comprehend professional practice. Other matters that have featured in the debate, such as whether advertising should be permitted and speculation over the mind-set of practitioners, are not eliminated by this emphasis. However, they are rendered subordinate to an evaluation of the technical quality of professional service and the preparedness of practitioners – individually, with regard to specific engagements, and collectively, with regard to the general standards of their profession – to accept responsibility for that service. The point is that the heart of professional practice is the exercise of expert authority in practical and significant contexts without informed invigilation. Efforts by sociologists of professions to identify and understand the ideals of professional practice have often tended to skirt around this main issue. No amount of altruistic intent, prohibitions or restrictions on advertising, or other ethical guidelines can remedy technical deficiencies in the quality of professional services or compensate for a failure to accept responsibility for those services.

This nomination of professional responsibility as the essential companion of professional authority prompts specification of an additional practice ideal. It concerns professional independence; a concept implied by professional authority but warranting individual specification and elaboration. Affirming that responsibility for the technical quality of professional services lies with the service providers is consequential to practitioner autonomy – that practitioners are unhindered by external influences that may detract from the quality of their work. This independence does not sanction capricious practices, but recognizes that professional work involves the application of specialized expertise to particular cases and that judgement underlies this process. Forces that interfere with the exercise of this judgement compromise the integrity of professional undertakings. This justifies, for example, a prohibition on medical practitioners having relationships of a personal or emotional kind with their patients. However, professional independence extends beyond the need for practitioners to have an objective state of mind to embrace also the technical aspects of their work.[2] Directives that, without robust justification, compel practitioners to apply certain procedures, or require the making of precise judgements about matters upon which insufficient evidence is available, are antonymic to professionalism. The grounds for enforcing the ideal of professional responsibility wane whenever practitioner autonomy is surrendered to extraneous influences. For these reasons, independence complements responsibility in defining the concomitants of professional authority within the setting of professional practice.

Accounting practice

This study has emphasized that elevated occupational authority is the essential outcome of professionalization and that the justification for this authority must be found primarily in occupational expertise. In the realm of professional practice – the application of such expertise – the ideals of responsibility and independence are the concomitants of professional authority. However, a distinguishing feature of the recent history of the accounting profession has been a concerted effort to avoid the burdens of professional responsibility. This has also coincided with an erosion of the independence of accounting practitioners as their work has been subjected to technical directives which have magnified the risks of accounting practice.

The evasion of professional responsibility within accounting commences at the very heart of practice in the form of efforts to avoid any general qualitative standard for financial information. Research by Chambers and Wolnizer (1991) reveals that the notion of regulating accounting information by a general specification of its required technical qualities has a long history. Provisions of this kind were a feature of early statutes and also the contractual and constitutive documents of business firms active in the United Kingdom during the seventeenth, eighteenth and nineteenth centuries. The recurring use of words such as 'regular', 'true', 'fair', 'proper' and 'necessary' (Chambers and Wolnizer 1991: 200–4) illustrates the nature of these provisions and provides the genealogy of the general qualitative standards – such as 'true and fair' – that came to be included in companies legislation. These findings provide not just a genealogy of the *use* of particular words but also their intended *meaning*. Thus, the conclusion of Chambers and Wolnizer (1991: 211) concerning that meaning has contemporary as well as historical interest:

> The material presented is considered to establish a *prima facie* case for two propositions: (a) that 'true and correct' and 'true and fair' and like terms are simply expressions in the vernacular of the intent that financial accounts and summaries shall be false to the dated financial facts of companies in no significant respect; (b) that in respect of property and other assets, the use of market selling prices, as in the ordinary course of business, and not cost prices, would give the required view of a dated state of affairs and dated profits or results.

The prospect of giving practical effect to legislative provisions intended to regulate the quality of accounting information emerges from these historical insights and related investigations: 'What may be said to be true and fair views of the states of affairs and of the periodical results of firms . . . are determinate by recourse to the theory of reasoned behaviour, accounting and legal dicta and empirical evidence' (Chambers and Wolnizer 1990: 353). However, instead of fostering such understanding the accounting profession has sought to avoid the onus of an effective general qualitative standard:

> Under the *true and fair* ethos, ethical behaviour by accountants necessitated that they produce financial information indicative of the financial characteristics it is held out to show. Few professional groups have as explicit an ethical charge presented to them as that, and few have had it embodied consistently (over 150 years) in legislation as widely used as the companies laws. One might have expected accountants and corporate managers to have jealously guarded that edict. Just the opposite has occurred. It has been abandoned.
>
> (Clarke, Dean and Oliver 1997: 251, emphasis in original)

Confronted by its failure to give effect to the 'true and fair' provision, the accounting profession has chosen simply to decamp. That is, not only has it sought to abandon this longstanding general qualitative standard, but done so without offering any robust replacement. Rather than testify to the presence or absence in financial reports of the significant and general qualities necessary to ensure that those reports can be relied upon to serve their widely attributed functions, it is proposed to offer only an opinion indicating whether prescribed rules have been complied with (McGregor 1992).[3]

This reluctance to endorse a general qualitative standard is a manoeuvre that eschews professional responsibility. It leaves the accounting profession without an equivalent to the generic and overriding quality specifications that exist in other professional fields: patient well-being in medicine, functional fitness in engineering, justice in law. However, this is only the most recent indication of the accounting profession's preparedness to accept the privileges of professional authority while seeking to diminish the attendant responsibilities. The whole history of the audit function has been characterized by the efforts of the accounting profession to circumscribe its duties (Sterling 1973a: 64–5; Wolnizer 1987: 179–86). Weaker words have been substituted for those with more robust connotations: certification of accounts giving way to an 'opinion'. Responsibility for fraud detection – once acknowledged as a fundamental purpose of auditing – is now substantially disclaimed. Idiosyncratic definitions have been invoked: verification coming to mean only testing for compliance with accounting rules. The claim that company managers should bear primary responsibility for financial statements is tirelessly reiterated. Rather than confront the need for technical reform, faith has been placed in institutional structures such as audit committees (Wolnizer 1995). These retreats form the foundation of the semantically curious manner in which auditing is represented as being defined and understood. Increasingly, this comprises detailed specifications of what auditing is not, and scant positive statements describing what it is. Thus, a review of official auditing pronouncements and the standard textbook literature yields a series of denials: that an audit does not permit conclusions to be drawn regarding fraud, the integrity of management, the viability of the organization, or the adequacy of the system of internal control. The restricted nature of the scope of an audit is similarly emphasized, leading to the inference that no absolute assurance about *anything* is provided. What is troubling about this list of negations is the clarity and vigour with which they are enunciated relative to the heavily qualified and tentative statements that purport to articulate what an audit does actually achieve. Professional services are said to pertain to matters of social importance and this creates an expectation that their purpose would, over time, come to be defined with confidence and precision. The reverse applies in connection with the audit function. In spite of its long history and being attributed such importance as to be mandated by law for certain classes of companies, the purpose of an audit remains only vaguely discernible in the ill-defined residual of increasingly expansive specifications of what it is not.

Not content with resiling from a clear specification of the function of an audit, the accounting profession has also sought to diminish its legal responsibility for audit work (Baxt 1987; Cohen 1987a; Gietzmann and Quick 1998; Godsell 1991; Grice 1993; Lee 1992; Lochner 1993; Monroe, Ng and Wellington 1992; Napier 1998; O'Malley 1993; Paton 1993; Power 1998; Rennie 1988; Schuetze 1993a; Small 1986a, 1986b; Smithers 1992). Underlying the campaign waged by professional accounting associations is the belief that the cause of the audit liability crisis is external to the accounting profession. For example, a president of the ICAA described outstanding legal claims against company auditors as:

> audacious attempts by aggrieved parties to claw back losses from ANY party believed to have money (or access to it), irrespective of their degree of responsibility. They represent an attack on the very existence of an independent and competent auditing profession, an attack it is vital we repel.
>
> (Smithers 1992: 60)

The plea is that accountants are being denied justice:

> Certainly the accountancy profession does not wish to escape its proper and equitable liability for negligence. We do however object to being unjustly liable for the negligence and incompetence of others and wish to restrict our liability within the limits which are commercially insurable at affordable cost and which represent a recognition of the contribution of all relevant parties to any damages award.
>
> (Smithers 1992: 61)

To petition for an artificial restriction on liability is to depart fundamentally from the ideal of professional responsibility. In the past, emphasis on this ideal was such that even conducting professional practice with the benefit of limited liability offered by incorporation was forbidden: 'Personal financial responsibility is the very essence of professional practice and operation of an accountancy business; therefore, the medium of a limited company is contrary to the concept of professional liability' (Irish 1972: 563). The kind of restricted liability being sought by the accounting profession – for example, in the form of a statutory cap – would not only diminish practitioners' responsibility, but provide them with a form of legal protection not usually available to the providers of more general goods and services. It defies the fundamental precept that, in recognition of the privileges granted to professional groups, more is demanded of the providers of professional services – not less.

The accounting profession's flight from responsibility – evident in its reluctance to embrace a general qualitative standard, continued retreat in defining auditors' duties and petitions for artificial restrictions on liability – has proceeded alongside a raft of attributions of blame. Thus, lobbying for removal of the 'true and fair' label has been justified on the ground that it has 'never been authoritatively defined by either the accounting profession or the courts' (McGregor 1992: 69). Given that the courts look to a profession itself to define its standards of acceptable practice, such an attribution of blame is untenable. Another argument presented is that 'seeking a meaning for the concept of "true and fair" is a futile exercise in that the concept defies definition in its own right' (McGregor 1992: 69). On what grounds truth and fairness – seemingly qualities beyond objection in connection with any professional service – defy definition in accounting remains unsaid. The temerity of the denial is revealed by research into the origins of 'true and fair' which is strongly suggestive of a clear intended meaning (Chambers and Wolnizer 1991). It is on the grounds of its claimed expertise that the accounting profession has been granted an exclusive responsibility for independently pronouncing on the truth and fairness of company accounts. Responsibility for defining 'true and fair' runs parallel to this privilege.

In addition to its attributions of blame, the accounting profession has sought solace in a claimed 'expectation gap': that the expectations of those relying on the work of professional accountants are unrealistic.[4] Thus, it has been said that 'many users misunderstand the auditor's role and responsibilities' and 'Users are unaware of the limitations of the audit function and confused about the distinction between the responsibilities of management and auditor' (Cohen 1987b: 6). The research study on the expectation gap sponsored by the ASCPA and ICAA (1994: 13) recommended that 'The Accounting Bodies should maintain an appropriate education and communication process to ensure that users of financial reports and critics of the Profession obtain the benefit of the views which support the Profession's position on current issues.'

When the presumption that the expectations gap is a consequence of others' ignorance is set aside in favour of consideration of technical accounting issues, the present inertia of the accounting profession becomes only further evident. The ASCPA and ICAA study (1994: 7) lists a range of criticisms concerning current financial reporting practices: the need to report on the basis of economic substance rather than legal form; the need for consistency in accounting policies adopted by and between reporting entities; the existence of too many optional accounting treatments; the need for current value rather than historical cost information; the need for timely information. The only substantive solution offered, however, was that 'A mature and well designed conceptual framework could be expected to deal with all of the above' (ASCPA and ICAA 1994: 7). On what grounds this faith is placed in a project that has neither delivered, nor shown evidence of delivering, substantive changes to accounting practice is left unspecified. Instead, there is an admission that significant change is not in fact being sought: 'In relation to concepts statements, the Working Party urges the Accounting Bodies and standard-setters to ensure that . . . change is managed strategically so as to mitigate the effects of far-reaching changes as much as possible' (ASCPA and ICAA 1994: 8).

Retreat from the ideals of professional practice thereby exists alongside a persistent complacency regarding present technical accounting practices. As stated by Zeff (1986: 131), 'The vitality of a professional literature depends not only on the efforts of academic researchers but also on the intellectual leadership exerted by professionals.' The view that 'accounting professionals have become a less fertile source of intellectual leadership in the affairs of the profession' (Zeff 1986: 132) is supported particularly by reference to professional accounting journals:

> an Australian professional journal, the *Australian Accountant*, was the vehicle for some of Chambers' path-breaking writing in the 1950s and 1960s. It is inconceivable that the journal would now publish comparable material.
>
> (Henderson, Peirson and Brown 1992: 355)

Instead of featuring robust debate over important technical accounting matters, professional accounting journals have come to bear little distinction from general business magazines. The array of tangential matters that receive prominence – holiday destinations, motor vehicle road tests, a variety of 'advertising features' – foster an impression that practitioners have no significant and critical interest in accounting matters.[5] Instead, a brief 'technical' column is provided that simply outlines and endorses each new official pronouncement that practitioners must obey. This apparent lack of intellectual vitality signifies a refusal to countenance the possibility that the recent and continuing traumas faced by the accounting profession – in particular audit failure and the associated liability crisis – may have a connection to present accounting technique.

Accounting rules and accounting practice

External pressures – such as growing complexity in commercial activity and a generally more litigious society – may have increased the challenge of accomplishing professional ideals within accounting practice. However, the very nature of professions renders them powerful institutions able to define and construct their own circumstances. Indeed, it is upon a premise of autonomy that professions are characterized and their need to be self-regulating abides. For these reasons it seems unlikely that the cause of the breakdown of the ideals of professional accounting practice can be attributed principally to external factors. A variety of contradictions offer preliminary evidence in support of this appraisal. First, while the authority of individual practitioners has been eroded, the power and size of the accounting profession as a whole appears to have progressed without serious impediment. This invites examination of why this enlarged macro-authority has not been matched at the individual practitioner level. Second, the accounting profession – perhaps above all other professions – has placed a premium on practitioner independence. Yet, the repeated apportioning of blame for accounting failures to company managers and other parties seems to suggest that accounting practitioners do not, or cannot, carry out their work independently. This is reinforced by the constancy of claims that accounting professionals are being made accountable for the failings of others. These implicit admissions of an inability to assert professional independence have arisen in spite of the ethical pronouncements of professional accounting associations containing detailed prescriptions on this matter. Third, and more generally, abnegation of the ideal of professional responsibility has occurred in the absence of any significant and critical examination of the technical aspects of accounting practice.[6] The auditor liability crisis and repeated evidence of the lack of serviceability of published financial statements have failed to provide a stimulus for change. Instead, the accounting profession has clung stubbornly to an unexamined presumption of its own competence. The consequence is that accounting continues to be in a state of almost perpetual crisis: 'Although all professions are from time to time subject to public scrutiny and criticism, the current situation in accountancy is unique because of its persistence and strength' (Lee 1996b: 168).

Developing from this rejection of the notion that the circumstances of the accounting profession are substantially determined and explained by factors beyond its control, the following discussion redirects attention to how present accounting technique effects deviations from the ideals of professional practice. That technique is now largely defined by accounting rules. This emphasis on rule application, magnified by the technical deficiencies of those rules, has eroded the professional authority and independence of accounting practitioners and induced a weakened sense of professional responsibility.

The deficiencies of accounting rules – made evident by a variety of inconsistencies – have been described earlier in this study (Chapter 4). Underlying these inconsistencies is a disjunction between the rules and actual commercial events and circumstances. Accounting rules, and by implication financial reports, are often based on imaginary concepts. As a consequence, replication of the consistency that abides within empirical information is foregone and the capacity to corroborate accounting data independently is sacrificed. These circumstances compromise not only the capacity of financial reports to serve as reliable financial instruments, but also the professional authority of accounting practitioners. A professional person should, in all situations, be able to explain and justify the technical procedures that he or she applies; to show evidence of being knowledgeable about the matters at hand. However, accounting standards and related statements mandate practices that lack theoretical justification. Regulatory fiat rather than cognition is what impels the actions of practitioners. How, for example, is an accounting practitioner to justify the application of the lower of cost and net realizable value rule to inventories? Certainly the rule can be justified by reference to an accounting standard that the practitioner may be obliged to comply with. But this carries no intellectual substance. It marks a retreat to mere formalism, with the practitioner reduced to being merely the agent of a rule-book. The point is that the lower of cost and net realizable value rule, along with a host of other prescriptions contained in accounting standards, is devoid of robust theoretical justification.[7] Practitioners who are coerced into applying those standards are not administering a professional kind of authority. They are, instead, reduced to being the servants of failed rule-making processes.

These problems, however, compound. Forced into an almost exclusive reliance on formally stated rules to justify particular accounting procedures, accounting practitioners are left without significant authority in connection with matters not subject to an accounting standard. To rely upon regulatory fiat to justify particular technical practices is to concede a lack of authority regarding matters that cannot be similarly substantiated.[8] Practitioner response to this dilemma appears to involve simply forsaking concern with matters not expressly covered by accounting standards. Thus, Walker (1993: 103) writes of an auditing culture in which accounting treatments are considered acceptable 'unless . . . specifically prohibited by legally enforceable requirements'. Under this ethos, and the de facto abandonment of the general qualitative standard of 'true and fair', accounting practice has descended into a rule-based contest.[9] Compliance with accounting standards has become an end in itself, rising above the consequences that such compliance is intended to achieve:

> Paradoxically, the best-case scenario from the Standard-setters' point of view – that there is *less* diversity in accounting practices now than in the past – possibly has done more to reduce the usefulness of accounting data than would have enhancing accountants' capacity to exercise their professional judgement on how to account for, and report on, the outcome of financial matters.
>
> (Clarke, Dean and Oliver 1997: 18, emphasis in original)

Thus, the proceduralism that presently characterizes accounting practice diminishes the professionalism of practitioners by eroding their capacity to make the judgements necessary to ensure that the products of their work have an express and demonstrable social utility. Practitioner duty is seen to terminate in the routinized task of checking that prescribed rules have been followed. The consequences of this forced abandonment of professional responsibility manifest further when, within the context of accounting as a rule-based contest, accounting standards are perceived as prescribing maximum requirements to be exploited through manoeuvres and interpretations intended only to deliver advantages to particular participants in the contest. As Chambers (1966a: 445) points out, 'Only by exceeding the general standard is a profession promoted.' The ethos of current accounting practice is contrary to this principle, with accounting practitioners engaging in and promoting creative interpretations of stipulated rules.[10]

Thus, the progenitors of what has been described as the 'accounting standard avoidance industry' are themselves members of the accounting profession

(Mitchell *et al.* 1991: 8; see also Briloff 1972, 1981, 1990, 1993; Mitchell *et al.* 1994; Naser 1993: ch. 12; Pasewark, Shockley and Wilkerson 1995; Shah 1996; Willmott 1990; Willmott, Sikka and Puxty 1994). Naser and Pendlebury's (1992: 116) survey of a sample of senior British accountants found that 72.7 per cent agreed or strongly agreed that the continued use of creative accounting posed 'a serious threat to the integrity of financial reporting'. However, 45.5 per cent of respondents also agreed or strongly agreed with the proposition that creative accounting constituted 'a legitimate business tool'.[11] The reduction of accounting to a rule-based contest thus appears to have turned accounting practitioners against their own discipline. 'Good' accounting is not presumed to subsist in the assurance that financial statements are characterized by objectivity and functional fitness, but rather in meeting the idiosyncratic preferences of client companies.[12] The technical deficiencies of present accounting standards are thus magnified by pedantic interpretations intended only to serve private interests. As active participants in this process, accounting practitioners compete against both the broader public interest and that of their occupation, fostering an alienation that confounds the whole concept of a profession as a unified occupational grouping (Belkaoui 1991: 85–8).

Even where accounting practitioners pursue the seemingly modest goal of trying to apply objectively the rules they are obliged to work with, the ideals of professional practice remain beyond reach. The reason is that the nature of these rules deprives practitioners of their independence, compelling them to make decisions about matters for which no reliable evidence is available. The most obvious of these concern the conjectures prescribed as the means of accounting for assets. Professional accountants, whether engaged in the preparation or audit of financial reports, are constantly required to speculate about the likelihood of 'future economic benefits' arising. Specific instances of this concern research and development expenditures, pre-production costs in the extractive industries, goodwill and income tax assets. The need to make these speculations also extends to all assets that are subject to depreciation charges: expected useful lives, residual values and patterns of use must be predicted. The requirement of AASB 1010 that non-current assets not be carried at more than 'recoverable amount' similarly forces practising accountants to surmise about what is unknown and unknowable. Cash flows are to be forecast and then, somehow, apportioned to individual assets or classes of assets.

An admission that such future oriented information is inherently speculative and incapable of being independently authenticated is contained in Australian Auditing Standard AUS 804 'The Audit of Prospective Financial Information':

> Prospective financial information relates to events and actions that have not yet occurred and may not occur. While evidence may be available to support the underlying assumptions, such evidence is itself generally future oriented and, therefore, speculative in nature, as distinct from the

evidence ordinarily available in the audit of historical financial information. The auditor is therefore not in a position to express an opinion as to whether the results shown in the prospective information will be achieved.

(AARF 1995, clause .09)

The qualifications contained in this paragraph – that future oriented information is speculative, incapable of being supported by firm evidence and cannot be audited – are entirely sensible. However, when future oriented information based on management predictions of 'future economic benefits' arising, or the cash flows needed to substantiate a 'recoverable amount', are incorporated in a statement of financial position, the qualifications are suddenly presumed not to apply. Those that bear the practical burden of this contradiction are accounting practitioners.

Being forced to attest to the truth and fairness of management forecasts and whether such forecasts achieve compliance with accounting standards, the professional authority and independence of accounting practitioners is imperilled: 'the products of anticipatory calculations cannot be independently authenticated' (Wolnizer 1987: 166). At best, the predictions of management can be subject only to some broad and vaguely specified evaluation of reasonableness. There are no technical means available by which practitioners can assert and exercise independent authority. The contrariety of professionalism is tolerated:

> To contend that managers shall have what they demand, where what they demand may prejudice the preservation of the interests of others or the exercise of judgement by others, is to forgo professional independence; to admit that intellectual or emotional involvement or self-interest dominate. Such a situation is the antithesis of professionalism; it is evidence of intellectual serfdom.
>
> (Chambers 1966b: 358)

The breakdown of the ideals of professional practice within accounting does not have its substantive origin in external forces. The core of the problem is *technical*, and any occupation that denies responsibility for its technical practices can have no valid claim to being a profession. Armed only with a rule-book, accounting practitioners are without an intellectual authority. The nature of the accounting practices prescribed in that rule-book – and, in particular, the need for anticipatory calculations – denies the possibility of professional independence being achieved. It is from these failings that the flight from professional responsibility in accounting has proceeded. As the cause of this malaise in accounting practice is technical, so must be its resolution. No amount of due process, psychological impartiality, altruistic endeavour, practitioner cooperation or other similar benefactions can compensate for deficiencies in a profession's technical practices. Only when accounting practitioners are the agents of a systematic body of ideas that allows them to arbitrate confidently on accounting matters can the ideals of professional practice be achieved.

Résumé and conclusion

Carr-Saunders and Wilson's (1933: 491) study of professions led them to conclude that 'the application of an intellectual technique to the ordinary business of life . . . is the chief distinguishing characteristic of the professions'. It is this realm of application – professional practice – that has been the subject of examination in this chapter. As a technology, accounting is relied upon to serve the ordinary business of life: 'The products of accounting are, or are expected to be, of practical use and consequence to recipients' (Chambers 1980: 174). However, present accounting practice is not guided by the application of an intellectual technique. Instead, it subsists in the application of accounting methods that carry only the endorsement of regulatory fiat.

This system breaks down the ideals of professional practice and imposes an invidious burden on accounting practitioners. They are expected to achieve the high standards of work performance rightly demanded in professional fields, yet their professional judgement and intellectual capacities are rendered subservient to the stipulations of a rule-book. Consequently, this rule-book form of accounting has not – despite common representations to the contrary – served to enhance the professional authority of accounting practitioners. Professional authority is a cognitive authority, not the authority of regulatory fiat. Applying particular accounting practices simply because they are mandated by accounting standards reduces accounting practice to a rule-based contest in which what is not proscribed is presumed to be sanctioned. As a result, not only is the authority of practising accountants diminished qualitatively (as it lacks cognitive vindication), but also limited quantitatively (as it is largely confined to extant rules).

It is in the application of present accounting standards that the authority of accounting practitioners is most seriously attenuated and the risks of practice most visibly distended. The need to comply with these standards is elevated over more general considerations pertaining to the exercise of professional judgement in financial reporting, even taking precedence over the general qualitative standard of 'true and fair'. Yet, in the application of these standards, accounting practitioners – whether engaged in the preparation or audit of financial reports – are consistently obligated to make conjectures that are fraught with risk. These pertain to such matters as the expected useful lives, pattern of use, residual values and recoverable amounts of assets, and the likelihood of 'future economic benefits' arising. Professional judgement does not intrude in attempts to resolve these contingencies as there is no reliable commercial or other evidence upon which to proceed. The consequences of these forced conjectures are not benign, with the record of history revealing them to be seriously erroneous in an abundance of instances. However, the accounting profession's response to the crises its technical practices catalyse has not comprised efforts to reform those practices. Instead, there has been a flight from professional responsibility. This is evident in opposition to a general qualitative standard for financial reporting, efforts to circumscribe the duties of auditors, and the petitioning for artificial restrictions on the extent of auditors' liability.

In aggregate, the three essential ideals of professional practice – authority, independence and responsibility – have been severely disabled within the professional accounting context. Remediation of this situation is not to be found in the issue of more technical rules of the kind that have contributed significantly to the present discomposure. Instead, the invigoration of professional accounting practice must proceed from advancement in professional accounting knowledge: a specification of the bounds and principles of accounting practice which provides a cognitive authority that accounting practitioners can independently administer and be accountable for. Fundamental in such reform is the need for accounting practice to embrace the empiricism that characterizes a system of instrumentation. This would elevate the independence of accounting practitioners and provide a means for escaping the debilitating inconsistencies that make evident the intellectual poverty and unserviceability of present accounting methods.

Practitioners themselves have an important role to play in achieving this reorientation. This requires an escape from the inertia evidenced by their present tolerance of a system that deprofessionalizes them and exposes them to substantial risk. Either lulled or overburdened by the impost of the regulatory statements they have to comply with, accounting practitioners no longer appear to be engaged in significant debate over the technical quality of the accounting information they either prepare or attest to: 'Accountants . . . submit to their rules with a meekness that makes sheep look like rugged individualists' (Gerboth 1987: 97). Thus, professional development in accounting has been reduced to comprehending each batch of new rules, rather than a conscientious and diligent evaluation of present practice and a search for the means by which it might be improved. Instances of practitioners actively competing against their discipline by engineering creative interpretations that further diminish the already limited serviceability of extant rules are far from unknown. These outcomes are symptomatic of a profession that not only lacks intellectual vitality but has become complacent about that lack. Only by redressing this intellectual malaise can the ideals of authority, independence and responsibility be invigorated within accounting practice. Proceeding from this enouncement, it is the possibility of advancing professional accounting knowledge which is considered in the next, and concluding, chapter.

9   Advancing professional accounting knowledge

> It is impossible to present a solid front against any group seeking to make accounting serve special ends in the absence of a coherent and consistent body of ideas.
>
> (Chambers 1960: 34)

Introduction

This study has described professions as occupation-based structures of authority which are relied upon to oversee specified domains within society and mediate interactions between actors within those domains. However, the presence of such authority has not been presumed to certify a fitness to administer it. Instead, investigation of the discharge of professional mandates has been advocated. This necessitates inquiry into the nature of the specialized knowledge that is widely presumed to provide the justification for the authority exercised by professions. The examination of the accounting profession pursued in this study has failed to find a firm cognitive grounding for the technical practices legitimated under its authority. Criteria derived from the consensual understanding that it is the function of accounting to provide factual and up-to-date financial information that serves as a reliable guide for financial choice and action have been adopted. In this way, and following Chambers (1992), accounting has been described as a system of financial instrumentation. As well as aiding in describing what the function of accounting is, this 'instrumentation' theme has been employed to articulate the essential concept of 'quality' – of functional fitness for purpose – within accounting. Instrumentation systems are measurement systems; they are established to provide accurate and timely representations of specified phenomena. The quality of a system of instrumentation subsists in the degree of correspondence between the information provided and the phenomena it purports to represent.

The design, implementation and operation of a reliable system of financial instrumentation are the substance of professional accounting knowledge. This requires specification of the commercial phenomena to be observed, how those observations can be represented in financial reports, and the means by which they can be independently authenticated. The essential theme of this study, however, is that the accounting profession has been, and continues to be, preoccupied with ensuring compliance with procedures rather than the serviceability of the products resulting from that compliance. This failure has been reinforced by the proliferation of formally stated accounting rules in recent decades. These rules consistently contravene the parameters of factual, dated financial statements through their failure to require observation of up-to-date commercial phenomena as their basic method. Rather, they prescribe methods of calculation that yield imaginary rather than descriptive quanta and which underlie the fundamental contradiction embedded in present accounting technique: accounting numbers are represented as being about particular entities when they often do not describe any element of the dated financial position and performance of those entities. Process has taken precedence over purpose, and rule-compliance has become an end in itself. The myriad of regulations applying to the preparation of financial statements have failed to make those statements a reliable guide for financial choice and action:

> Accounting practice enjoys a peculiar insulation from the conventional idea in Western law that consumers may presume goods and services to possess the characteristics making them fit for the uses commonly made of them. Why accounting retains this exception is impossible to understand.
>
> (Clarke, Dean and Oliver 1997: 242)

The adverse consequences of the accounting rules that have proliferated in recent decades extend beyond their direct failure to deliver adequate discipline over accounting practice. Far from being a mechanism of reform, these regulations have created a barrier to reform through their disabling effects on the usual means of progress within professional fields. As accounting has evolved as a rule-based rather than knowledge-based discipline, the discourse of accounting researchers has neglected the central practice issue of 'how best to account'. Instead, increasingly sophisticated methods have been applied to the otiose task of describing what is already well known: that in the absence of an effective regulatory force the quality of accounting information will be compromised by self-interest and opportunism. Debate on how to overcome the unreliability and unserviceability of present financial reporting practices remains on the fringe of academic inquiry. Similarly, within accounting education, the outputs of accounting rule-making have been accepted supinely in spite of their defects. The result is a mundane process of learning in which procedures carrying only institutional endorsement predominate. Students of accounting are thus indoctrinated into the conventional accounting wisdom and its ritual of compliance with rules, rather than being exposed to the challenges of finding ever more serviceable ways of representing and measuring the dated financial features of firms. In turn, accounting practitioners – educated and practised in the application of official pronouncements – are unlikely to seek and apply reliable knowledge in the manner expected of a professional occupation.

Accounting is a comparatively young profession but its failings cannot be excused indefinitely on the grounds of its youthfulness. The greater problem is that the accounting profession is travelling on the wrong path. Rule-making of the kind that dominates the accounting profession does not, and cannot, provide the means for leaving behind an epistemological infancy. The only valid means of substantiating professional accounting authority is a body of specialist knowledge that serves as the primary mediating force within the accounting domain. It is the possibility of such knowledge that is the principal focus of the remainder of this chapter, commencing in the next section with an outline of the expected features of a body of professional accounting knowledge. This is followed by an attempt to illustrate how some general, cognitively derived principles offer a much greater prospect for overcoming the basic flaws of conventional accounting practice than the abundance of specific rules that have been promulgated in recent decades. In particular, two matters neglected in the development of present accounting rules are explored. The first of these concerns the fact that any item of information is bound to a temporal dimension; it will relate to either the past, present or future. The second is that items of information with differing temporal dimensions are distinct in terms of their implications for decision-making processes and their capacity to be independently corroborated. These observations and their corollaries are argued to establish a firm basis for eliminating many of the contradictions embedded in present accounting technique. Consideration is then given to the possible consequences for the accounting profession if it continues to excuse rather than endeavour to improve the technical quality of financial reports.

Features of a body of professional accounting knowledge

While the basic features of knowledge-based statements have been outlined earlier in this study (Chapter 4), they are deserving of brief recapitulation for the purpose of helping describe the expected features of a body of professional accounting knowledge. Consistency is the overriding criterion. Knowledge-based statements must correspond with what is true and cohere with each other. As professional knowledge is relied upon in the governance of human conduct, this requirement for consistency takes on added significance. Inconsistencies in professional knowledge do not just reside in the abstract – as curiosities in textbooks or academic discourse – but translate into confused and misguided behaviour. As Chambers (1969/1957: 371) explains, a theory of accounting would have consistency as its most distinguishing feature:

> Such a theory will be internally consistent, since it proceeds by logical steps to reasoned conclusions. It will also be consistent with the characteristics of the entities for which accounts are kept and with the environment in which those entities operate.

Thus, the development of accounting knowledge must be driven by a search for contradictions and the means by which they can be eliminated. This is an ongoing task: 'the quest for knowledge must be endlessly self-revising' (Tarnas 1996: 396). Consequently, no body of knowledge – professional or otherwise – can ever be presumed complete and beyond refinement. The practical repercussions of this are evident. In medical practice second opinions may be sought in connection with complex or unusual conditions. Advice provided by legal practitioners may vary when their interpretations of complex statutes or case-law differ. Alternative means for resolving engineering problems may be proposed. In accounting, however, contradictory practices are ubiquitous and endorsed.[1]

Conventional accounting rules have served to institutionalize these inconsistencies rather than contribute to their elimination. Indeed, accounting is not comprehended, practised or taught as a coherent and disciplined system, but as a collection of individually determined rules. Accounting standards are developed as discrete projects that proceed unconstrained by any rigorous theoretical framework. The outcome has been a proliferation of standards that enshrine contradictory ideas and legitimate inconsistent practices. Progress within a discipline occurs when ideas can be connected, when they cohere with other ideas or contribute to eliminating contradictions. As Chambers (1980: 171) points out, to tolerate an internally inconsistent body of ideas is 'anti-rational, anti-scientific and anti-intellectual'.

Consistency between the individual elements is the first quality to be sought within a body of professional accounting knowledge. However, a second condition of consistency must also obtain. This study has emphasized that bodies of professional knowledge are not purely abstract systems; they must have application in the practical setting of human affairs. Hence, while imaginary numbers may be held in contemplation within an abstract system of mathematics they are necessarily discarded within engineering and other fields involving the pursuit of practical ends. Therefore, the second condition of consistency that must obtain in connection with a body of professional knowledge concerns the need for an empirical foundation: the system must be derived from, and correspond to, real-world contexts. There can be no contradiction of 'what is'. Except for the reporting of cash and claims to and against cash, conventional accounting practices rarely satisfy this condition. Changes in prices and price-levels (and hence the dated significance of all monetary amounts) are either ignored altogether or dealt with on an ad hoc basis, in spite of the existence of price changes and their significance for informed decision making being everywhere apparent in the commercial environment. Aggregations yielding sums that are descriptive of no commercial phenomena are sanctioned and mandated. Only by chance are statements of financial position descriptive of the actual financial position of firms as at their date, or do reported profit figures coincide with the actual financial performance of the entities they are appended to.

In summary, the structural bounds of a body of professional accounting knowledge are defined by dual conditions of consistency. First, the individual elements must not be in contradiction of each other. Second, the individual elements must correspond with the empirical context – the commercial environment – that constitutes the domain of the accounting discipline. There is a supervening connection between these two conditions, as temporally unified descriptions of phenomena must cohere with each other. The function of accounting is to describe – as a system of instrumentation – the pertinent financial features of entities in a manner that facilitates informed decision making about those entities. This requires the specification of what those features are and the means by which they can be represented in financial reports in a manner that does not violate the conditions of consistency and correspondence that have been described.

Accounting information, time and decision making

In the professional and academic literature, it is asserted repeatedly that accounting is concerned with the provision of information that is technically useful for decisions that involve allocating scarce resources and making accountability evaluations. However, extant practices are not guided by any systematic exposition of the conditions under which financial statements attain this usefulness. The resulting uncertainty is at the foundation of much of the disarray in accounting practice, with the link between the prescriptions of accounting standards and informed action asserted rather than demonstrated. It has been argued in this study that the technical quality of accounting information can only be advanced when the justification for prescribed practices extends beyond regulatory fiat to encompass explanation of how their combined application yields information that is coherent and systematically connected to the functions it is expected to serve.

The information content of particular statements may pertain to real or imagined situations and be of either of three temporal dimensions: what was (the past), what is (the present), and what might be (the future).[2] These categories of information are fundamentally dissimilar. First, they are not generally substitutive. A report on yesterday's weather cannot be presumed descriptive of today's weather, nor predictive of future weather patterns. Similarly, the previous month's price of a commodity cannot be assumed to provide a reliable guide to present or future prices. The temporal dimension attaching to a statement can only be transformed by the passing of time itself, and then only unidirectionally. A prediction about the future can only become a description of what is, if and when the passage of time allows the prediction to be presently verified.[3] Similarly, a description of what is can only become a description of what was when the present has moved to the past. A description of what was, however, cannot be resurrected to be a description of what is. Synoptically, all statements have a temporal dimension and only time itself permits these dimensions to be transgressed.

Second, statements having different temporal dimensions do not possess common degrees of veracity. An imagined future situation cannot presently be corroborated; it is personalized and exists only within an actor's mind. There is no evidential matter against which it can be authenticated.[4] However, a statement describing a present situation has the potential to be corroborated by an independent observer. In the case of statements describing past events, independent corroboration is dependent on sufficient evidence surviving. Thus, the accuracy of a prediction for the following day's maximum temperature cannot presently be corroborated. However, a statement of the current temperature can; by applying an appropriate measuring instrument (a thermometer) to the relevant phenomenon (air temperature). Statements concerning previous maximum temperatures cannot similarly be corroborated by reference to primary evidence. Instead, secondary evidence must be sought; archival documents which record the results of past observations. Thus, statements possessing different temporal dimensions vary in terms of their reliability and their capacity to be independently verified.

Third, while statements pertaining to each of the past, present and future may be useful – in that each may have implications for human choice and action – the role of each is different. Statements about the past might describe trends that enhance our understanding of the present and which inform our expectations about the future: a football team's winning streak in recent games might inform assessments of its potential for continued success. However, some statements about the past may have only historical and artefactual value: the previous week's lottery numbers cannot logically be used as a guide to predict those that will win in the current week. The usefulness of factual statements about the present subsists in revealing capacities for action: a football coach may analyse a team's present line-up to identify changes designed to deliver competitive advantages. In making such choices, imagined future states will be contemplated – for example, the expected outcome of particular team strategies and tactics. Human activity is thus guided by statements that pertain to each of the past, present and future. But these categories of statements guide human action in quite distinct ways. The usefulness of statements describing what was, is restricted to circumstances in which they can reasonably be inferred to have predictive value. Statements describing what is, delineate actual potentialities for action. Statements drawn from contemplations about the future are necessarily imaginary and personal, but such conjectures may be useful for ranking possible courses of action.

Of these different kinds of statements it is those pertaining to present facts which provide the universal foundation for informed action. All future outcomes are constrained by what the present makes possible, and without a knowledge of present circumstances there is no reliable basis upon which possible future courses of action can be identified and evaluated. Expectations not shaped by an understanding of present facts will be realized only by chance. For a discipline that is consistently defined through the juxtaposition of the terms 'information', 'useful' and 'decision making', appreciation and application of these ideas take on special significance. Yet little regard is had for them in conventional accounting practice.

A statement of financial position is a dated statement, conventionally headed as being 'as at' a particular time. Section 295(2) of the *Australian Corporations Act* specifies that time: 'as at the end of the year'. The temporal dimension specified is unambiguous. Beyond the heading to the statement, however, the accounting profession – both through its conventional practices and the formal rules it has endorsed – has seen fit to make the statement of financial position a repository for information of different temporal dimensions. The methods used to value assets, for example, are variously descriptive of events from a variety of past dates (historical costs), descriptive of the present (cash and cash-like balances), or anticipatory (present values and 'recoverable amounts'). Belying both the heading that they are reported under ('as at' a specified date) and statutory requirements (to show the state of affairs as at the end of an accounting period), the elements of conventionally prepared statements of financial position are temporally heterogeneous. A variety of distinct attributes are quantified using measurement units that are of different significance on account of changes in the purchasing power of money. Recently promulgated definitions of assets perpetuate rather than remedy this confusion. The SAC4 definition provides that the distinguishing feature of an asset is 'future economic benefits' (AARF and AASB 1995a: para. 14). However, the criteria for asset recognition require that 'the asset possesses a cost or other value that can be measured reliably' (para. 38). The 'idea' of an asset thereby resides in the future, but its quantification may be drawn from a past event and expressed in the unique purchasing power unit applying on the date of that event.

The consequences of a statement of financial position failing to embrace a single temporal dimension are profound. First, it means that the statement is incoherent and unintelligible. The aggregate figures it presents are neither descriptive of what was nor what is and are therefore not empirical. Nor, however, are the aggregates prospective. Instead, items of information pertaining to each of the past, present and future are combined as if they could be presumed to be substitutive.[5] Second, the statement cannot be independently and meaningfully audited. While some elements may be independently corroborated, others cannot. Third, conventionally prepared balance sheets have no logical connection to decision-making processes. Individual elements in the statement variously describe past actions, define present circumstances, or anticipate future outcomes. The aggregation of these elements cannot yield a factual and up-to-date guide for financial choice and action.

If a statement of financial position is to be coherent, subject to an approbative statement regarding its veracity, and to provide a reliable guide for decision-making processes, it must embrace a single temporal dimension. A representation of financial position for a dynamic entity can only be momentary: as at a specified date. The choice, then, lies in representing financial position as at some past date, the present, or in projecting to some future date. Any of these choices may give rise to a statement with a single – and therefore coherent – temporal dimension. Of these, only statements pertaining to the past or present are empirical; that is, descriptive of phenomena and capable of being independently authenticated. Any projected statement of financial position will be constituted by conjectures that are personal and unable to be presently verified.

The law relating to companies has long provided the temporal specification for dated statements of financial position: they are to be prepared as at the end of an annual accounting period. Empowered to give practical effect to this prescription (and its intention – see Chambers and Wolnizer 1990, 1991), the accounting profession has consistently condoned and promoted accounting practices that contravene it. With the exceptions of cash, payables and receivables the individual elements of a conventional statement of financial position are generally not true to the dated nature of the statement. Redress of this circumstance is possible.[6] In the case of liabilities, it requires the reporting of legally enforceable obligations existing at balance date at their legally enforceable amounts. Similarly, assets must be defined and represented by a single empirical attribute measured at the balance sheet date. For non-monetary assets – that is, assets which are not cash or fixed claims to cash – there is only one such attribute of a financial character: the selling prices (market values or current cash equivalents) prevailing at the date for which financial position is to be determined.[7] These are universal values – all non-monetary assets have a current cash equivalent, even if it be zero.[8] The current cash equivalents of non-monetary assets also have universal relevance to the exordial decision pertaining to all such assets: whether they are to be held or released to the market place.[9] The use of market prices in the valuation of non-monetary assets permits aggregation with cash on hand and contractual entitlements to receive cash, yielding a measurement of the total cash that can be accessed by the conversion of an entity's assets. No cost-based quantification can similarly be added logically to cash on hand and cash receivable from third parties. The concept of assets here envisaged departs from the presently popular notion that an asset – as a 'future economic benefit' – is simply a conjecture about the future. Instead, assets would comprise 'only real things, not abstractions' (Schuetze 1993b: 69). Similarly, the valuation of assets would be guided by phenomena – up-to-date market prices in the case of non-monetary assets – rather than the violable processes of calculation and prediction that currently obtain.

A statement prepared on the basis outlined – assets defined and measured in terms of current cash equivalents, and liabilities defined and measured as legally enforceable obligations existing at balance date expressed in money terms – would deliver a broad range of other advances over extant practice. The statement of financial position would have a robust theoretical link to the decision-making processes it is expected to serve as it would delineate an entity's present capacity for action and adaptive behaviour within its dynamic environment. Aggregations contained in the statement would be valid and yield sums of practical significance: a comparison between total assets and total liabilities would be indicative of present debt-paying capacity. Being empirical, the statement would have the capacity to be audited by recourse to independent evidence. Moreover, determination of the financial position of firms in the manner suggested would pave the way for a meaningful calculation of periodic profit. The measure of equity contained in the balance sheet would have an empirical referent, being a general capacity to command resources. Comparison of successive dated measures of equity – adjusted for distributions and capital contributions and after allowing for general price level movements – would reveal changes in this capacity that could sensibly be described as profits or losses.

The accounting principles outlined are the corollaries of a simple proposition that is supportable on practical, cognitive and legal grounds: that a statement of financial position should include only information that is true to the dated nature of the statement. Adopted as a guiding principle, this would offer much greater potential for the reform of accounting than that delivered by the array of present accounting rules which have perpetuated and often compounded the incoherence of company statements of financial position. In addition, the style of accounting here envisaged would enable accounting practitioners to conduct their work in a professional manner. It would not relieve them of the need to make judgements, but provide firm theoretical and practical foundations upon which judgements could proceed. The application of present accounting standards necessitates many decisions but typically they are of a speculative nature, involving, for example, assessments of the likelihood of 'future economic benefits' arising. Such decisions do not involve accountants and auditors in exercising professional authority. Instead, conjectures supplant professional judgement and the opinions of company managers are put beyond rigorous scrutiny.

Rescuing the statement of financial position from its current incoherence requires that its temporal bounds be narrowed to exclude all information of a kind that is not contemporaneous with its dated specification. Such a reform would establish the foundation for the effective measurement and monitoring of the financial state and progress of firms from time to time. Assessments of rates of return, debt-paying capacity and financial flexibility could be made on the basis of up-to-date readings that are factually and continuously descriptive of the actual phenomena that determine these variables, rather than crude and often misleading proxies.

Accounting as a profession: prospects and challenges

The future of accounting as a professional occupation is bleak. Willmott, Sikka and Puxty's (1994: 73) predictions concerning the accounting profession in the United Kingdom resonate across national boundaries:

> For the UK accounting industry the balmy days of self-regulation, indulged by a weak and permissive state, are fast fading as the profession's claims and capacity to provide effective self-regulation are more severely

tested and found wanting. Numerous minor reforms have been introduced in a forlorn attempt to plug some of the holes. But the ship of self-regulation continues to sink. She is probably holed beyond repair. . . .

As the industrialisation of accounting becomes more conspicuous, the scale of accounting and audit failure becomes chronic . . . pressures will mount to make more fundamental changes in the structure of regulation. In response, the profession will seek to placate its critics by rehearsing its willingness to introduce reforms. However, the self-interest of the membership, a dependence upon clients and inadequate resources will ensure that the reforms are cosmetic. Eventually, though, the pressures upon the ship of self-regulation will become too great, financially and commercially, for its present structure to tolerate. At this point the captains of the accounting industry will reluctantly support their critics in recommending that the ship of self-regulation be scuttled, to be replaced by a more independent and accountable regulatory body.

Like observations are becoming more widespread and discussions of the 'deprofessionalization' of accounting abound (Baker 1993; Belkaoui 1991; Cooper *et al.* 1994; Dezalay 1997; Hanlon 1994, 1997; Most 1993; Pasewark, Shockley and Wilkerson 1995; Richardson 1997; Sikka, Willmott and Lowe 1989; Tweedie 1993; Velayutham 1996; Willmott 1990; Willmott, Sikka and Puxty 1994; Willmott and Sikka 1997). Moreover, these perspectives are not necessarily in contradiction of how representatives of the accounting profession perceive its future. Consider, for example, the recent musings of an Executive Director of the ICAA:

[What] is once again coming into question is who regulates the profession. It is, in fact, becoming a topic of debate and some disagreement. We must discuss this issue and listen to the range of views that exist, if we are able to find an acceptable balance between the crucial roles of regulator and representative, and sometimes defender, of our members. . . .

In today's climate, however, we are in reality a co-regulator of our profession alongside the government regulators. . . . Some of the questions now being asked are: Should we only be a representative of the members, not a regulator? Should we be more self-regulating? Or, should we cooperate more closely with the government regulators as a true co-regulator of the profession?

(Harrison 1995: 90)

Professionalism in accounting, it seems, has moved to an uncertain and disputatious stage. Standards of performance have been deemed unsatisfactory and only an equivocal acceptance of responsibility for those standards demonstrated. According to Most (1993: 10):

Many social institutions have suffered a loss of status and credibility in the last quarter of the twentieth century. In some cases this has been due to a failure to adapt, but in others there has been an apparent decline in standards of performance, to a level below society's expectations. This appears to have been the case in public accounting.

This 'decline in standards of performance', however, has coincided with the era in which the accounting profession has been effusive in promulgating and endorsing formal statements of standards. It is this incongruity – of a decline in professional performance standards being overseen by a massive expansion of regulatory statements – that has been the focus of inquiry in this study. It has been shown that regulatory statements, no matter how abundant and stringently enforced, which lack a sound cognitive basis can only diminish rather than advance professional performance. The detrimental effects of present accounting rules have been shown to extend beyond the immediacies of technical practice to weaken the whole epistemic infrastructure of the accounting profession.

The significance of these matters reaches beyond just the self-interest of accountants. As explained by Naser (1993: 1), accounting is of great importance to orderly social and economic functioning:

> The environment of accounting consists of social-economic-political-legal conditions, restraints and influences that vary over time. Accounting is not important because it is a product of its environment, but rather because it reshapes its environment and plays a significant role in the conduct of economic, social, political, legal and organizational decisions and actions. It provides information for the re-evaluation of social, political and economic objectives as well as the relative costs and, more specifically, publicly reported accounting numbers influence the distribution of scarce resources.

Growing recognition of the importance of accounting information has not, however, been accompanied by progress in ensuring that the technical quality of that information is commensurate with the significance of the purposes it is expected to serve. It is on this ground that present regulatory structures – which have placed faith in the expertise of the accounting profession – have failed.

Abandonment of reliance on professional authority, however, does not provide a solution as it leaves unanswered the questions of what agency should play the principal regulatory role and how a more serviceable form of accounting will be prescribed. In the absence of leadership from the profession, government prescription of the specifications for financial reports may be the only alternative (Chambers 1973b: 219; Chambers, Ramanathan and Rappaport 1978: 97; Chambers and Wolnizer 1990: 366). The following additions to the statutes governing companies have been proposed:

> No balance sheet shall be deemed to give a true and fair view of the state of affairs of a company unless the amounts shown for the assets are the

money amounts or the best available approximations to the net selling prices in the ordinary course of business of those assets in their state and condition as at the date of the balance sheet.

No profit and loss account shall be deemed to give a true and fair view of the profit or loss of a company unless that profit or loss is so calculated as to include the effects during the year of changes in the net selling prices of assets and of changes in the general purchasing power of the unit of account.

(Chambers, Ramanathan and Rappaport 1978: 97)

These proposals do not – and are not intended to – obviate the need for expert practitioners and their exercise of professional judgement. On the contrary, they offer a framework for the invigoration of accounting as a professional occupation. Accounting would be transformed into a rigorous (empirical) process of measurement – of financial instrumentation – rather than remaining a calculationary (and arbitrary) system. The judgements required to be made by practitioners would be based on observations of commercial phenomena such as prices, price-changes and legally enforceable obligations. Auditing would become the rigorous safeguard it was intended to be. It would entail checking the representations in financial statements against independent evidence and auditors would be required to make professional judgements about the adequacy and reliability of that evidence.

In the absence of a coherent and rigorous theoretical framework, the specification of individual rules for each and every kind of financial instrument and transaction, whether in statute, professional standards or other regulatory dicta, is to little avail. This is so for a variety of reasons. First, the dynamic and complex nature of the commercial environment suggests that such rule-making will constantly be in deficit as it lags behind the continued evolution of business practices. Second, this deficit is likely to be accentuated by the willingness of participants in commercial activity to structure transactions with the intention of circumventing the rules or taking advantage of their flexibility. Third, a 'rule-book' style of accounting is likely to foster a tendency to interpret what has not been precisely proscribed as having being condoned. Fourth, and being the cumulation of the foregoing factors, a constant expansion and amendment of technical rules is likely to result in higher compliance costs but greater risk that non-compliance will pass undetected. These scenarios are already evident in contemporary accounting practice which is increasingly characterized by a 'rule-book' style of regulation.

On these grounds, the case for seeking to rely on occupational self-regulation – with practitioners bringing discipline to accounting practice through the responsible application of a coherent set of ideas about accounting – is a potentially attractive one. At present, however, it is apparent that the accounting profession has not responded to the challenges presented by this form of arrangement. Rather than seeking to define and improve their expertise within a clearly defined boundary, accountants have embarked on a crusade to extend their territory:

> the industrialization of accounting is a consequence of the diversification of product lines, including every conceivable form of consultancy, that have little connection with what was once (but is no longer) core exper-tise. Major firms are no longer [only] providers of 'professional services', such as receivership or accounting and audit. They are also sellers of actuarial services, software packages, asset valuations, legal services, opinion polls, executive recruitment, pensions and insurances. They even undertake to lay golf courses and print T-shirts and badges for client companies.
>
> (Willmott, Sikka and Puxty 1994: 61)

According to Power (1997: 124), 'it has now become difficult to define precisely what an accountant is other than trivially in terms of membership of a professional body'. The warning of Chambers (1966b: 358) has not been heeded:

> The professional is an expert in a strictly bounded field. His role in society is acknowledged only because he professes in a bounded field. He is not expected to be an expert in other fields. As evidence, we may note that if an expert presumes to pronounce in other fields, even his prestige in his own becomes questioned if not tarnished.

Of greatest concern regarding the propensity of the accounting profession to venture outside its traditional bounds is its willingness to do so without regard for the state of its home territory. The chairman of a task force established by the ICAA and ASCPA has proclaimed that 'Accountants are measurers; they're great process builders and if you have a process for establishing a measurement, you can actually take that process into a number of different industries' (cited in Gettler 1997: B5). On these grounds it is contended that accountants are qualified to engage in such activities as evaluating the quality of educational processes and determining appropriate levels for factory emissions (Gettler 1997). Auditing expertise is now said to extend to environmental matters (Power 1997). These claims for expanding the jurisdiction of accounting are contradicted by reference to the state of the traditional output – audited financial reports – of accountants' work. But what is even more disconcerting is that such claims suggest a present satisfaction with technical practices that are demonstrably flawed. The accounting profession has *not* developed systematic measuring processes that are applicable to financial information. Instead, the determination of the periodic financial position and progress of firms proceeds in an undisciplined manner, incorporating arbitrary choices and conjectures that are antithetical to the rigorous and empirical process of measurement.

The misplaced faith that accountants have in their technical practices constitutes a fundamental impediment to advancing the professional warrant of the accounting occupation. Underlying these circumstances is the continuing acceptance of an incomplete notion of 'quality' within the accounting domain; the belief that 'quality' obtains from compliance with rules per se rather than the serviceability of the information yielded by applying those rules. Thus, rule-compliance has evolved to be an end rather than a means, and continued growth in the number and status of rules accepted as a comforting prop. An authentic accounting professionalism, however, must derive from a body of reliable accounting knowledge.

Résumé and conclusion

The charges of all professional groups are onerous and subsist in the responsible and self-directed application of specialized expertise to matters of significance in the conduct of human affairs. The charge given to the accounting profession has been to actuate longstanding provisions in companies legislation requiring the reporting and authentication of the financial position and progress of firms. Complexities and volatilities in commercial activity, incentives and propensities for secrecy and obfuscation, conflicting interests among affected parties and the severity of the consequences of misjudgements conspire to ensure that the lot of an accounting professional is not an easy one. But it is precisely these pressures – and those of a congruent nature in other fields – that create the need for professions. Professions are relied upon to mediate such pressures in a manner that protects and enhances the public interest. Qualification to undertake this role must derive from an occupational group's specialist expertise and demonstrated commitment to apply it responsibly.

The authority of the accounting profession will lack justification until professional accounting knowledge is sufficiently well-developed to provide a robust framework for mediating the conflicting interests and differential capacities of actors within the accounting domain. The rapid and continuing increase in the number of formal accounting rules issued during recent decades is indicative of the accounting profession's present struggle to administer its authority. But expressing conventional ideas in formal statements and endowing them with mandatory status cannot compensate for deficits in professional knowledge. On the contrary, this accounting by official decree has distracted attention from the search for, and application of, the knowledge necessary to vindicate the professional claim of accountants. Such knowledge would be characterized by dual conditions of consistency. First, its individual elements would not be in contradiction of each other. Second, there would be no violation of the relevant empirical context in which accounting is expected to function; financial reports would be descriptive of commercial phenomena at their date.

Redressing the chaotic means by which the financial position of companies is currently purported to be represented has been nominated as an essential starting point for the advancement of professional accounting knowledge. In particular, giving practical effect to the temporal specification for statements of financial position that has been provided for in legislation applying to companies – that they reveal financial position as at the end of each annual accounting period – would provide the foundation for a thorough reform of accounting technique. It would make possible the elimination of many of the inconsistencies of current practices, enable the audit function to operate as the rigorous safeguard it was intended to be, and establish a coherent theoretical link between accounting information and its posited role of aiding accountability evaluations and financial decision making. In addition, successive dated statements of financial position embracing coherent temporal specifications would yield the opportunity to calculate and report comprehensible and verifiable measures of wealth changes.

In the continued absence of progress in reforming the technical quality of financial statements, the status and privileges currently enjoyed by the accounting profession warrant the scrutiny that continued financial reporting debacles threaten to precipitate. The demise of accounting as a professional occupation would, of course, represent a lost opportunity for accountants. In part, this would be a consequence of forsaking the prestige and tangible rewards that are the usual companions of professional status. Of more importance, however, would be a diminished sense of occupational accomplishment and worth. The social contribution of work remains a core means by which people construct meaning in their lives. Seeking membership of an occupational group that contributes in significant ways to social well-being is a noble aspiration; career achievements within such an occupation a worthy source of pride. To forsake the pursuit of professionalism is to compromise these possibilities.

The adverse consequences of accounting failing as a profession extend beyond just the immediate interests of accountants. Professional authority is relied upon as a particular kind of disciplinary mechanism, and the complexity, importance and dynamic nature of the commercial environment mark it as a domain warranting the self-regulatory oversight of a professional group. The experiment in recent decades of attempting to govern accounting information through the continued promulgation of technical rules that are not developed from firm cognitive foundations stands as further testimony to this need. A coherent body of accounting knowledge that defines the boundaries of acceptable practice through the expression of unequivocal principles and definitions offers the most promising prospect for providing financial reports with the demonstrable fitness for use that users of such reports are entitled to expect:

> Knowledge of the subject (theory) gives cohesion and consistency to practice. It cannot eliminate measures which have no other justification than expedience or custom, but as knowledge increases and becomes more widely accepted among practitioners, they may take steps to minimize

the dependence of the art on rules and conventions which are inconsistent with reason.

(Chambers 1969/1957: 367)

In even the most favourable circumstances, progress of this kind may take considerable time. However, present contentment with the imposition by regulatory fiat of demonstrably defective technical practices has stifled the possibility of such progress. To break free of this inertia and pursue an intellectual foundation for accounting practice is the challenge that still confronts the accounting profession. Indeed, it is upon this challenge that the future of accounting as a profession rests.

Notes

1 Matters in conflict

1 This presupposes the existence of an independent reality that can be apprehended and described objectively, and that 'truth' in accounting and other domains is thereby an empirical concept. It is acknowledged that this is now sometimes considered a contentious claim. As summarized by Lynch (1998: 220), 'the postmodern sceptic takes ascriptions of truth as essentially actions of power and domination; the function of truth is political rather than epistemic'. Such views have exerted some influence within the accounting literature. Ingram and Rayburn (1989: 59), for example, state: 'Unfortunately, truth from an accounting perspective is not an empirical fact to be discovered; it is a subjective understanding to be manufactured and agreed upon.' This matter is examined in more detail in Chapter 6. For the present, it is noted that comprehensive defences of the possibility of truth having an empirical foundation may be found in BonJour (1985), Goldman (1988), Ziman (1968, 1978) and, with specific references to the social sciences, Kincaid (1996).

2 Examples of these rules include: the accounting standards issued by the Australian Accounting Standards Board (AASB) and its predecessor the Accounting Standards Review Board (ASRB); the accounting standards set out in the handbook of the Canadian Institute of Chartered Accountants (CICA); the accounting standards issued by the Financial Accounting Standards Board (FASB) in the United States; the Statements of Standard Accounting Practice (SSAP) and Financial Reporting Standards (FRS) issued in the United Kingdom; and the standards issued by the International Accounting Standards Board (IASB). In this study the terms 'accounting rules', 'accounting standards' and others of similar purport are used to refer generally to pronouncements of this kind. These are distinguished from general qualitative regulations, such as 'true and fair', which have long been specified in legislation applying to companies. This distinction is not just one of origin, but of kind. The legislative provision of 'true and fair' specifies an overall quality standard for company accounts. It is an *output* standard. However, the accounting rules that have been referred to are *input* standards that typically specify only how particular elements of financial statements are to be accounted for. They do not specify – individually or collectively – any particular quality standard for the financial reports they are applied to. While references to Australian pronouncements, situations and institutions are emphasized in this study, the findings are considered to be generalizable, particularly among Anglo-American countries.

3 Examples include inventory flow assumptions and the treatment of intangible assets. The arbitrary nature of the prescriptions contained in accounting standards on these matters is evident from inconsistencies across different standard setting jurisdictions. Thus, while the last-in-first-out inventory flow assumption is permitted under FASB rules, it is prohibited by the AASB. In the United States, the maximum amortization

period for goodwill was set at 40 years; in Australia it is 20 years. Within the United Kingdom, goodwill can be treated as having an indefinite life and therefore not be subject to amortization.

4 The volume of technical accounting rules has now apparently reached such a level that breaches are viewed as inevitable. A 1996 survey of annual reports undertaken by The Institute of Chartered Accountants in Australia (ICAA) found that more than half contained departures from accounting standards. A representative of the ICAA commented that 'The multiplicity of disclosure requirements is such that it is almost inevitable that some won't be met' ('One in four annual reports queried' 1996: 85; see also Belkaoui and Jones 1996: 121–4; Boymal 1988; Hepp and McRae 1982; Larson and Kelley 1984; Lee, Larson and Chenok 1983).

5 To permit preservation of the chronology of ideas, two dates are shown for references accessed in a re-published form. The first identifies the date of re-publication as per the list of references and the second the date of original publication.

2 Professions: their nature, roles and responsibilities

1 As the subject of this chapter is 'professions', an obligation of definition is acknowledged. The issue of defining professions is discussed throughout this chapter which also develops and justifies the conception of profession that will be used in this study.

2 The magnitude of discord within the study of professions is such to have itself become a focus of inquiry, with the literature containing various explanations for the perceived lack of progress and proposals for how the study of professions should proceed (Atkinson and Delamont 1990; Barber 1963; Freidson 1986: ch. 2; Johnson 1972; Klegon 1978; Saks 1983; Torstendahl 1990).

3 A notable exception was George Bernard Shaw, whose character Sir Patrick Cullen in the play *The Doctor's Dilemma* opines that 'All professions are conspiracies against the laity' (1932/1906: 106). In a lengthy 'Preface on doctors' published with the play, Shaw foreshadowed many of the arguments that would be pursued by radical writers on the professions some 70 years later. The 'object of the medical profession', he asserted, was 'to secure an income for the private doctor; and to this consideration all concern for science and public health must give way when the two come into conflict' (1932/1906: 28).

4 Although not published in English until 1957, Durkheim's *Professional Ethics and Civil Morals* originated from a series of lectures first presented late in the nineteenth century.

5 Outside of the sociology literature trait models have endured with greater persistence, particularly in publications authored by representatives of occupational groups claiming professional status. For examples within the accounting literature, see Cottell and Perlin 1990: 18; Jeffery 1995; Leung and Cooper 1995: 5; Windal and Corley 1980: 8–11; for a more general illustration see Benson 1981. Trait models have also remained in favour with textbook writers (for example, Gul *et al.* 1997: 7–9; Gay and Simnett 2000: 43–4).

6 The widespread questioning of the nature of professions initiated by sociologists in the 1970s lagged behind that of economists. Milton Friedman in *Capitalism and Freedom* (1962) vigorously questioned the social desirability of occupational licensing, claiming that it lessened competition. The American Medical Association, he contended, was 'a trade union that can limit the number of people who can enter' (1962: 150).

7 For example, Boreham (1983: 702) states that Carr-Saunders and Wilson 'wrote in a style better characterized by advocacy rather than by description or evaluation'.

8 The 'problem' of professions that do not operate within markets has been a recurring and unresolved issue in the literature. Carr-Saunders and Wilson (1933: 3) state: 'We . . . omit the Church and the Army. The former is left out because all those

functions related to the ordinary business of life, education among them, which used to fall to the Church, have been taken over by other vocations. The functions remaining to the Church are spiritual, and we are only concerned with the professions in their relation to the ordinary business of life. The Army is omitted, because the service which soldiers are trained to render is one which it is hoped they will never be called upon to perform.' Wilensky (1964: 141) claims that the clergy has been 'established solidly' as a profession since the late middle ages and acknowledges that the military also provides professional careers. However, both the clergy and the military are excluded from the author's analysis of the process of professionalization (1964: 142). Larson (1977: xvii), nominating that the main focus of her study would be 'the constitution of professional markets' was content to note that this would determine 'the exclusion of professions like the military and the clergy, which do not transact their services on the market'.

9 Haug and Sussman (1973: 89) appear to find more commonalities than differences between professionalization and unionism, contending that both are 'processes by which members of an occupation seek to achieve collective upward mobility'. According to Selander (1990: 142) the distinction between a profession and a trade union is simply one of underlying motivation: 'Traditional professionalization as upward, collective social mobility differs from trade-unionist strategies because its purpose is to cross class boundaries, which is not the case for trade-unionist strategies.'

10 Salient examples are readily available in connection with accounting. For example, the sociologist Turner (1995: 136) states: 'Because accountancy has a direct relationship to capitalist processes, accountancy lacks the element of indeterminacy which is essential to the professional relationship.' In contrast, the accountants Booth and Cocks (1990b: 402) explain how the accounting profession has avoided such a situation 'by constructing standards to preserve the need for judgement'. Turner's conclusion that the accountant 'housed within the accountancy firm or within the larger corporation . . . does not control their work situation' (1995: 136) differs from that of fellow sociologist Freidson (1986: 162–3): 'large accounting firms have emphasized personal autonomy on the part of the full-fledged employee'. Johnson's (1972: 18) description of accountancy as 'not highly advanced in the process of professionalisation' is, as will be discussed in Chapter 3, contrary to the majority of other commentators.

11 Roth (1974: 17) even suggests that the sociology of professions literature may have been influenced by sociologists' concern with their *own* status: 'they too are in an occupation on the make and they have an interest in seeing how they can increase their score in relation to other occupations'. Phillips' (1973) analysis of sociology's standing as a profession suggests that the interest referred to by Roth may be an anxiety-laden one (see also Lynch and Bogen 1997).

12 The influence of Weber and Marx on the study of professions poignantly draws attention to the extent to which the literature has been shaped by ideology. As Burrage (1990: 1) notes, 'two of sociology's founding fathers said virtually nothing about the professions. For Marx they were not significant participants in the class conflicts of capitalist societies. . . . Weber ignored them altogether'.

13 Economists have shown a greater inclination for investigating the rationales for professional monopolies (for example, Shaked and Sutton 1981).

14 Difficulty in defining the subject of their inquiries appears to have all but exasperated sociologists of the professions, with the clear tendency in the recent literature being to either avoid the issue or offer only a very broad definition. Freidson (1986: 16), for example, describes professionals as the 'the agents of formal knowledge' but reverts to the use of census classifications for the more practical task of identifying professions. Abbott (1983: 856) notes that 'There is much to lose and little to gain by insisting on a precise definition.' In a later work he followed his own advice, offering 'the very loose definition that professions are occupational groups applying somewhat abstract knowledge to particular cases' (Abbott 1988: 8). Macdonald (1995: 1), with

similar reservations, found the same resolution, using the word 'professions' 'as a kind of shorthand, not as a closely defined technical term'.

15 This is not intended to imply that the technical quality of professional services and ethical behaviour in the provision of those services are entirely separate issues. The maintenance of competence, for example, may itself be construed as an ethical responsibility. However, in many instances ethical responsibilities are independent of the actual service being supplied. This would include, for example, the preservation of client confidentiality.

16 Finnis (1990: 176, emphasis in original) defines authority in the following terms: 'A person treats something (for example, an opinion, a pronouncement, a map, an order, a rule . . .) as authoritative if and only if he treats it as giving him sufficient reason for believing or acting in accordance with it *notwithstanding* that he himself cannot otherwise see good reason for so believing or acting, or cannot evaluate the reasons he can see, or sees some countervailing reason(s), or would otherwise (i.e. in the absence of what it is that he is treating as authoritative) have preferred not so to believe or act.'

17 This conception does not provide a completely clear demarcation between professions and other occupational groups, nor is it intended to. As suggested by other writers (Barber 1963; Greenwood 1966/1957; Wilensky 1964), professionalization should be understood in terms of a general tendency rather than an absolute concept.

18 Various evaluations of the 'performance' of accounting as a profession have been made in recent years (Baker 1993; Booth and Cocks 1990b; Briloff 1990; Byington and Sutton 1991; Fogarty *et al.* 1997; Mitchell *et al.* 1991, 1994; Pasewark, Shockley and Wilkerson 1995; Puxty, Sikka and Willmott 1997; Robson *et al.* 1994; Sikka and Willmott 1995a, 1995b; Sikka, Willmott and Lowe 1989; Turner and Jensen 1987; Willmott 1990; Willmott, Puxty and Cooper 1993; Willmott, Sikka and Puxty 1994). However, these studies have typically been concerned with the *behaviour* of accounting professionals within the context of claims to serve the public interest. They have generally not had as a central focus the issue of whether the accounting profession possesses a sufficiently strong knowledge mandate to render it capable of effectively serving and protecting the public interest in terms of the technical aspects of accounting practice.

3 Accounting as a profession

1 For example, in the case of *Pacific Acceptance Corporation Ltd v. Forsyth and Others* (92 WN (1970) NSW 239: 74), Moffitt, J. made the following comment concerning the technical standards of auditors' work: 'now, as formerly, standards and practices adopted by the profession to meet current circumstances provide a sound guide to the court in determining what is reasonable'.

2 Further discussion on this matter is contained in Chapter 5.

3 Unlike the other references listed, Brown was apparently not commissioned by an accounting organization. However, he noted in his preface that the idea for his work had 'been heartily approved of by the Scottish Societies of Accountants' and that contributors to the volume considered that they were 'rendering a service to the profession' (1968/1905: vii).

4 Given the variety of connotations attaching to the words 'profession' and 'professional', it is perhaps inevitable that the term 'professionalization' also lacks a precise and singular meaning. In this discussion 'professionalization' is used to describe the process by which accountants acquired the elevated occupational authority that has been described earlier in the chapter. As such, the term is not used here to imply a necessary fitness to administer that authority. Rather, the acquisition of occupational authority and the discharge of the responsibilities that accompany that authority are viewed as separate issues.

5 Walker (1996) draws attention to the fragility of social exclusiveness as a professionalization strategy, evidencing how the public exposure of the dishonourable actions of 'a single practitioner could potentially inflict considerable damage on the reputation of the occupation' (1996: 29). That 'single practitioner' in the case of the Society of Accountants in Edinburgh was one Donald Smith Peddie, whose serious and, most importantly, very visible recreant behaviour caused the Society to act 'expeditiously to institute regulations to uphold public confidence in the profession' (1996: 30).

6 The struggle can be traced back to the first known Australian accounting association, the Adelaide Society of Accountants, formed in 1885 (Chua and Poullaos 1993: 700).

7 Abbott (1988: 29) nominates the railroad professions and psychological mediums as examples of 'professional deaths'.

4 The nature of accounting rules

1 The point is that expertise in interpreting and applying regulatory statements per se is not an accounting expertise, but the clearly established province of the legal profession.

2 Popper's emphasis on falsifiability in the construction of theoretical systems has often been accorded more attention than his affirmation of the need for consistency (see, for example, Hines 1988b). However, as pointed out by Popper (1968: 92), the conditions of consistency and falsifiability 'are to a large extent analogous'. More specifically: 'Statements which do not satisfy the condition of consistency fail to differentiate between any two statements within the totality of all possible statements. Statements which do not satisfy the condition of falsifiability fail to differentiate between any two statements within the totality of all possible empirical basic statements' (1968: 92).

3 This does not demand that the system will be 'perfect', as a body of knowledge that is complete and without scope for improvement represent only a theoretical ideal. Rather, the expectation is that a body of professional knowledge be practically robust; that is, without fundamental or incapacitating contradictions.

4 This is routinely overlooked in accounting textbooks which typically define accounting in terms of the definitions provided in Box 4.1, but then devote chapters to procedures and regulations applicable to individual accounting issues without giving any consideration to how these individual treatments combine to yield serviceable financial reports. This issue is considered further in Chapter 7.

5 Thus, frameworks for the analysis and interpretation of financial statements are constructed invariably around these or similar variables. For example, Gaffikin (1993: ch. 19) emphasizes the analysis of operating performance and financial strength; Peirson and Ramsay (1996: chs 22 and 23) short-term financial position, long-term financial structure and operating performance; Wise *et al.* (1998: ch. 19) liquidity, profitability, long-term solvency and cash flow adequacy.

6 The relevant AASB standards are: AASB 1013 'Accounting for goodwill', AASB 1036 'Borrowing costs', AASB 1022 'Accounting for the extractive industries', AASB 1011 'Accounting for research and development costs', and AASB 1009 'Construction contracts'.

7 'Recoverable amount' is defined in AASB 1010, in relation to an asset, as 'the net amount that is expected to be recovered through the cash inflows and outflows arising from its continued use and subsequent disposal' (para. 12.1).

8 Houghton and Walawski (1992) demonstrate how professional accountants differ in the meanings they attach to contingency terms contained in accounting standards and statements of accounting concepts.

9 In the event of this algorithm yielding a negative number it is to be disclosed as a liability and described as 'the amount due to customers for contract work' (para. 10.1).

10 This is demonstrated by the findings of Begum and West's (1996) survey of the valuation practices of a sample of Australian companies.

11 As Martin (1989: 246) states: 'The identification and promulgation of a conceptual framework in accounting has taken on the character of a search for the Holy Grail. Millions of dollars have been expended in the United States and in other western countries in attempting to set forth the objectives, assumptions and basic definitions of accounting.'

12 Hines (1989, 1991) attributes an alternative function: 'conceptual frameworks may be seen to be a *political resource* in the conflict over the control of occupational territory' (1989: 85, emphasis in original). Richardson (1988, 1990) presents a similar argument with regard to accounting rule-making in general: 'the accounting profession appears to achieve its social rewards by committing itself to particular responses to accounting issues' (1988: 393).

13 The meaning attached to the term 'real-world' follows that provided by Lee (1993: 16): 'the physically observable and verifiable environment in which human beings are located'.

14 The suggestion that concepts statements are 'the residual of the standard-setting process' is emphasized by Hines (1991: 315) in her evaluation of the FASB's conceptual framework. Evidence that supports this interpretation is available particularly in connection with the issue of measurement. The FASB in *Statement of Accounting Concepts No. 5* 'Recognition and Measurement in Financial Statements of Business Enterprises' states: 'this concepts Statement characterizes present practice as based on different [measurement] attributes. Rather than attempt to select a single attribute and force changes in practice so that all classes of assets and liabilities use that attribute, this concepts Statement suggests that use of different attributes will continue' (FASB 1984: para. 70). A similar outcome has been predetermined in connection with the measurement 'building block' of the Australian conceptual framework, with the retention of the modified historical cost system being signalled for the foreseeable future (AASB and PSASB 1994). Conflict between the stated and actual function of concepts statements is also suggested by their present subordination to accounting standards.

15 Evidence of this confusion is revealed by continuing reference to 'intangible assets', as if they were a separate category. Under the SAC4 definition it would seem that *all* assets are intangible. Nobody has ever seen or laid hands on a future economic benefit.

16 The source of this dictionary definition and those that follow is the *New Shorter Oxford English Dictionary*. Chambers' (1991a: 40) review of the etymology of the word asset is conclusive: 'Any description of assets that fails to make reference to the spending or debt-paying power they represent bypasses the financial significance of assets.'

17 Schuetze's comment was made with reference to the FASB definition of assets: 'Assets are probable future economic benefits obtained or controlled by a particular entity as a result of past transactions or events' (FASB 1985: para. 25). The substance of this definition is the same as that contained in SAC4.

18 The *New Shorter Oxford English Dictionary* offers the following definition of control: 'The act or power of directing or regulating; command, regulating influence'. It is difficult to envisage, in most business settings, how future economic benefits could be directed, regulated or commanded.

19 The *New Shorter Oxford English Dictionary*, for example, includes the following definitions of the word obligation: 'The action of constraining oneself by promise or contract to a particular course of action . . .', 'A binding agreement . . .', 'the condition of being morally or legally bound . . .', 'what one is bound to do'. In each instance the emphasis is on binding rather than elective or possible courses of action.

20 Not surprisingly, Patel and Day (1996) report that student participants in a research experiment had significant difficulty in understanding SAC4.

5 Explaining the proliferation of accounting rules

1 It is reiterated that the term 'accounting rules' is used in this study as a generic description for formally prescribed methods of accounting. It is not intended to embrace general qualitative standards for accounting information, such as 'true and fair', nor prescriptions that are concerned purely with matters of disclosure. This directs emphasis away from statutes applying to companies. Gibson (1971: 1) notes that 'The first statutes facilitating the incorporation of companies had little to say about the information to be made available to investors.' Subsequent developments in company law have tended to mandate disclosures rather than prescribe methods of accounting: 'while at times great effort has been expended in securing the disclosure of specific information, there has been little attempt in Australia to define the quantitative basis of measurement underlying the published "facts" ' (Gibson 1971: 3–4).

2 The requirement to comply with accounting standards is contained in section 296(1) of the *Australian Corporations Act*.

3 These comprised the Institute of Chartered Accountants of Scotland, the Institute of Chartered Accountants in Ireland, the Association of Chartered Certified Accountants, the Chartered Institute of Management Accountants and the Chartered Institute of Public Finance and Accountancy.

4 Concerns about the quality of accounting principles re-emerged in the views of a Chief Accountant of the SEC almost 60 years later (Schuetze 1993a, 1993b, 1994).

5 The Dominion Association of Chartered Accountants was the forerunner to the CICA.

6 This lack of consensus is reflected in the early history of the law relating to incorporated entities. For example, the requirements for a compulsory audit contained in the 1844 legislation were abandoned in the *Companies Act of 1856*, although provisions for the voluntary appointment of an auditor were maintained. In the *Companies Act of 1900* a return was made to mandatory audit appointments (Lee 1979: 154). As Peirson and Ramsay (1983: 287–8) state, 'The question of whether to introduce compulsory requirements regarding the preparation and content of . . . accounts, and for their distribution to shareholders was debated frequently in the United Kingdom in the latter half of the nineteenth century and the early decades of the twentieth century.'

7 Other writers concur with this proposition. Langfield-Smith (1990: 6) states that 'The need for accounting standards is generally accepted.' The conclusion of Godfrey, Hodgson and Holmes (1997: 354) is that 'market mechanisms will not be able to achieve a socially optimal equilibrium price for accounting information'. These authors base this finding on public good and monopoly arguments, the perceived inability of users to agree on what information should be disclosed, and accountants' inability to agree on how that information should be derived.

8 This is reflected in recently issued AASB standards having an often lengthy appendix headed 'Development of the standard'. These appendices outline the various steps undertaken in the process of standard setting and are consonant with the notion that accounting rule-makers consider their accountability to be contingent upon the processes they have undertaken rather than the technical quality of the output they produce. This is further evident in the contrast between the lengthy 'Development of the standard' appendices and the paucity of words offered in defence of the actual technical prescriptions contained in accounting standards.

9 This is not to imply, of course, that the administration of this test would be free of judgement. As with other professions, judgement is a necessary aspect of accounting practice. However, there is a difference in kind about making a professional judgement about something that exists and for which evidence may be collected (for example, the market value of an asset) and conjecturing about abstractions (for example, deferred research and development costs).

10 For example, prescribing a method and maximum period for amortizing goodwill may ensure that different firms calculate amortization expense in the same way. However, it provides no assurance that the expense (or the remaining unamortized cost) calculated for a particular firm is an accurate description of any feature of that firm.

6 Professionalism, accounting rules and accounting discourse

1 For example, AASB 1008 'Leases' and AASB 1028 'Employee benefits' require that certain assets and liabilities be valued on the basis of present value calculations. Examples of industry-specific standards include AASB 1022 'Accounting for the extractive industries' and AASB 1023 'Financial reporting of general insurance activities'.

2 The impotence of the present rule-based approach to regulating accounting information has been exposed repeatedly in recent years through its inability to deal, on a timely basis, with new forms of commercial transactions such as derivatives and other exotic financial instruments (Hancock 1994).

3 It is acknowledged that the field of engineering involves employing a knowledge of physics and other sciences in the pursuit of practical ends, demonstrating how a combination of disciplines may yield a level of professional authority beyond that attainable within a single discipline.

4 The source of this etymology is the *New Shorter Oxford English Dictionary*.

5 Even the medical profession has found that it is not immune from these pressures, with increasing community attention being directed to 'alternative' medical treatments such as naturopathy and homoeopathy in recent years. Motivating this action has been the dissatisfaction of some members of the public with 'conventional' medicine and the apparent elusiveness of cures for some medical conditions.

6 This is not intended to imply that all research findings should be expected to have an immediate and significant impact on practice. The processes of evaluation, replication and refinement necessary for the yielding of reliable knowledge may take considerable time. In addition, the case for 'pure' research is not denied. The salient point is that professions are charged with overseeing matters of practical and recurring importance in the conduct of human affairs. Over time then, there is a legitimate expectation that some general but robust connection between scholarly discourse and professional practice should be observable.

7 Chambers (1966b) portrays continuing business firms as adaptive entities and thus challenges the relevance of cost-based values for assets. Tabart-Gay and Wolnizer (1997) offer empirical evidence drawn from the Australian banking industry that is in accord with this perspective.

8 For example, the disclosure of supplementary current cost information was mandatory for certain classes of companies in the United States from 1976 to 1986. In the United Kingdom SSAP 16, issued in 1980 and withdrawn in 1985, also mandated current cost disclosures. Within Australia, a statement of accounting practice (SAP1) recommending the disclosure of supplementary financial statements prepared on a current cost basis was issued in 1983 and remains in place (Godfrey, Hodgson and Holmes 1997: 147–51).

9 For example, Brown, Izan and Loh (1992: 36) 'argue' that 'managers are not indifferent to how and when they revalue their firm's assets'. Similarly, Whittred and Chan (1992: 72) conclude: 'Asset revaluations are a form of voluntary accounting policy choice (i.e. of the valuation base for certain assets). Our discussion and results point to the endogeneity of such choices.'

10 In spite of this, Watts and Zimmerman in their ten year review of positive accounting theory (1990: 138) describe accounting choice studies as 'promising'. Consideration of the other major form of research embraced by positive accounting theorists

– market reaction studies – has not been pursued here on the basis of the admission of Watts and Zimmerman (1990: 138) that such studies 'are probably relatively weak tests of the theory' (see also Chambers 1965; Lev 1989).

11 While the origins of positive accounting theory are commonly traced to the late 1960s (Watts and Zimmerman 1986: 5), its rise to prominence became most evident in the 1970s. This coincided with or shortly followed important developments that, as described in Chapter 4, firmly established the accounting profession's reliance on the promulgation of technical accounting rules such as accounting standards. The Accountancy Research Foundation in Australia was established in 1965, but became most active in the development of accounting standards following its reorganization and renaming as the AARF in 1974. The FASB was established in 1973, the same year that the Accounting Standards Committee was established in Canada. In the United Kingdom the Accounting Standards Steering Committee was established in 1970.

12 Consistent with this observation, Llewellyn (1996: 112, emphasis in original) argues that 'interpretive and critical accounting researchers should now reconnect with accounting as a practice and be prepared to present theories *for* practice rather than restricting their research to theories *about* practice'.

13 Accounting education, of course, played a major role in promoting this acceptance (see Chambers 1994).

7 Professionalism, accounting rules and accounting education

1 More specifically, the emphasis in this chapter is on undergraduate university programmes that provide an entrée to professional employment in accounting and programmes administered by accounting associations that lead to professional qualifications such as 'CPA' and 'Chartered Accountant'.

2 Aristotle is said to have proclaimed that 'Educated men are as much superior to uneducated men as the living are to the dead.'

3 As will be discussed later in the chapter, criticisms of this kind have been made of accounting education. However, criticisms of the opposite kind – that accounting education lacks sufficient theoretical emphasis – have also been frequent.

4 Although the inquiries cited relate specifically to either Australia or the United States, Abdolmohammadi, Novin and Christopher (1997) show that many concerns about accounting education are common to both countries. Similarly, Tinker and Koutsoumadi (1997: 463) identify 'a great deal of commonality' between accounting education in North America, Australia and the United Kingdom.

5 The situation varies slightly in the United States where the CPA Examination is often undertaken during the last year of university study (Zeff 1989b: 167).

6 The need to assess students accentuates this problem. Consider, for example, the requirements of AASB 1012 pertaining to the translation of financial statements denominated in a foreign currency. If the foreign operation is 'self-sustaining' the 'current rate' method of translation is required to be used. If the foreign operation is 'integrated' the 'temporal' method is to be applied. In reality, distinguishing between 'self-sustaining' and 'integrated' operations is often likely to be very subjective and in some instances either classification might be able to be defended. However, an examination question in which both methods are 'right' will not directly help in discriminating between students. Hence, educators may turn to questions in which the need for clearly right and clearly wrong answers is given priority over the realities of the commercial environment.

8 Professionalism, accounting rules and accounting practice

1 It is also, to some extent, now an obsolete portrayal. Prohibitions on advertising, for example, are now much less evident in the ethical codes of professions.

2 This is emphasized by Wolnizer (1987: 129, emphasis in original): 'Professionalism entails not only the character of professional persons and the observable features of their associations, but the *function* or *technical object* to be served by them.' Thus, in the case of auditing: 'the mental attitude of auditors *per se* should not be the focus of the professional prescriptions on independence. The essential issue is whether the function of auditing has been served; whether accounts have been independently authenticated' (Wolnizer 1987: 129).

3 Claims (for example, McGregor 1992) that accounting rules have made the general qualitative standard of 'true and fair' redundant are unsustainable on a variety of grounds. First, since the rules do not cover all accounting matters, the absence of a general qualitative standard would mean that significant elements of accounting practice would not be subject to *any* qualitative standard. Second, the technical deficiencies of existing rules make it imprudent to abandon other – and potentially more effective – regulatory devices. Third, and perhaps most importantly, a proliferating array of specific rules (such as accounting standards) does not, in principle, obviate the need for an all-embracing general qualitative standard. Specific regulations applying to the individual components of a motor vehicle, for example, do not make redundant concerns about the *overall* quality of the product in terms of its safety and fitness for use.

4 More recently the term 'expectations gap' has also been applied to encompass deficient professional performance. This expansion of the meaning of the term appears to have developed from the perspectives contained in academic writings (for example, Porter 1993). Hence, in *A Research Study on Financial Reporting and Auditing – Bridging the Expectation Gap*, commissioned by the ASCPA and ICAA (1994: 3), the expectations gap is described as having two components: 'the difference between the expectations of users and the reasonable standard of financial reporting and auditing which the Profession can be expected to deliver' and 'the difference between the reasonable standard of financial reporting and auditing which the profession can be expected to deliver and the services which are being delivered by the Profession'.

5 Advertisements for *Charter*, the official journal of the ICAA, have included the following statement: 'Oh, yes and we do squeeze in a few pages on accounting and auditing topics.'

6 Instead, a familiar and well-rehearsed routine of *appearing* to take action has been repeated. Thus, in reviewing *A Research Study on Financial Reporting and Auditing – Bridging the Expectation Gap*, Hogan (1994: 63) commented that 'Failure to explore issues to which attention has been drawn time and time again is the major weakness.' Porter's (1996: 134) review of the same study expresses regret that the members of the working party which authored the study were 'all drawn from the accounting profession and thus conditioned to seeing the external financial reporting arena through similarly blinkered eyes'. In a similar vein, Willmott, Sikka and Puxty (1994) chastise the accounting profession within the United Kingdom for pursuing only cosmetic reforms to professional practice.

7 Typically, the application of the lower of cost and net realizable value rule will result in an individual firm's inventories being partly valued on an assigned cost basis and partly at net realizable value. The aggregate amount thus calculated for inventory has no empirical meaning; it describes no property of the inventories. Further, the asymmetrical nature of the lower and cost rule can only be understood in terms of a deliberate advocacy of bias, rather than the objectivity that might reasonably be expected in connection with an independent professional service.

8 The situation is explained by Hall (1987: 41): 'Every experienced auditor, I am sure, has heard a client – or even, I dislike admitting, one of his associates – argue that some novel accounting must be acceptable because it is not specifically forbidden. "Show me the rule that says I can't do it", is an argument sometimes heard.'

9 A survey of Australian auditing firms by Deegan, Kent and Lin (1994) found that over half the respondents did not implement separate procedures to check for whether financial statements provided a 'true and fair' view. The authors conclude: 'Many audit firms do not implement any audit procedures other than those used to test compliance with the Corporations Law (apart from the requirement to present true and fair accounts) and accounting standards because they believe that compliance with these requirements should lead to a true and fair view' (1994: 11).

10 For example, Hall (1987: 41) writes of a 'search for loopholes that rules seem to foster. To some, the rules seem almost a challenge to find ways to get around them. This gamesmanship would be almost enticing, perhaps, if it were not so subversive to the very thrust of financial reporting – to tell it as it is'.

11 Thus, at least a significant number of respondents who perceived creative accounting to be a serious threat to the integrity of financial reporting also considered it to be a legitimate business tool.

12 Mitchell *et al.* (1991: 8, with their emphasis preserved) cite an audit tender document prepared by a major accounting firm which refers to 'an acknowledged track record in *constructive accounting solutions*' and further stated 'our experience and expertise in financial reporting will enable us to contribute to your discussion of . . . how to best present your results and balance sheet'. The same authors also cite an admission from the chairman of a major firm of being involved in the 'industry' of accounting standards avoidance. Within this milieu, accounting firms are said to compete against each other in terms of the extent to which they will tolerate idiosyncratic accounting practices, giving rise to so-called 'opinion shopping' (Mitchell *et al.* 1991: 25; Gay and Simnett 2000: 84).

9 Advancing professional accounting knowledge

1 'Diversity' has even been described as a basic 'assumption' of financial accounting practice: 'an assumption that accounting procedures could differ between businesses even if those businesses were similar' (Henderson, Peirson and Brown 1992: 87).

2 This clearly invokes a linear and unidirectional conception of time in which the future becomes the present and then the past. Although this conception of time is not universal, alternative understandings do not appear to eliminate its basic elements. See, for example, Asechemie (1995) and Ezzamel and Robson (1995: 150).

3 Accordingly, attempts in accounting practice to calculate the 'present value' of expected future cash flows do not, and cannot, transform conjectures about the future to descriptions of the present. Such calculations merely involve changing the unit of quantification, in the same way in which amounts expressed in Australian dollars might be converted to New Zealand dollars.

4 Wolnizer's (1987: 45) examination of information quality generally and in accounting particularly concludes: 'The basis of quality assurance is independently observable and testable evidence that a product's actual condition and performance corresponds with that represented in its specifications.' Excluded from the province of quality assurance are personal and conjectural statements: 'At any point in time we can only discover what was or is the case. The subjects of these discoveries are, in general, independently observable (non-personal) objects and events. We describe as *independently testable* those statements which depict the past or present state or relation between non-personal properties of objects and events' (1987: 12–13, emphasis in original).

5 Conventional depreciation calculations compound this problem. Where an asset is valued at depreciated historical cost, an observation of the past is subject to modification on account of expectations regarding the duration and pattern of future use and residual value. As a result, the net amounts ('book' or 'written down' values) recorded for such assets are eternally non-empirical. That is, they never can be statements of what was or what is because they can never correspond to phenomena. The

'idea' they represent is a purely imaginary one, being some unallocated portion of an acquisition cost.

6 The prescriptions which follow derive from, and endorse, the system of Continuously Contemporary Accounting developed by Chambers (1966b, 1970c, 1974).

7 The concept of 'current replacement cost' has been excluded from consideration here on the grounds that it does not describe a feature of an asset to be reported in a balance sheet. Instead, it describes the cost of some other asset which, more likely than not, will never be an asset of the entity. Moreover, current replacement cost lacks universality, having – by definition – no application in connection with assets that are 'irreplaceable'.

8 This is not to imply that the market prices of non-monetary assets will in all cases necessarily be readily ascertainable. The markets for certain kinds of items may operate only sporadically, compromising the opportunity for timely market observations. This does not deny the existence of market prices but admits that, in some restricted instances, the discovery of those prices might not proceed without some difficulty. To deny the general availability of market prices would be to deny the existence of the fundamental information that informs commercial activity. Several studies have revealed the availability of up-to-date market prices in connection with a broad range of commodities (Foster 1969; Gray 1975; McKeown 1971; Wolnizer 1977, 1983).

9 Chambers and Wolnizer (1991: 211) draw attention to the rich and documented history of the importance of up-to-date selling prices in commercial activity: 'to give any other valuations than up-to-date money equivalents of assets would violate the trust which others do, and must, place in the solvency and the financial substance represented in financial statements of companies that operate under the cover of limited liability'.

References

Statutes

Australia

Australian Corporations and Securities Legislation (2002) Sydney: CCH.

Canada

Canadian Business Corporations Act and Regulations (1998) Toronto: Thomson.

United Kingdom

Act for the Registration, Incorporation and Regulation of Joint Stock Companies, 7 and 8 Vict., c.110, 1844.
Joint Stock Companies Act, 19 and 20 Vict., c.47, 1856.
Companies Act, 11 and 12 Geo. 6, c.38, 1948.

Court case

Pacific Acceptance Corporation Ltd v. Forsyth and Others 1970, 92 WN (NSW) 29.

Accounting regulatory pronouncements and related statements

Australia

Australian Accounting Research Foundation (1995) *Auditing Standard* AUS 804 'The audit of prospective financial information'.
Australian Accounting Research Foundation and Accounting Standards Review Board (1990) *Statement of Accounting Concepts* SAC2 'Objective of general purpose financial reporting'.
Australian Accounting Research Foundation and Australian Accounting Standards Board (1995a) *Statement of Accounting Concepts* SAC4 'Definition and recognition of the elements of financial statements'.
Australian Accounting Research Foundation and Australian Accounting Standards Board (1995b) *Policy Statement* 5 'The nature and purpose of statements of accounting concepts'.
Australian Accounting Standards Board, AASB 1008 'Leases' (reissued October 1998).

Australian Accounting Standards Board, AASB 1009 'Construction contracts' (reissued December 1997).

Australian Accounting Standards Board, AASB 1010 'Recoverable amount of non-current assets' (reissued December 1999).

Australian Accounting Standards Board, AASB 1011 'Accounting for research and development costs' (as amended August 1991).

Australian Accounting Standards Board, AASB 1012 'Foreign currency translation' (as amended August 1991).

Australian Accounting Standards Board, AASB 1013 'Accounting for goodwill' (reissued June 1996).

Australian Accounting Standards Board, AASB 1019 'Inventories' (reissued March 1998).

Australian Accounting Standards Board, AASB 1020 'Income taxes' (reissued December 1999).

Australian Accounting Standards Board, AASB 1021 'Depreciation' (reissued August 1997).

Australian Accounting Standards Board, AASB 1022 'Accounting for the extractive industries' (as amended August 1991).

Australian Accounting Standards Board, AASB 1023 'Financial reporting of general insurance activities' (reissued November 1996).

Australian Accounting Standards Board, AASB 1028 'Accounting for employee entitlements' (issued March 1994).

Australian Accounting Standards Board, AASB 1028 'Employee benefits' (as amended June 2001).

Australian Accounting Standards Board, AASB 1036 'Borrowing costs' (issued December 1997).

Australian Accounting Standards Board, AASB 1041 'Revaluation of non-current assets' (issued December 1999).

Australian Accounting Standards Board (2002) *Policy Statement 4* 'International convergences and harmonisation policy'.

Australian Accounting Standards Board and Public Sector Accounting Standards Board (1994) *Proposed Program for the Development of Concepts on Measurement of the Elements of Financial Statements*.

Australian Society of Certified Practising Accountants and The Institute of Chartered Accountants in Australia (1995) APS1 'Conformity with Accounting Standards and UIG Consensus Views'.

United States of America

Accounting Principles Board (1970) *Statement No. 4* 'Basic concepts and accounting principles underlying financial statements of business enterprises', New York: American Institute of Certified Public Accountants.

Financial Accounting Standards Board (1984) *Statement of Financial Accounting Concepts No. 5* 'Recognition and measurement in financial statements of business enterprises'.

Financial Accounting Standards Board (1985) *Statement of Financial Accounting Concepts No. 6* 'Elements of financial statements'.

Books and articles

Abbott, A. (1983) 'Professional ethics', *American Journal of Sociology*, 88(5): 855–85.

Abbott, A.D. (1988) *The System of Professions: An Essay on the Division of Expert Labor*, Chicago: University of Chicago Press.

Abdolmohammadi, M., Novin, A. and Christopher, T. (1997) 'A comparative study of the problems facing education and practice of accounting in Australia and the United States', *Accounting Research Journal*, 10(1): 99–108.

Accounting Education Change Commission (1990) *Position Statement No. 1* 'Objectives of education for accountants'.

Accounting in Higher Education: Report of the Review of the Accounting Discipline in Higher Education ('Mathews Report') (1990) 3 vols, Canberra: Australian Government Publishing Service.

Albrecht, S. (1997) 'U.S. educators look to the big picture', *Australian Accountant*, 67(4): 52–4.

Albrecht, W.S. and Sack, R.J. (2000) *Accounting Education: Charting the Course Through a Perilous Future* (Accounting Education Series, vol. 16), Sarasota: American Accounting Association.

Allen, K. (1991) 'In pursuit of professional dominance: Australian accounting 1953–1985', *Accounting, Auditing and Accountability Journal*, 4(1): 51–67.

American Accounting Association (1966) *The American Accounting Association: Its First Fifty Years*, Sarasota: American Accounting Association.

American Accounting Association Committee on Concepts and Standards for External Financial Reports (1977) *Statement on Accounting Theory and Theory Acceptance*, Sarasota: American Accounting Association.

American Accounting Association Committee on the Future Structure, Content, and Scope of Accounting Education (1986) 'Future accounting education: preparing for the expanding Profession' ('Bedford Report'), *Issues in Accounting Education*, 1(1): 168–95.

American Accounting Association Committee to Prepare a Statement of Basic Accounting Theory (1966) *A Statement of Basic Accounting Theory*, Sarasota: American Accounting Association.

Annisette, M. (1999) 'Importing accounting: the case of Trinidad and Tobago', *Accounting, Business and Financial History*, 9(1): 103–33.

Annisette, M. (2000) 'Imperialism and the professions: the education and certification of accountants in Trinidad and Tobago', *Accounting, Organizations and Society*, 25(7): 631–59.

Aranya, N. (1974) 'The influence of pressure groups on financial statements in Britain', *Abacus*, 10(1): 3–12.

Archer, S. (1997) 'The ASB's exposure draft statement of principles: a comment', *Accounting and Business Research*, 27(3): 229–41.

Arrington, C.E. (1990) 'Intellectual tyranny and the public interest: the quest for the grail and the quality of life', *Advances in Public Interest Accounting*, 3: 1–16.

Arrington, C.E. and Francis, J.R. (1989) 'Letting the chat out of the bag: deconstruction, privilege and accounting research', *Accounting, Organizations and Society*, 14(1/2): 1–28.

Arrington, C.E. and Francis, J.R. (1993) 'Accounting as a human practice: the appeal of other voices', *Accounting, Organizations and Society*, 18(2/3): 105–6.

Arrington, C.E. and Schweiker, W. (1992) 'The rhetoric and rationality of accounting research', *Accounting, Organizations and Society*, 17(6): 511–33.

Asechemie, D.P.S. (1995) 'Accounting, time and African philosophy', *Advances in Public Interest Accounting*, 6: 19–33.

Atkinson, P. and Delamont, S. (1990) 'Professions and powerlessness: female marginality in the learned occupations', *The Sociological Review*, 38(1): 90–110.

'Australian Accountancy Profession Joint Submission' (1982) (Submission to National Companies and Securities Commission regarding the establishment of an Accounting Standards Review Board), reprinted in *The Australian Accountant*, 52(5): 308–10.

Australian Society of Accountants (1962) *History of the Australian Society of Accountants and its Antecedent Bodies: 1887 to 1962*, Melbourne: Australian Society of Accountants.

Australian Society of Certified Practising Accountants (1991) ASA 2 'History of the Society', *Members' Handbook*, Melbourne: Australian Society of Certified Practising Accountants.

Australian Society of Certified Practising Accountants and The Institute of Chartered Accountants in Australia (1994) *A Research Study on Financial Reporting and Auditing – Bridging the Expectation Gap*, Melbourne and Sydney: Australian Society of Certified Practising Accountants and The Institute of Chartered Accountants in Australia.

Baer, W.C. (1986) 'Expertise and professional standards', *Work and Occupations*, 13(4): 532–52.

Bailey, D. (1992) 'The attempt to establish the Russian accounting profession 1875–1931', *Accounting, Business and Financial History*, 2(1): 1–23.

Baker, C.R. (1993) 'Self-regulation in the public accounting profession: the structural responses of the large public accounting firms to a changing environment', *Accounting, Auditing and Accountability Journal*, 6(2): 68–80.

Barber, B. (1963) 'Some problems in the sociology of professions', *Daedalus*, 92(4): 669–88.

Baxt, R. (1987) 'Should auditors have limited liability?', *The Chartered Accountant in Australia*, 57(7): 65–6.

Baxter, W.T. (1994, originally published 1979) 'Accounting standards – boon or curse?', in S.A. Zeff and B.G. Dharan (eds) *Readings and Notes on Financial Accounting*, 4th edn, New York: McGraw-Hill.

Bedford, N.M. (1978) 'The impact of a priori theory and research on accounting practice', in A.R. Abdel-khalik and T.F. Keller (eds) *The Impact of Accounting Research on Practice and Disclosure*, Durham: Duke University Press.

Begum, R. and West, B. (1996) 'Non-current asset valuation: an Australian Survey', *Charter*, 67(1): 49–51.

Belkaoui, A. (1991) 'The context of the contemporary accounting profession', *Advances in Public Interest Accounting*, 4: 83–97.

Belkaoui, A.R. and Jones, S. (1996) *Accounting Theory*, Sydney: Harcourt Brace.

Benson, H. (1981) 'The professions and the community', *The Australian Accountant*, 51(4): 239–44.

Benston, G.J. (1976) 'Public (U.S.) compared to private (U.K.) regulation of corporate financial disclosure', *The Accounting Review*, 51(3): 494–8.

Benston, G.J. (1980) 'The establishment and enforcement of accounting standards: methods, benefits and costs', *Accounting and Business Research*, 11(41): 51–60.

Benston, G.J. (1982a) 'An analysis of the role of accounting standards for enhancing corporate governance and social responsibility', *Journal of Accounting and Public Policy*, 1(1): 5–17.

Benston, G.J. (1982b) 'Accounting and corporate accountability', *Accounting, Organizations and Society*, 7(2): 87–105.

Bevis, H.W. (1966) 'Progress and poverty in accounting thought', *Journal of Accountancy*, 122(1): 34–40.

Birkett, W.P. and Walker, R.G. (1971) 'Response of the Australian accounting profession to company failures in the 1960s', *Abacus*, 7(2): 97–136.

Birkett, W.P. and Walker, R.G. (1972) 'Professional ideas on research in accounting: Australia, 1930–49', *Abacus*, 8(1): 35–60.

Blake, J. (1995) *Accounting Standards*, 5th edn, London: Pitman.

Bloom, R. and Naciri, M.A. (1989) 'Accounting standard setting and culture: a comparative analysis of the United States, Canada, England, West Germany, Australia, New Zealand, Sweden, Japan and Switzerland', *The International Journal of Accounting*, 24(1): 70–97.

Bloom, R., Heymann, H.G., Fuglister, J. and Collins, M. (1994) *The Schism in Accounting*, Westport: Quorum Books.

Blough, C.G. (1937) 'The need for accounting principles', *The Accounting Review*, 12(1): 30–6.

Boland, L.A. and Gordon, I.M. (1992) 'Criticizing positive accounting theory', *Contemporary Accounting Research*, 9(1): 142–70.

BonJour, L. (1985) *The Structure of Empirical Knowledge*, Cambridge: Harvard University Press.

Booth, P. and Cocks, N. (1990a) 'Critical research in accounting standard setting', *Journal of Business Finance and Accounting*, 17(4): 511–28.

Booth, P. and Cocks, N. (1990b) 'Power and the study of the accounting profession', in D.J. Cooper and T.M. Hopper (eds) *Critical Accounts*, London: Macmillan.

Boreham, P. (1983) 'Indetermination: professional knowledge, organization and control', *The Sociological Review*, 31(4): 693–718.

Boymal, D.G. (1988) 'The application of accounting standards to small business', *The Chartered Accountant in Australia*, 58(7): 49–51.

Boys, P. (1994) 'The origins and evolution of the accountancy profession', in W. Hapgood (ed.) *Chartered Accountants in England and Wales: A Guide to Historical Records*, Manchester: Manchester University Press.

Brewer, L. (1996) 'Bureaucratic organisation of professional labour', *Australian and New Zealand Journal of Sociology*, 32(3): 21–38.

Bricker, R.J. and Previts, G.J. (1990) 'The sociology of accountancy: a study of academic and practice community schisms', *Accounting Horizons*, 4(1): 1–14.

Brief, R.P. (1975) 'The accountant's responsibility in historical perspective', *The Accounting Review*, 50(2): 285–97.

Briloff, A.J. (1972) *Unaccountable Accounting*, New York: Harper and Row.

Briloff, A.J. (1981) *The Truth About Corporate Accounting*, New York: Harper and Row.

Briloff, A.J. (1990) 'Accountancy and society. A covenant desecrated', *Critical Perspectives on Accounting*, 1(1): 5–30.

Briloff, A.J. (1993) '*Unaccountable Accounting* revisited', *Critical Perspectives on Accounting*, 4(4): 301–35.

Briston, R.J. and Kedslie, M.J.M. (1986) 'Professional formation: the case of Scottish accountants – some corrections and some further thoughts', *The British Journal of Sociology*, 37(1): 122–30.

Briston, R.J. and Kedslie, M.J.M. (1997) 'The internationalization of British Professional Accounting: the role of the examination exporting bodies', *Accounting, Business and Financial History*, 7(2): 175–94.

Broadbent, J. (1995) 'The values of accounting and education: some implications of the creation of visibilities and invisibilities in schools', *Advances in Public Interest Accounting*, 6: 69–98.

Brown, P. and Howieson, B. (1998) 'Capital markets research and accounting standard setting', *Accounting and Finance*, 38(1): 5–28.

Brown, P., Izan, H.Y. and Loh, A.L. (1992) 'Fixed asset revaluations and managerial incentives', *Abacus*, 28(1): 36–57.

Brown, P. and Tarca, A. (2001) 'Politics, process and the future of Australian Accounting Standards', *Abacus*, 37(3): 267–96.

Brown, R.B. (ed.) (1968, originally published 1905) *History of Accounting and Accountants*, London: Frank Cass and Company.

Buckley, J.W. (1980) 'Policy models in accounting: a critical commentary', *Accounting, Organizations and Society*, 5(1): 49–64.

Burchell, S., Clubb, C. and Hopwood, A.G. (1985) 'Accounting in its social context: towards a history of value added in the United Kingdom', *Accounting, Organizations and Society*, 10(4): 381–413.

Burchell, S., Clubb, C., Hopwood, A., Hughes, J. and Nahapiet, J. (1980) 'The roles of accounting in organizations and society', *Accounting, Organizations and Society*, 5(1): 5–27.

Burkett, G. and Knafl, K. (1974) 'Judgement and decision making in a medical speciality', *Sociology of Work and Occupations*, 1(1): 82–109.

Burns, D.C. and Haga, W.J. (1977) 'Much ado about professionalism: a second look at accounting', *The Accounting Review*, 52(3): 705–15.

Burrage, M. (1990) 'Introduction: the professions in sociology and history', in M. Burrage and R. Torstendahl (eds) *Professions in Theory and History: Rethinking the Study of the Professions*, London: Sage.

Burrows, G. (1996) *The Foundation: A History of the Australian Accounting Research Foundation 1966–91*, Melbourne: Australian Accounting Research Foundation.

Byington, J.R. and Sutton, S.G. (1991) 'The self-regulating profession: an analysis of the political monopoly tendencies of the audit profession', *Critical Perspectives on Accounting*, 2(4): 315–30.

Byrne, G. (1937) 'To what extent can the professional practice of accounting be reduced to rules and standards?', *Journal of Accountancy*, 54(5): 364–79.

Canning, J.B. (1978, originally published 1929) *The Economics of Accountancy*, New York: Arno.

Caplow, T. (1966, originally published 1954) 'The sequence of professionalization', in H.M. Vollmer and D.L. Mills (eds) *Professionalization*, Englewood Cliffs: Prentice-Hall.

Carey, J.L. (1968) 'What is the professional practice of accounting?', *The Accounting Review*, 43(1): 1–9.

Carey, J.L. (1969) *The Rise of the Accounting Profession: From Technician to Professional*, New York: American Institute of Certified Public Accountants.

Carey, J.L. and Doherty, W.O. (1966) *Ethical Standards of the Accounting Profession*, New York: American Institute of Certified Public Accountants.

Carnegie, G.D. (1993) 'The Australian Institute of Incorporated Accountants', *Accounting, Business and Financial History*, 3(1): 61–80.

Carnegie, G.D. and Edwards, J.R. (2001) 'The construction of the professional accountant: the case of the Incorporated Institute of Accountants, Victoria (1886)', *Accounting, Organizations and Society*, 26(4/5): 301–25.

Carnegie, G.D. and Parker, R.H. (1996) 'The transfer of accounting technology to the southern hemisphere: the case of William Butler Yaldwyn', *Accounting, Business and Financial History*, 6(1): 23–49.

Carnegie, G.D. and Parker, R.H. (1999) 'Accountants and empire: the case of co-membership of Australian and British accountancy bodies, 1885 to 1914', *Accounting, Business and Financial History*, 9(1): 77–102.

Carr-Saunders, A.M. (1966, originally published 1928) 'Professions: their organization and place in society', in H.M. Vollmer and D.L. Mills (eds) *Professionalization*, Englewood Cliffs: Prentice-Hall.

Carr-Saunders, A.M. and Wilson, P.A. (1933) *The Professions*, Oxford: Oxford University Press.

Chambers, R.J. (1955) 'Blueprint for a theory of accounting', *Accounting Research*, 6(1): 17–25.

Chambers, R.J. (1960) 'The conditions of research in accounting', *The Journal of Accountancy*, 110(6): 33–9.

Chambers, R.J. (1965) 'Financial information and the securities market', *Abacus*, 1(1): 3–30.

Chambers, R.J. (1966a) 'A matter of principle', *The Accounting Review*, 41(3): 443–57.

Chambers, R.J. (1966b) *Accounting, Evaluation and Economic Behavior*, Englewood Cliffs: Prentice-Hall.

Chambers, R.J. (1969, originally published 1957) 'Detail for a blueprint', in R.J. Chambers *Accounting, Finance and Management*, Sydney: Butterworths.

Chambers, R.J. (1969, originally published 1965) 'Professional education and the Vatter Report', in R.J. Chambers, *Accounting, Finance and Management*, Sydney: Butterworths.

Chambers, R.J. (1969, originally published 1967) 'University education in accounting: developments in an Australian university', in R.J. Chambers, *Accounting, Finance and Management*, Sydney: Butterworths.

Chambers, R.J. (1970a) 'Accounting research and technology', paper presented in Monterrey Institute of Technology, Mexico and reprinted in R.J. Chambers and G.W. Dean (eds) *Chambers on Accounting Volume III: Accounting Theory and Research*, New York and London: Garland.

Chambers, R.J. (1970b) 'Varieties of accounting research', paper presented in Monterrey Institute of Technology, Mexico and reprinted in R.J. Chambers and G.W. Dean (eds) *Chambers on Accounting Volume III: Accounting Theory and Research*, New York and London: Garland.

Chambers, R.J. (1970c) 'Second thoughts on Continuously Contemporary Accounting', *Abacus*, 6(1): 39–55.

Chambers, R.J. (1972) 'The anguish of accountants', *The Australian Accountant*, 42(4): 154–61.

Chambers, R.J. (1973a) 'Accounting principles or accounting policies?', *The Journal of Accountancy*, 135(5): 48–53.

Chambers, R.J. (1973b) *Securities and Obscurities: A Case for Reform of the Law of Company Accounts*, Sydney: Gower.

Chambers, R.J. (1974) 'Third thoughts', *Abacus*, 10(2): 129–37.

Chambers, R.J. (1975) 'A critical examination of Australian accounting standards', *Abacus*, 11(2): 136–52.

Chambers, R.J. (1979) 'Usefulness – the vanishing premise in accounting standard setting', *Abacus*, 15(2): 71–92.

Chambers, R.J. (1980) 'The myths and the science of accounting', *Accounting, Organizations and Society*, 5(1): 167–80.

Chambers, R.J. (1987) 'Accounting education for the twenty-first century', *Abacus*, 23(2): 97–106.

Chambers, R.J. (1991a) *Foundations of Accounting*, Geelong: Deakin University Press.

Chambers, R.J. (1991b) 'Metrical and empirical laws in accounting', *Accounting Horizons*, 5(4): 1–15.

Chambers, R.J. (1992) 'Accounting as financial instrumentation', *Economica Aziendale*, 11(3): 439–51.

Chambers, R.J. (1993) 'Positive accounting theory and the PA cult', *Abacus*, 29(1): 1–26.

Chambers, R.J. (1994) 'Historical cost – tale of a false creed', *Accounting Horizons*, 8(1): 76–89.

Chambers, R.J. (1996) 'Ends, ways, means and conceptual frameworks', *Abacus*, 32(2): 119–32.

Chambers, R.J., Ramanathan, T.S. and Rappaport, H.H. (1978) *Company Accounting Standards (Report of the Accounting Standards Review Committee)*, Ultimo, New South Wales: N.S.W. Government Printer.

Chambers, R.J. and Wolnizer, P.W. (1990) 'A true and fair view of financial position', *Company and Securities Law Journal*, 8(6): 353–68.

Chambers, R.J. and Wolnizer, P.W. (1991) 'A true and fair view of position and results: the historical background', *Accounting, Business and Financial History*, 1(2): 197–213.

Chandler, R.A. (1997) 'Judicial views on auditing from the nineteenth century', *Accounting History*, NS 2(1): 61–80.

Cherns, A.B. (1978) 'Alienation and accountancy', *Accounting, Organizations and Society*, 3(2): 105–14.

Cheung, K. (1994) 'Auditor surveillance: the ASC's role', *Charter*, 65(11): 48–9.

Child, J. and Fulk, J. (1982) 'Maintenance of occupational control: the case of professions', *Work and Occupations*, 9(2): 155–92.

Chisholm, R.M. (1989) *Theory of Knowledge*, 3rd edn, Englewood Cliffs: Prentice Hall.

Christenson, C. (1983) 'The methodology of positive accounting', *The Accounting Review*, 58(1): 1–22.

Chua, W.F. (1986a) 'Radical developments in accounting thought', *The Accounting Review*, 61(4): 601–32.

Chua, W.F. (1986b) 'Theoretical constructions of and by the real', *Accounting, Organizations and Society*, 11(6): 583–98.

Chua, W.F. (1988) 'Of gods and demons, science and ideology', *Advances in Public Interest Accounting*, 2: 29–46.

Chua, W.F. (1996) 'Teaching and learning only the language of numbers – monolingualism in a multilingual world', *Critical Perspectives on Accounting*, 7(1/2): 129–56.

Chua, W.F. and Clegg, S. (1990) 'Professional closure: the case of British nursing', *Theory and Society*, 19(2): 135–72.

Chua, W.F. and Poullaos, C. (1993) 'Rethinking the profession–state dynamic: the case of the Victorian Charter attempt, 1885–1906', *Accounting, Organizations and Society*, 18(7/8): 691–728.

Chua, W.F. and Poullaos, C. (1998) 'The dynamics of closure amidst the construction of market, profession, empire and nationhood: an historical analysis of an Australian accounting association, 1886–1903', *Accounting, Organizations and Society*, 23(2): 155–87.

Clarke, F.L., Dean, G.W. and Oliver, K.G. (1997) *Corporate Collapse: Regulatory, Accounting and Ethical Failure*, Cambridge: Cambridge University Press.

Cogan, M.L. (1953) 'Toward a definition of profession', *Harvard Educational Review*, 23(1): 33–50.

Cohen, G.A. (1987a) 'Yes, the company auditor should have limited liability', *The Chartered Accountant in Australia*, 57(8): 73.

Cohen, G.A. (1987b) 'The audit expectation gap', *The Chartered Accountant in Australia*, 58(3): 6.

Collett, P. (1995) 'Standard setting and economic consequences: an ethical issue', *Abacus*, 31(1): 18–30.

Collins, R. (1979) *The Credential Society: An Historical Sociology of Education and Stratification*, New York: Academic Press.

Collins, R. (1990) 'Market closure and the conflict theory of the professions', in M. Burrage and R. Torstendahl (eds) *Professions in Theory and History: Rethinking the Study of the Professions*, London: Sage.

Committe, B.E. (1990) 'The delegation and privatization of financial accounting rule-making authority in the United States of America', *Critical Perspectives on Accounting*, 1(2): 145–66.

Cooper, D. and Hopper, T. (1987) 'Critical studies in accounting', *Accounting, Organizations and Society*, 12(4/5): 407–14.

Cooper, D. and Hopper, T. (1990) 'Stimulating research in critical accounts', in D.J. Cooper and T.M. Hopper (eds) *Critical Accounts*, London: Macmillan.

Cooper, D. and Sherer, M. (1984) 'The value of corporate accounting reports: arguments for a political economy of accounting', *Accounting, Organizations and Society*, 9(3/4): 207–32.

Cooper, D., Puxty, T., Robson, K. and Willmott, H. (1994) 'Regulating accountancy in the UK: episodes in a changing relationship between the state and the profession', in A.G. Hopwood and P. Miller (eds) *Accounting as Social and Institutional Practice*, Cambridge: Cambridge University Press.

Cooper, K. (1996) 'From charlatan to doyen: the legitimization of Australian accountancy', in A.J. Richardson (ed.) *Disorder and Harmony: 20th Century Perspectives on Accounting History* (Selected Papers from the 7th World Congress of Accounting Historians), Vancouver: CGA-Canada Research Foundation.

Cottell, P.G. and Perlin, T.M. (1990) *Accounting Ethics*, New York: Quorum Books.

Coutts, J.A. and Roberts, J. (1995) 'Segregation: a patriarchal strategy in the professions', *Advances in Public Interest Accounting*, 6: 99–131.

Crompton, R. (1987) 'Gender and accountancy: a response to Tinker and Neimark', *Accounting, Organizations and Society*, 12(1): 103–10.

Davidson, S. and Anderson, G.D. (1987) 'The development of accounting and auditing standards', *Journal of Accountancy*, 163(5): 110–27.

Davis, S.W., Menon, K. and Morgan, G. (1982) 'The images that have shaped accounting theory', *Accounting, Organizations and Society*, 7(4): 307–18.

Davis, S.W. and Sherman, W.R. (1996) 'The Accounting Education Change Commission: a critical perspective', *Critical Perspectives on Accounting*, 7(1/2): 158–89.

Day, M.M. (1995) 'Ethics of teaching critical: feminisms on the wings of desire', *Accounting, Auditing and Accountability Journal*, 8(3): 97–112.

Deegan, C., Kent, P. and Lin, C.J. (1994) 'True and fair view: a study of Australian auditors' application of the concept', *Australian Accounting Review*, 4(7): 2–12.

Demski, J.S. (1973) 'The general impossibility of normative accounting standards', *The Accounting Review*, 48(4): 718–23.

Demski, J.S. (1976) 'An economic analysis of the Chambers' normative standard', *The Accounting Review*, 51(3): 653–56.

Demski, J.S. (1988) 'Positive accounting theory: a review', *Accounting, Organizations and Society*, 13(6): 623–9.

Dent, M. (1993) 'Professionalism, educated labour and the state: hospital medicine and the new managerialism', *The Sociological Review*, 41(2): 244–73.

Derber, C. (ed.) (1982) *Professionals as Workers: Mental Labour in Advanced Capitalism*, Massachusetts: G.K. Hall.

Dezalay, Y. (1995) ' "Turf battles" or "class struggles": the internationalization of the market for expertise in the "professional society" ', trans. G. Burchell, *Accounting, Organizations and Society*, 20(5): 331–44.

Dezalay, Y. (1997) 'Accountants as "new guard dogs" of capitalism: stereotype or research agenda?', trans. P. Miller, *Accounting, Organizations and Society*, 22(8): 825–9.

Dillard, J.F. (1991) 'Accounting as a critical social science', *Accounting, Auditing and Accountability Journal*, 4(1): 8–28.

Dingwall, R. (1976) 'Accomplishing profession', *The Sociological Review*, 24(2): 331–49.

Dominion Association of Chartered Accountants (1950) *Annual Report*.

Dow, K.J. and Feldman, D.A. (1997) 'Current approaches to teaching intermediate accounting', *Issues in Accounting Education*, 12(1): 61–75.

Duman, D. (1979) 'The creation and diffusion of a professional ideology in nineteenth century England', *The Sociological Review*, 27(1): 113–38.

Durkheim, E. (1957) *Professional Ethics and Civil Morals*, trans. C. Brookfield, London: Routledge and Kegan Paul.

Dyckman, T.R. (1974) 'Public accounting: guild or profession?', in R.R. Sterling (ed.) *Institutional Issues in Public Accounting*, Lawrence: Scholars Book Co.

Dyckman, T.R., Gibbins, M. and Swieringa, R.J. (1978) 'Experimental and survey research in financial accounting: a review and evaluation', in A.R. Abdel-khalik and T.F. Keller (eds) *The Impact of Accounting Research on Practice and Disclosure*, Durham: Duke University Press.

Edwards, E.O. and Bell, P.W. (1961) *The Theory and Measurement of Business Income*, Berkeley: University of California Press.

Edwards, J.R. (1989) *A History of Financial Accounting*, London: Routledge.

Elliott, P. (1972) *The Sociology of the Professions*, London: Macmillan.

Engel, G.V. and Hall, R.H. (1973) 'The growing industrialization of the professions', in E. Freidson (ed.) *The Professions and Their Prospects*, Beverly Hills: Sage Publications.

English, L. (1988) 'Accounting standards: a new order?', *Australian Accountant*, 58(11): 30–7.

Eraut, M. (1994) *Developing Professional Knowledge and Competence*, London: Falmer Press.

Ezzamel, M. and Robson, R. (1995) 'Accounting in time: organizational time reckoning and accounting practice', *Critical Perspectives on Accounting*, 6(2): 149–70.

Fallshaw, R. (1993) 'Getting it wrong by following the rules' (letter), *Business Review Weekly*, 26 March: 105.

Feller, B. (1973) 'Developing accounting standards', *The Australian Accountant*, 43(10): 600–1.

Feller, B. (1974) 'Accounting standards – objectives, problems, achievements', *The Australian Accountant*, 44(7): 392–401.

Feyerabend, P. (1988) *Against Method*, revised edn, London: Verso.

Finnis, J.M. (1990) 'Authority', in J. Raz (ed.) *Authority*, Oxford: Basil Blackwell.

Fogarty, T.J. (1994) 'Structural-functionalism and financial accounting: standard setting in the US', *Critical Perspectives on Accounting*, 5(3): 205–26.

Fogarty, T.J. (1997) 'The education of accountants in the U.S.: reason and its limits at the turn of the century', *Critical Perspectives on Accounting*, 8(1/2): 45–68.

Fogarty, T.J., Hussein, M.E.A. and Ketz, J.E. (1994) 'Political aspects of financial accounting standard setting in the USA', *Accounting, Auditing and Accountability Journal*, 7(4): 24–46.

Fogarty, T.J., Zucca, L.J., Meonske, N. and Kirch, D.P. (1997) 'Proactive practice review: a critical case study of accounting regulation that never was', *Critical Perspectives on Accounting*, 8(3): 167–87.

Foster, G.J. (1969) 'Mining inventories in a current price accounting system', *Abacus*, 5(2): 99–118.

Freedman, M. (1988) 'Functionalism', in A. Bullock, O. Stallybrass and S. Trombley (eds) *The Fontana Dictionary of Modern Thought*, London: Fontana.

Freidson, E. (1973a) 'Foreword', in E. Freidson (ed.) *The Professions and Their Prospects*, Beverly Hills: Sage Publications.

Freidson, E. (1973b) 'Professions and the occupational principle', in E. Freidson (ed.) *The Professions and Their Prospects*, Beverly Hills: Sage.

Freidson, E. (1983) 'The theory of professions: state of the art', in R. Dingwall and P. Lewis (eds) *The Sociology of the Professions*, London: Macmillan.

Freidson, E. (1986) *Professional Powers: A Study of the Institutionalization of Formal Knowledge*, Chicago: University of Chicago.

Freidson, E. (1994) *Professional Reborn: Theory, Prophecy and Policy*, Cambridge: Polity Press.

Friedman, M. (1953) *Essays in Positive Economics*, Chicago: University of Chicago Press.

Friedman, M. (1962) *Capitalism and Freedom*, Chicago: University of Chicago Press.

Gaffikin, M.J.R. (1988) 'Legacy of the Golden Age', *Abacus*, 24(1): 16–36.

Gaffikin, M.J.R. (1993) *Principles of Accounting*, 3rd edn, Sydney: Harcourt Brace.

Gallhofer, S. and Haslam, J. (1996) 'Analysis of Bentham's Chrestomathia, or towards a critique of accounting education', *Critical Perspectives on Accounting*, 7(1/2): 13–31.

Gambling, T. (1977) 'Magic, accounting and morale', *Accounting, Organizations and Society*, 2(2): 141–51.

Gangolly, J.S. and Hussein, M.E.A. (1996) 'Generally accepted accounting principles: perspectives from philosophy of law', *Critical Perspectives on Accounting*, 7(4): 383–407.

Gavens, J.J., Carnegie, G.D. and Gibson, R.W. (1989) 'Company participation in the Australian accounting standards setting process', *Accounting and Finance*, 29(2): 47–58.

Gavens, J.J. and Gibson, R.W. (1992) 'An Australian attempt to internationalize accounting professional organizations', *The Accounting Historians Journal*, 19(2): 79–102.

Gay, G. and Simnett, R. (2000) *Auditing and Assurance Services in Australia*, Sydney: McGraw-Hill.

Gerboth, D.L. (1973) 'Research, intuition, and politics in accounting inquiry', *The Accounting Review*, 48(3): 475–82.

Gerboth, D.L. (1978) 'The conceptual framework: not definitions, but professional values', *Accounting Horizons*, 1(3): 1–8.

Gerboth, D.L. (1987) 'The accounting game', *Accounting Horizons*, 1(4): 96–9.

Gettler, L. (1997) 'Accounting firms take new steps into internet territory', *The Age*, 24 November: B5.

Gibson, K. and Goyen, M. (1996) 'Financial measurement and Australian accounting standards', *Accounting Research Journal*, 9(1): 56–73.

Gibson, R.W. (1971) *Disclosure by Australian Companies*, Melbourne: Melbourne University Press.

Gibson, R.W. (1979) 'Development of corporate accounting in Australia', *Accounting Historians Journal*, 6(2): 23–38.

Gibson, R.W. (1980) 'The public comment procedures in the setting of accounting standards', in D.M. Emanuel and I.C. Stewart (eds) *Essays in Honour of Trevor R. Johnston*, Auckland: University of Auckland.

Gieryn, T.F., Bevins, G.M. and Zehr, S.C. (1985) 'Professionalization of American scientists: public science in the creation/evolution trials', *American Sociological Review*, 50(3): 392–409.

Gietzmann, M.B. and Quick, R. (1998) 'Capping auditor liability: the German experience', *Accounting, Organizations and Society*, 23(1): 81–103.

Gillian, M. (1995) 'The accounting standard-setting process in Australia: a preparer's perspective', *Australian Accounting Review*, 5(2): 23–5.

Godfrey, J., Hodgson, A. and Holmes, S. (1997) *Accounting Theory*, 3rd edn, Brisbane: John Wiley.

Godsell, D. (1991) 'Auditors' legal liability and the expectation gap', *Australian Accountant*, 61(1): 22–8.

Goldman, A.H. (1988) *Empirical Knowledge*, Berkeley: University of California Press.

Goldstein, J. (1984) 'Foucault among the sociologists: the "disciplines" and the history of the professions', *History and Theory*, 23(2): 170–92.

Goode, W.J. (1960) 'Encroachment, charlatanism, and the emerging profession: psychology, sociology, and medicine', *American Sociological Review*, 25(6): 902–14.

Gray, R.H. (1995) 'Being social while being accountants – Centre for Social and Environmental Accounting Research', *Accounting Forum*, 19(2/3): 253–8.

Gray, S.J. (1975) 'Price changes and company profits in the securities market', *Abacus*, 11(1): 71–85.

Greenwood, E. (1966, originally published 1957) 'Attributes of a profession', in H.M. Vollmer and D.L. Mills (eds) *Professionalization*, Englewood Cliffs: Prentice-Hall.

Grice, B. (1993) 'From the president', *Charter*, 64(4): 45.

Gul, F.A., Teoh, H.Y., Andrew, B.H. and Schelluch, P. (1997) *Theory and Practice of Australian Auditing*, 4th edn, Melbourne: Nelson.

Guy, D.M., Alderman, C.W. and Winters, A.J. (1996) *Auditing*, 4th edn, Fort Worth: Harcourt Brace.

Hall, R.H. (1983) 'Theoretical trends in the sociology of occupations', *Sociological Quarterly*, 24(1): 5–23.

Hall, W.D. (1987) *Accounting and Auditing: Thoughts on Forty Years in Practice and Education*, Chicago: Arthur Andersen.

Halliday, T.C. (1985) 'Knowledge mandates: collective influence by scientific, normative and syncretic professions', *British Journal of Sociology*, 36(3): 421–47.

Halliday, T.C. (1987) *Beyond Monopoly*, Chicago: University of Chicago.

Halmos, P. (1973) 'Introduction', in P. Halmos (ed.) *Professionalization and Social Change*, Keele: University of Keele.

Hamlyn, D.W. (1970) *The Theory of Knowledge*, London: Macmillan.

Hammond, T. and Oakes, L.S. (1992) 'Some feminisms and their implications for accounting practice', *Accounting, Auditing and Accountability Journal*, 5(3): 52–70.

Hancock, P. (1994) 'Accounting for financial instruments: an overview', *Australian Accounting Review*, 4(2): 3–12.

Hanlon, G. (1994) *The Commercialisation of Accountancy: Flexible Accumulation and the Transformation of the Service Class*, London: Macmillan.

Hanlon, G. (1997) 'Commercialising the service class and economic restructuring – a response to my critics', *Accounting, Organizations and Society*, 22(8): 843–55.

Harding, N. and McKinnon, J. (1997) 'User involvement in the standard-setting process: a research note on the congruence of accountant and user perceptions of decision usefulness', *Accounting, Organizations and Society*, 22(1): 55–67.

Harrison, G.L. and McKinnon, J.L. (1986) 'Culture and accounting change: a new perspective on corporate reporting regulation and accounting policy formulation', *Accounting, Organizations and Society*, 11(3): 233–52.

Harrison, S. (1995) 'On balance', *Charter*, 66(3): 90.

Haug, M.R and Sussman, M.B. (1973) 'Professionalization and unionism: a jurisdictional dispute?', in E. Freidson (ed.) *The Professions and Their Prospects*, Beverly Hills: Sage Publications.

Hegarty, J. (1997) 'Accounting for the global economy: is national regulation doomed to disappear?', *Accounting Horizons*, 11(4): 75–90.

Henderson, S. (1985) 'The impact of financial accounting standards on auditing', *Australian Accountant*, 55(3): 50–3.

Henderson, S. (1988) 'Have accounting standards been worthwhile?', *Accounting Forum*, 12(2): 5–10.

Henderson, S. (1993) 'Financial accounting in Australia: retrospect and prospect, *Accounting Forum*, 17(2): 4–18.

Henderson, S. and Peirson, G. (1978) 'Does accounting research matter?', *Accounting and Business Research*, 9(33): 25–33.

Henderson, S. and Peirson, G. (1998) *Issues in Financial Accounting*, 8th edn, Melbourne: Longman.

Henderson, S., Peirson, G. and Brown, R. (1992) *Financial Accounting Theory: Its Nature and Development*, 2nd edn, Melbourne: Longman Cheshire.

Hepp, G.W. and McRae, T.W. (1982) 'Accounting standards overload: relief is needed', *Journal of Accountancy*, 153(5): 52–62.

Hines, R. (1983) 'Economic consequences of accounting standards: a good reason for a representative ASRB', *The Chartered Accountant in Australia*, 54(1): 24–7.

Hines, R. (1987) 'Financial accounting standard setting: from truth to due process', *The Chartered Accountant in Australia*, 58(1): 30–3.

Hines, R. (1988a) 'Financial accounting: in communicating reality, we construct reality', *Accounting, Organizations and Society*, 13(3): 251–62.

Hines, R. (1988b) 'Popper's methodology of falsificationism and accounting research', *The Accounting Review*, 64(4): 657–62.

Hines, R. (1989) 'Financial accounting knowledge, conceptual framework projects and the social construction of the accounting profession', *Accounting, Auditing and Accountability Journal*, 2(2): 72–92.

Hines, R. (1991) 'The FASB's conceptual framework, financial accounting and the maintenance of the social world', *Accounting, Organizations and Society*, 16(4): 313–31.

Hines, R. (1992) 'Accounting: filling the negative space', *Accounting, Organizations and Society*, 17(3/4): 313–41.

Hogan, W. (1994) 'Accounting introspection', *Australian Accounting Review*, 4(2): 54–64.

Hogler, R.L., Hunt, H.G. and Wilson, P.A. (1996) 'Accounting standards, health care and retired American workers: an institutional critique', *Accounting, Organizations and Society*, 21(5): 423–39.

Hope, T. and Gray, R. (1982) 'Power and policy making: the development of an R&D standard', *Journal of Business Finance and Accounting*, 9(4): 531–57.

Hopper, T., Annisette, M.A., Dastoor, N., Uddin, S.N. and Wickramasinghe, D.P. (1995) 'Some challenges and alternatives to positive accounting research: introduction', in S. Jones, C. Romano and J. Ratnatunga (eds) *Accounting Theory: A Contemporary Review*, Sydney: Harcourt Brace.

Hopper, T., Storey, J. and Willmott, H. (1987) 'Accounting for accounting: towards the development of a dialectical view', *Accounting, Organizations and Society*, 12(5): 437–56.

Hoskin, K.W. and Macve, R.H. (1986) 'Accounting and the examination: a genealogy of disciplinary power', *Accounting, Organizations and Society*, 11(2): 105–36.

Hoskin, K.W. and Macve, R.H. (1994) 'Writing, examining, disciplining: the genesis of accounting's modern power', in A.G. Hopwood and P. Miller (eds) *Accounting as Social and Institutional Practice*, Cambridge: Cambridge University Press.

Houghton, K.A. and Walawski, J.B. (1992) 'Asset recognition and probabilistic judgements', *Australian Accounting Review*, 1(3): 2–9.

House, E.R. (1993) *Professional Evaluation: Social Impact and Political Consequences*, Newbury Park: Sage.

Howieson, B. (1996) 'Whither financial accounting research: a modern-day Bo-Peep?', *Australian Accounting Review*, 6(1): 29–36.

Humphrey, R. (1997) 'The competitive imperative of harmonisation with international accounting standards', *Australian Accounting Review*, 7(2): 27–9.

Hunt, H.G. and Hogler, R.L. (1993) 'An institutional analysis of accounting growth and regulation in the United States', *Accounting, Organizations and Society*, 18(4): 341–60.

Ijiri, Y. (1972) 'The nature of accounting research', in R.R. Sterling (ed.) *Research Methodology in Accounting*, Houston: Scholars Book Co.

Ingram, R.W. and Rayburn, F.R. (1989) 'Representational faithfulness and economic consequences: their roles in accounting policy', *Journal of Accounting and Public Policy*, 8(1): 57–68.

(The) Institute of Chartered Accountants in England and Wales (1966) *The History of the Institute of Chartered Accountants in England and Wales and its Founder Bodies 1870–1965*, London: Institute of Chartered Accountants in England and Wales.

(The) Institute of Chartered Accountants of Scotland (1961) *The Institute's Future Policy*, Edinburgh: The Institute of Chartered Accountants of Scotland.

(The) Institute of Chartered Accountants of Scotland (1984, originally published 1954) *A History of the Chartered Accountants of Scotland From the Earliest Times to 1954*, New York and London: Garland.

Irish, R. (1972) *Auditing*, 4th edn, Sydney: Law Book Company.

Jamous, H. and Peloille, B. (1970) 'Professions or self-perpetuating systems? Changes in the French university-hospital system', in J.A. Jackson (ed.) *Professions and Professionalization*, Cambridge: Cambridge University Press.

Jeffery, B. (1995) 'From the President', *Australian Accountant*, 65(2): 3.

Jensen, M.C. and Meckling, W.H. (1976) 'Theory of the firm: managerial behaviour, agency costs and ownership structure', *Journal of Financial Economics*, 3(4): 305–60.

Jensen, R.E. and Arrington, C.E. (1983) 'Accounting education: turning wrongs into rights in the 1980s', *Journal of Accounting Education*, 1(1): 5–18.

Johnson, P. (1995) 'Towards an epistemology for radical accounting: beyond objectivism and relativism', *Critical Perspectives on Accounting*, 6(6): 485–509.

Johnson, T. (1972) *Professions and Power*, London: Macmillan.

Johnson, T. (1973) 'Imperialism and the professions: notes on the development of professional occupations in Britain's colonies and the new states', in P. Halmos (ed.) *Professionalization and Social Change*, Keele: University of Keele.

Johnson, T. (1980) 'Work and power', in G. Esland and G. Salaman (eds) *The Politics of Work and Power*, Milton Keynes: Open University Press.

Johnson, T. (1982) 'The state and the professions: peculiarities of the British', in A. Giddens and G. Mackenzie (eds) *Social Class and the Division of Labour: Essays in Honour of Ilya Neustadt*, Cambridge: Cambridge University Press.

Jonsson, S. (1991) 'Role making for accounting while the state is watching', *Accounting, Organizations and Society*, 16(5/6): 521–46.

Jourdain, P.E. (1960) 'The nature of mathematics', in J.R. Newman (ed.) *The World of Mathematics*, London: George Allen and Unwin.

Kam, V. (1990) *Accounting Theory*, 2nd edn, New York: John Wiley.

Kaplan, A. (1973) *The Conduct of Inquiry: Methodology for Behavioral Science*, Aylesbury: Intertext.

Kaplan, R.S. (1978) 'The information content of financial accounting numbers: a survey of empirical evidence', in A.R. Abdel-khalik and T.F. Keller (eds) *The Impact of Accounting Research on Practice and Disclosure*, Durham: Duke University Press.

Kedslie, M.J.M. (1990a) *Firm Foundations: The Development of Professional Accounting in Scotland*, Hull: Hull University Press.

Kedslie, M.J.M. (1990b) 'Mutual self interest – a unifying force; the dominance of societal closure over social background in the early professional accounting bodies', *The Accounting Historians Journal*, 17(2): 1–19.

Kerr, A., Cunningham-Burley, S. and Amos, A. (1997) 'The new genetics: professionals' discursive boundaries', *The Sociological Review*, 45(2): 279–303.

Kessler, L. (1972) 'The struggle for the establishment of accounting principles and standards in the U.S.A.', *The Australian Accountant*, 42(10): 379–82.

Kincaid, H. (1996) *Philosophical Foundations of the Social Sciences: Analyzing Controversies in Social Research*, Cambridge: Cambridge University Press.

Kinney, W.R. (1989) 'The relation of accounting research to teaching and practice: a "positive" view', *Accounting Horizons*, 3(1): 119–24.

Kirkham, L.M. and Loft, A. (1993) 'Gender and the construction of the professional accountant', *Accounting, Organizations and Society*, 18(6): 507–58.

Klegon, D. (1978) 'The sociology of professions: an emerging perspective', *Sociology of Work and Occupations*, 5(3): 259–83.

Klumpes, P. (1995) 'Competition between professions: developing an Australian life insurance accounting standard', *Pacific Accounting Review*, 7(2): 1–28.

Krever, H.K. (1978) 'Professional education', in P. Slayton and M.J. Trebilcock (eds) *The Professions and Public Policy*, Toronto: University of Toronto.

Kropp, J. and Johnston, B. (1996) 'International convergence of accounting standards', *Accounting Forum*, 19(4): 283–90.

Kuhn, T.S. (1970) *The Structure of Scientific Revolutions*, 2nd edn, Chicago: University of Chicago Press.

Langenderfer, H.Q. (1987) 'Accounting education's history – a 100-year search for identity', *Journal of Accountancy*, 163(5): 302–31.

Langfield-Smith, I. (1990) 'Enforcing accounting standards in Australia', *Company and Securities Law Journal*, 8(1): 5–25.

Larson, K.D. and Holstrum, G.L. (1973) 'Financial accounting standards in the United States: 1973–?', *Abacus*, 9(1): 3–15.

Larson, M.S. (1977) *The Rise of Professionalism: A Sociological Analysis*, Berkeley: University of California Press.

Larson, R.E. and Kelley, T.P. (1984) 'Differential measurement in accounting standards: the concept makes sense', *Journal of Accountancy*, 158(5): 78–90.

Laughlin, R. (1995) 'Empirical research in accounting: alternative approaches and a case for "middle-range" thinking', *Accounting, Auditing and Accountability Journal*, 8(1): 63–87.

Laughlin, R.C. and Puxty, A.G. (1983) 'Accounting regulation: an alternative perspective', *Journal of Business Finance and Accounting*, 10(3): 451–79.

Laughlin, R.C. and Puxty, A.G. (1984) 'Accounting regulation: an alternative perspective: a reply', *Journal of Business Finance and Accounting*, 11(4): 593–6.

Lavoie, D. (1987) 'The accounting of interpretations and the interpretation of accounts: the communicative function of "The Language of Business" ', *Accounting, Organizations and Society*, 12(6): 579–604.

Lee, B.Z., Larson, R.E. and Chenok, P.B. (1983) 'Issues confronting the accounting profession', *Journal of Accountancy*, 156(5): 78–85.

Lee, T. (1979) 'A brief history of company audits: 1840–1940', in T.A. Lee and R.H. Parker (eds) *The Evolution of Corporate Financial Reporting*, Sunbury-on-Thames: Thomas Nelson.

Lee, T. (1989) 'Education, practice and research in accounting: gaps, closed loops, bridges and magic accounting', *Accounting and Business Research*, 19(75): 237–53.

Lee, T. (1990a) 'A systematic view of the history of the world of accounting', *Accounting, Business and Financial History*, 1(1): 73–107.

Lee, T. (ed.) (1990b) *The Closure of the Accounting Profession* (2 vols), New York and London: Garland.

Lee, T. (1991) 'A review essay: professional foundations and theories of professional behaviour', *The Accounting Historians Journal*, 18(2): 193–203.

Lee, T. (1992) 'The audit liability crisis: they protest too much!', *Accountancy*, 110(1192): 102.

Lee, T. (1993) *Corporate Audit Theory*, London: Chapman and Hall.

Lee, T. (1994) 'Financial reporting quality labels: the social construction of the audit profession and the expectation gap', *Accounting, Auditing and Accountability Journal*, 7(2): 30–49.

Lee, T. (1995a) 'Shaping the US academic accounting profession: the American Accounting Association and the social construction of a professional elite', *Critical Perspectives on Accounting*, 6(3): 241–61.

Lee, T. (1995b) 'The professionalization of accountancy: a history of protecting the public interest in a self-interested way', *Accounting, Auditing and Accountability Journal*, 8(4): 48–69.

Lee, T. (1996a) 'Identifying the founding fathers of public accountancy: the formation of The Society of Accountants in Edinburgh', *Accounting, Business and Financial History*, 6(3): 315–35.

Lee, T. (1996b) 'A history of the professionalisation of accountancy in the UK and the US', in T.A. Lee, A. Bishop and R.H. Parker (eds) *Accounting History From the Renaissance to the Present*, New York and London: Garland.

Lee, T. (1997) 'The editorial gatekeepers of the accounting academy', *Accounting Auditing and Accountability Journal*, 10(1): 11–30.

Leftwich, R. (1980) 'Market failure fallacies and accounting information', *Journal of Accounting and Economics*, 2(3): 193–211.

Lehman, C. (1992) ' "Herstory" in accounting: the first eighty years', *Accounting, Organizations and Society*, 17(3/4): 261–85.

Lehman, C. and Tinker, T. (1987) 'The "real" cultural significance of accounts', *Accounting, Organizations and Society*, 12(5): 503–22.

Leisenring, J.L. and Johnson, L.T. (1994) 'Accounting research: on the relevance of research to practice', *Accounting Horizons*, 8(4): 74–9.

Leung, P. and Cooper, B. (1995) *Professional Ethics: A Survey of Australian Accountants*, Melbourne: Australian Society of Certified Practising Accountants.

Lev, B. (1989) 'On the usefulness of earnings and earnings research: lessons and directions from two decades of empirical research', *Journal of Accounting Research*, 27(supplement): 153–91.

Lewis, C.I. (1970) 'Knowledge as justified true belief', in C. Landesman (ed.) *The Foundations of Knowledge*, Englewood Cliffs: Prentice Hall.

Linn, R. (1996) *Power, Progress and Profit: A History of the Australian Accounting Profession*, Melbourne: Australian Society of Certified Practising Accountants.

Llewellyn, S. (1996) 'Theories for theorists or theories for practice? Liberating academic accounting research', *Accounting, Auditing and Accountability Journal*, 9(4): 112–18.

Lochner, P.R. (1993) 'Accountants' legal liability: a crisis that must be addressed', *Accounting Horizons*, 7(2): 92–6.

Loft, A. (1986) 'Towards a critical understanding of accounting: the case of cost accounting in the U.K., 1914–1925', *Accounting, Organizations and Society*, 11(2): 137–69.

Loft, A. (1994) 'Accountancy and the First World War', in A.G. Hopwood and P. Miller (eds) *Accounting as Social and Institutional Practice*, Cambridge: Cambridge University Press.

Lowe, E.A., Puxty, A.G. and Laughlin R.C. (1983) 'Simple theories for complex processes: accounting policy and the market for myopia', *Journal of Accounting and Public Policy*, 2(1): 19–42.

Lowe, T., Gallhofer, S. and Haslam, J. (1991) 'Theorising accounting regulation in a global context: insights from a study of accounting in the Federal Republic of Germany', *Advances in Public Interest Accounting*, 4: 143–77.

Lynch, M. (1998) 'Coherence, truth and knowledge', *Social Epistemology*, 12(3): 217–25.

Lynch, M. and Bogen, D. (1997) 'Sociology's asociological "core": an examination of textbook sociology in light of the sociology of scientific knowledge', *American Sociological Review*, 62(3): 481–93.

Macdonald, K.M. (1984) 'Professional formation: the case of the Scottish accountants', *The British Journal of Sociology*, 35(2): 174–89.

Macdonald, K.M. (1985) 'Social closure and occupational registration', *Sociology*, 19(4): 541–56.

Macdonald, K.M. (1987) 'Professional formation: a reply to Briston and Kedslie', *The British Journal of Sociology*, 38(1): 106–11.

Macdonald, K.M. (1995) *The Sociology of the Professions*, London: Sage.

Macdonald, K.M. and Ritzer, G. (1988) 'The sociology of the professions: dead or alive?', *Work and Occupations*, 15(3): 251–72.

MacNeal, K. (1970, originally published 1939) *Truth in Accounting*, Lawrence: Scholars Book Co.

MacNeal, K. (1977, originally published 1939) 'What's wrong with accounting?', in W.T. Baxter and S. Davidson (eds) *Studies in Accounting*, London: The Institute of Chartered Accountants in England and Wales.

Maddox, H. (1993) *Theory of Knowledge*, Castlemaine: Freshet.

Makkai, T. (1991) 'The formation and evolution of professional engineering values', *The Australian and New Zealand Journal of Sociology*, 27(3): 332–50.

Martin, C. (1989) 'ASRB – current thinking and accounting standards update', in *ASCPA Victorian State Congress Speakers' Papers*, Melbourne: Australian Society of Certified Practising Accountants.

Margavio, G.W. (1993) 'The savings and loan debacle: the culmination of three decades of conflicting regulation, deregulation and re-regulation', *The Accounting Historians Journal*, 20(1): 1–31.

Mathews, M.R. (1994) 'A comment on Lewis, Humphrey and Owen. Accounting and the social: a pedagogic perspective', *British Accounting Review*, 26(1): 91–7.

Mathews, M.R. (2001) 'Whither (or wither) accounting education in the new millennium', *Accounting Forum*, 25(4): 380–404.

Mathews, M.R. and Perera, M.H.B. (1996) *Accounting Theory and Development*, 3rd edn, Melbourne: Thomas Nelson.

Mattessich, R. (1984) 'The scientific approach to accounting', in R. Mattessich (ed.) *Modern Accounting Research: History, Survey and Guide*, Vancouver: Canadian Certified General Accountants' Research Foundation.

Matthews, D., Anderson, M. and Edwards, J.R. (1997) 'The rise of the professional accountant in British Management', *Economic History Review*, 50(3): 407–29.

Mautz, R.K. (1974) 'Where do we go from here?', *The Accounting Review*, 49(2): 353–60.

May, R.G. and Sundem, G.L. (1976) 'Research for accounting policy: an overview', *Accounting Review*, 51(4): 747–63.

McGregor, W. (1989) 'The new standard bearer', *Chartered Accountant*, 60(8): 48–9.

McGregor, W. (1992) 'True and fair view – an accounting anachronism', *Australian Accountant*, 62(1): 68–9.

McGregor, W.J. (1995) 'The setting of accounting standards in Australia: an evolving structure', *Australian Accounting Review*, 5(2): 17–22.

McKeown, J.C. (1971) 'An empirical test of a model proposed by Chambers', *The Accounting Review*, 46(1): 12–29.

McSweeney, B. (1997) 'The unbearable ambiguity of accounting', *Accounting Organizations and Society*, 22(7): 691–712.

Meiksins, P.F. and Watson, J.M. (1989) 'Professional autonomy and organizational constraint: the case of engineers', *The Sociological Quarterly*, 30(4): 561–85.

Merino, B.D. (1993) 'An analysis of the development of accounting knowledge: a pragmatic approach', *Accounting, Organizations and Society*, 18(2/3): 163–85.

Merino, B.D. and Neimark, M.D. (1982) 'Disclosure regulation and public policy: a sociohistorical reappraisal', *Journal of Accounting and Public Policy*, 1(1): 33–57.

Miller, M.C. (1995) 'The credibility of Australian financial reporting: are the co-regulation arrangements working?', *Australian Accounting Review*, 5(2): 3–16.

Miller, P. (1990) 'On the interrelations between accounting and the state', *Accounting, Organizations and Society*, 15(4): 315–38.

Miller, P., Hopper, T. and Laughlin, R. (1991) 'The New Accounting History: an introduction', *Accounting, Organizations and Society*, 16(5/6): 395–403.

Miller, P. and Napier, C. (1993) 'Genealogies of calculation', *Accounting, Organizations and Society*, 18(7/8): 631–47.

Millerson, G. (1964) *The Qualifying Associations: A Study in Professionalization*, London: Routledge and Kegan Paul.

Mitchell, A., Puxty, A., Sikka, P. and Willmott, H. (1991) *Accounting for Change: Proposals for Reform of Audit and Accounting*, London: Fabian Society.

Mitchell, A., Puxty, T., Sikka, P. and Willmott, H. (1994) 'Ethical statements as smokescreens for sectional interests: the case of the U.K. accountancy profession', *Journal of Business Ethics*, 13(1): 39–51.

Monroe, G.S., Ng, J. and Wellington, A.J. (1992) 'Limiting auditors' liability: the potential consequences', *Australian Accounting Review*, 1(4): 16–26.

Montagna, P.D. (1973) 'The public accounting profession', in E. Freidson (ed.) *The Professions and Their Prospects*, Beverly Hills: Sage Publications.

Montagna, P.D. (1974a) *Certified Public Accountants: A Sociological View of a Profession in Change*, Houston: Scholars Book Co.

Montagna, P.D. (1974b) 'Public accounting: the dynamics of occupational change', in R.R. Sterling (ed.) *Institutional Issues in Public Accounting*, Lawrence: Scholars Book Co.

Montagna, P.D. (1986) 'Accounting rationality and financial legitimation', *Theory and Society*, 15(1/2): 103–38.

Montagna, P.D. (1991) 'Accounting elites and accounting theory', *Accounting, Organizations and Society*, 16(1): 93–9.

Moore, J.F and Cooper, K.A. (1994) 'The consolidation of a profession: 1880–1906', *Accounting History*, 6(2): 17–32.

Moore, J.F. and Gaffikin, M. (1994) 'The early growth of corporations leading to the empowerment of the accounting profession, 1600–1855', *Accounting History*, 6(2): 46–66.

Moore, W.E. (1970) *The Professions: Roles and Rules*, New York: Russell Sage Foundation.

Morgan, G. (1988) 'Accounting as reality construction: towards a new epistemology for accounting practice', *Accounting, Organizations and Society*, 13(5): 477–85.

Morgan, G. and Willmott, H. (1993) 'The new accounting research: on making accounting more visible', *Accounting, Auditing and Accountability Journal*, 6(4): 3–36.

Most, K.S. (1993) *The Future of the Accounting Profession: A Global Perspective*, Westport: Quorum Books.

Mouck, T. (1992) 'The rhetoric of science and the rhetoric of revolt in the "story" of positive accounting theory', *Accounting, Auditing and Accountability Journal*, 5(4): 35–56.

Mouck, T. (1993) 'The "revolution" in financial reporting theory: a Kuhnian interpretation', *The Accounting Historians Journal*, 20(1): 33–57.

Mumford, E. (1983) *Medical Sociology*, New York: Random House.

Murphy, R. (1984) 'The structure of closure: a critique and development of the theories of Weber, Collins and Parkin', *The British Journal of Sociology*, 35(4): 547–67.

Mustard, J.F. (1978) 'Health professional education', in P. Slayton and M.J. Trebilcock (eds) *The Professions and Public Policy*, Toronto: University of Toronto.

Napier, C.J. (1998) 'Intersections of the law and accountancy: unlimited auditor liability in the United Kingdom', *Accounting, Organizations and Society*, 23(1): 105–28.

Naser, K. (1993) *Creative Financial Accounting: Its Nature and Use*, New York: Prentice Hall.

Naser, K. and Pendlebury, M. (1992) 'A note on the use of creative accounting', *British Accounting Review*, 24(2): 111–18.

(*The*) *New Shorter Oxford English Dictionary* (1993) Oxford: Oxford University Press.

Nobes, C. (1991) 'Cycles in UK standard setting', *Accounting and Business Research*, 21(83): 265–74.

Ogan, P. and Ziebart, D.A. (1991) 'Corporate reporting and the accounting profession: an interpretive paradigm', *Journal of Accounting Auditing and Finance*, 6(3): 387–406.

Okcabol, F. and Tinker, T. (1990) 'The market for positive theory: deconstructing the theory for excuses', *Advances in Public Interest Accounting*, 3: 71–95.

Okcabol, F. and Tinker, T. (1993) 'Dismantling financial disclosure regulations: testing the Stigler-Benston hypothesis', *Accounting, Auditing and Accountability Journal*, 6(1): 10–38.

O'Leary, T. and Boland, R.J. (1987) 'Self-regulation, public interest and the accounting profession', *Research in Accounting Regulation*, 1: 103–21.

Olson, W.E. (1982) *The Accounting Profession: Years of Trial: 1969–1980*, New York: American Institute of Certified Public Accountants.

O'Malley, S.F. (1993) 'Legal liability is having a chilling effect on the auditor's role', *Accounting Horizons*, 7(2): 82–7.

'One in four annual reports queried' (1996) *Business Review Weekly*, October 7: 85.

Orlikowski, W.J. (1988) 'The data processing occupation: professionalization or proletarianization?', *Research in the Sociology of Work*, 4: 95–124.

Paisey, C. and Paisey, N.J. (1996) 'Continuing professional education: pause for reflection?', *Critical Perspectives on Accounting*, 7(1/2): 103–26.

Panozzo, F. (1997) 'The making of the good academic accountant', *Accounting, Organizations and Society*, 22(5): 447–80.

Parker, L.D. (1987) 'An historical analysis of ethical pronouncements and debate in the Australian accounting profession', *Abacus*, 23(2): 122–40.

Parker, R.H. (1961) 'Australia's first accountancy body – The Adelaide Society of Accountants', *The Chartered Accountant in Australia*, 32(6): 337–40.

Parker, R.H. (1989) 'Importing and exporting accounting: the British experience', in A.G. Hopwood (ed.) *International Pressures for Accounting Change*, London: Prentice Hall.

Parker, R.H. and Morris, R.D. (2001) 'The influence of U.S. GAAP on the harmony of accounting measurement policies of large companies in the U.K. and Australia', *Abacus*, 37(3): 297–328.

Parker, R.H., Peirson, C.G. and Ramsay, A.L. (1987) 'Australian accounting standards and the law', *Company and Securities Law Journal*, 5(4): 231–46.

Parkin, F. (1979) *Marxism and Class Theory: A Bourgeois Critique*, New York: Columbia University Press.

Pasewark, W.R., Shockley, R.A. and Wilkerson, J.E. (1995) 'Legitimacy claims of the auditing profession *vis-a-vis* the behaviour of its members: an empirical examination', *Critical Perspectives on Accounting*, 6(1): 77–94.

Patel, C. and Day, R. (1996) 'The influence of cognitive style on the understandability of a professional accounting pronouncement', *British Accounting Review*, 28(2): 139–54.

Paton, G. (1993) 'From the president', *Australian Accountant*, 63(10): 1.

Paton, W.A. (1962, originally published 1922) *Accounting Theory: With Special Reference to the Corporate Enterprise*, Chicago: Accounting Studies Press.

Paton, W.A. (1967) 'Some reflections on education and professoring', *The Accounting Review*, 42(1): 7–23.

Paton, W.A. (1971) 'Earmarks of a profession – and the APB', *Journal of Accountancy*, 131(1): 37–45.

Paton, W.A. and Littleton, A.C. (1940) *An Introduction to Corporate Accounting Standards*, Sarasota: American Accounting Association.

Pavalko, R.M. (1971) *Sociology of Occupations and Professions*, Itasca: F.E. Peacock.

Peasnell, K.V. and Williams, D.J. (1986) 'Ersatz academics and scholar-saints: the supply of financial accounting research', *Abacus*, 22(2): 121–35.

Peirson, G. and Ramsay, A. (1983) 'A review of the regulation of financial reporting in Australia', *Company and Securities Law Journal*, 1(5): 286–300.

Peirson, G. and Ramsay, A. (1996) *Financial Accounting: An Introduction*, Melbourne: Longman.

Peltzman, S. (1976) 'Toward a more general theory of regulation', *The Journal of Law and Economics*, 19(2): 211–40.

Perkin, H. (1989) *The Rise of Professional Society: England Since 1880*, London: Routledge.

Perks, R.W. (1993) *Accounting and Society*, London: Chapman and Hall.

Phillips, D.L. (1973) 'Sociologists and their knowledge: some critical remarks on a profession', in E. Freidson (ed.) *The Professions and Their Prospects*, Beverly Hills: Sage Publications.

Popper, K. (1968) *The Logic of Scientific Discovery*, revised edn, London: Hutchinson.

Porter, B.A. (1993) 'An empirical study of the audit expectation–performance gap', *Accounting and Business Research*, 24(93): 49–68.

Porter, B.A. (1996) 'Review of *A Research Study on Financial Reporting and Auditing – Bridging the Expectation Gap*', *Accounting Horizons*, 10(1): 130–5.

Posner, R.A. (1974) 'Theories of economic regulation', *Bell Journal of Economics and Management Science*, 5(2): 335–57.

Poullaos, C. (1993) 'Making profession and state, 1907 to 1914: the ACPA's first charter attempt', *Abacus*, 29(2): 196–229.

Poullaos, C. (1994) *Making the Australian Chartered Accountant*, New York and London: Garland.

Power, M. (1991) 'Educating accountants: towards a critical ethnography', *Accounting, Organizations and Society*, 16(4): 333–53.

Power, M. (1994) 'The audit society', in A.G. Hopwood and P. Miller (eds) *Accounting as Social and Institutional Practice*, Cambridge: Cambridge University Press.

Power, M. (1997) *The Audit Society: Rituals of Verification*, Oxford: Oxford University Press.

Power, M. (1998) 'Auditor liability in context', *Accounting, Organizations and Society*, 23(1): 77–9.

Prandy, K. (1965) *Professional Employees: A Study of Scientists and Engineers*, London: Faber and Faber.

Preston, A.M., Cooper, D.J., Scarborough, D.P. and Chilton, R.C. (1995) 'Changes in the code of ethics of the U.S. accounting profession, 1917 and 1988: the continual quest for legitimation', *Accounting, Organizations and Society*, 20(6): 507–46.

Prior, A.N. (1967) 'Correspondence theory of truth', in *The Encyclopedia of Philosophy*, New York: Crowell Collier and Macmillan.

Puxty, T., Sikka, P. and Willmott, H. (1994) '(Re)forming the circle: education, ethics and accountancy practices', *Accounting Education*, 3(1): 77–92.

Puxty, A., Sikka, P. and Willmott, H. (1997) 'Mediating interests: the accountancy bodies' responses to the McFarlane Report', *Accounting and Business Research*, 27(4): 323–40.

Puxty, A.G., Willmott, H.C., Cooper, D.J. and Lowe, T. (1987) 'Modes of regulation in advanced capitalism: locating accounting in four countries', *Accounting, Organizations and Society*, 12(3): 273–91.

Quinton, A. (1967) 'Knowledge and belief', in *The Encyclopedia of Philosophy*, New York: Crowell Collier and Macmillan.

Rahman, A.R. (1992) *The Australian Accounting Standards Review Board: The Establishment of its Participative Review Process*, New York and London: Garland.

Rahman, A.R., Ng, L.W. and Tower, G.D. (1994) 'Public choice and accounting standard setting in New Zealand: an exploratory study', *Abacus*, 30(1): 98–117.

Ramirez, C. (2001) 'Understanding social closure in its cultural context: accounting practitioners in France (1920–1939)', *Accounting, Organizations and Society*, 26(4/5):
391–418.

Rennie, K. (1988) 'Liability of auditors', *The Chartered Accountant in Australia*, 58(8): 8.

Richardson, A.J. (1987a) 'Accounting as a legitimating institution', *Accounting,
Organizations and Society*, 12(4): 341–55.

Richardson, A.J. (1987b) 'Professionalization and intraprofessional competition in the
Canadian accounting profession', *Work and Occupations*, 14(4): 591–615.

Richardson, A.J. (1988) 'Accounting knowledge and professional privilege', *Accounting,
Organizations and Society*, 13(4): 381–96.

Richardson, A.J. (1989a) 'Canada's accounting elite: 1880–1930', *Accounting Historians
Journal*, 16(1): 1–19.

Richardson, A.J. (1989b) 'Corporatism and intraprofessional hegemony: a study of regulation and internal social order', *Accounting, Organizations and Society*, 14(5/6): 415–31.

Richardson, A.J. (1990) 'Accounting knowledge and professional privilege: a replication
and extension', *Accounting, Organizations and Society*, 15(5): 499–501.

Richardson, A.J. (1997) 'Social closure in dynamic markets: the incomplete professional
project in accountancy', *Critical Perspectives on Accounting*, 8(6): 635–53.

Roberts, J. and Coutts, J.A. (1992) 'Feminization and professionalization: a review of an
emerging literature on the development of accounting in the United Kingdom',
Accounting, Organizations and Society, 17(3/4): 379–95.

Robson, K. and Cooper, D. (1990) 'Understanding the development of the accountancy
profession in the United Kingdom', in D.J. Cooper and T.M. Hopper (eds) *Critical
Accounts*, London: Macmillan.

Robson, K., Willmott, H., Cooper, D. and Puxty, T. (1994) 'The ideology of professional
regulation and the markets for accounting labour: three episodes in the recent history
of the U.K. accountancy profession', *Accounting, Organizations and Society*, 19(6): 527–53.

Roslender, R. (1990a) 'The accountant in the class structure', *Advances in Public Interest
Accounting*, 3: 195–212.

Roslender, R. (1990b) 'Sociology and management accounting research', *British
Accounting Review*, 22(4): 351–72.

Roslender, R. (1992) *Sociological Perspectives on Modern Accountancy*, London: Routledge.

Roslender, R. (1996) 'Critical accounting and the labour of accountants', *Critical Perspectives on Accounting*, 7(4): 461–84.

Roth, J.A. (1974) 'Professionalism: the sociologist's decoy', *Sociology of Work and
Occupations*, 1(1): 6–23.

Roy, R.H. and MacNeill, J.H. (1967) *Horizons for a Profession: The Common Body of
Knowledge for Certified Public Accountants*, New York: American Institute of Certified
Public Accountants.

Rueschemeyer, D. (1983) 'Professional autonomy and the social control of expertise', in
R. Dingwall and P. Lewis (eds) *The Sociology of the Professions: Lawyers, Doctors and Others*,
London: Macmillan.

Russell, B. (1973, originally published 1940) *An Inquiry into Meaning and Truth*,
Harmondsworth: Penguin.

Saggers, S., Grant, J., Woodhead, M. and Banham, V. (1994) 'The professionalisation of
mothering: family day care', *The Australian and New Zealand Journal of Sociology*, 30(3):
273–87.

Saks, M. (1983) 'Removing the blinkers? A critique of recent contributions to the sociology of the professions', *The Sociological Review*, 31(1): 1–21.

Saudagaran, S.M. (1996) 'The first course in accounting: an innovative approach', *Issues
in Accounting Education*, 11(1): 83–94.

Saul, J.R. (1997) *The Unconscious Civilization*, Melbourne: Penguin Books.

Schipper, K. (1994) 'Academic accounting research and the standard setting process',
Accounting Horizons, 8(4): 61–73.

Schuetze, W.P. (1993a) 'The liability crisis in the U.S. and its impact on Accounting', *Accounting Horizons*, 7(2): 88–91.

Schuetze, W.P. (1993b) 'What is an asset?', *Accounting Horizons*, 7(3): 66–70.

Schuetze, W.P. (1994) 'A mountain or a molehill', *Accounting Horizons*, 8(1): 69–75.

Schuetze, W.P. (2001) 'What are assets and liabilities? Where is true north? (Accounting that my sister would understand)', *Abacus*, 37(1): 1–25.

Scruton, R. (1996) *Modern Philosophy: An Introduction and Survey*, London: Mandarin.

Seal, W., Sucher, P. and Zelenka, I. (1996) 'Post-socialist transition and the development of an accountancy profession in the Czech Republic', *Critical Perspectives on Accounting*, 7(4): 485–508.

Selander, S. (1990) 'Associative strategies in the process of professionalization: professional strategies and the scientification of occupations', in M. Burrage and R. Torstendahl (eds) *Professions in Theory and History: Rethinking the Study of the Professions*, London: Sage.

Shackleton, K. (1995) 'Scottish chartered accountants: internal and external political relationships, 1853–1916', *Accounting, Auditing and Accountability Journal*, 8(2): 18–46.

Shackleton, K. (1999) 'Gender segregation in Scottish chartered accountancy: the deployment of male concerns about the admission of women, 1900–25', *Accounting, Business and Financial History*, 9(1): 135–56.

Shah, A.K. (1996) 'Creative compliance in financial reporting', *Accounting, Organizations and Society*, 21(1): 23–39.

Shaked, A. and Sutton, J. (1981) 'The self-regulating profession', *Review of Economic Studies*, 48(2): 217–34.

Shapiro, B.P. (1997) 'Objectivity, relativism, and truth in external financial reporting: what's really at stake in the disputes?', *Accounting, Organizations and Society*, 22(3): 165–85.

Sharpe, M. (1998) 'Looking for harmony: building a global framework', *Australian Accountant*, 68(2): 16–18.

Shaw, G.B. (1932, originally published 1906) *The Doctor's Dilemma* (including 'Preface on doctors'), London: Constable and Company.

Shaw, K.E. (1987) 'Skills, control and the mass professions', *The Sociological Review*, 35(4): 775–94.

Shearer, T.L. and Arrington, C.E. (1993) 'Accounting in other wor(l)ds: a feminism without reserve', *Accounting, Organizations and Society*, 18(2/3): 253–72.

Sikka, P. (1987) 'Professional education and auditing books: a review article', *British Accounting Review*, 19(3): 291–304.

Sikka, P. and Willmott, H. (1995a) 'The power of "independence": defending and extending the jurisdiction of accounting in the United Kingdom', *Accounting, Organizations and Society*, 20(6): 547–81.

Sikka, P. and Willmott, H. (1995b) 'Illuminating the state-professions relationship: accountants as Department of Trade and Industry Investigators', *Critical Perspectives on Accounting*, 6(4): 341–69.

Sikka, P. and Willmott, H. (1997) 'Practising critical accounting', *Critical Perspectives on Accounting*, 8(1/2): 149–65.

Sikka, P., Willmott, H. and Lowe, T. (1989) 'Guardians of knowledge and public interest: evidence and issues of accountability in the UK accountancy profession', *Accounting, Auditing and Accountability Journal*, 2(2): 47–71.

Slayton, P. (1978) 'Professional education and the consumer interest: A framework for inquiry', in P. Slayton and M.J. Trebilcock (eds) *The Professions and Public Policy*, Toronto: University of Toronto.

Small, B. (1986a) 'Limitation of accountant's liability: the present position', *The Chartered Accountant in Australia*, 56(7): 12.

Small, B. (1986b) 'Civil liability of company auditors', *The Chartered Accountant in Australia*, 56(8): 11.

Smith, A. (1952, originally published 1776) *An Inquiry into the Nature and Causes of the Wealth of Nations*, Chicago: William Benton.

Smithers, D. (1992) 'President's message', *Charter*, 63(8): 60–1.

Solomons, D. (1978) 'The politicization of accounting', *Journal of Accountancy*, 146(5): 65–72.

Solomons, D. (1983) 'The political implications of accounting and accounting standard setting', *Accounting and Business Research*, 13(50): 107–18.

Sprouse, R.T. (1983) 'Standard setting: the American experience', in M. Bromwich and A.G. Hopwood (eds) *Accounting Standards Setting: An International Perspective*, London: Pitman.

Sprouse, R.T. (1988) 'Commentary on financial reporting', *Accounting Horizons*, 2(4): 121–7.

Stamp, E. (1980) *Corporate Reporting: Its Future Evolution*, Toronto: Canadian Institute of Chartered Accountants.

Stamp, E. (1985) 'The politics of professional accounting research: some personal reflections', *Accounting, Organizations and Society*, 10(1): 11–23.

'Statements on recommended accounting practice' (1971) *The Australian Accountant*, 41(6): 245.

Sterling, R.R. (1970) *Theory of the Measurement of Enterprise Income*, Lawrence: University Press of Kansas.

Sterling, R.R. (1972) 'Introduction', in R.R. Sterling (ed.) *Research Methodology in Accounting*, Houston: Scholars Book Co.

Sterling, R.R. (1973a) 'Accounting power', *Journal of Accountancy*, 135(1): 61–7.

Sterling, R.R. (1973b) 'Accounting research, education and practice', *Journal of Accountancy*, 136(3): 44–52.

Sterling, R.R. (1975a) 'Professional schools of accounting: some academic questions', in A.H. Bizzell and K.D. Larson (eds) *Schools of Accountancy: A Look at the Issues*, New York: American Institute of Certified Public Accountants.

Sterling, R.R. (1975b) 'Toward a science of accounting', *Financial Analysts Journal*, September–October: 28–36.

Sterling, R.R. (1976) 'Accounting at the crossroads', *The Journal of Accountancy*, 142(2): 82–7.

Sterling, R.R. (1977) 'Accounting in the 1980s', in N.M. Bedford (ed.) *The Council of Arthur Young Professors*, University of Illinois.

Sterling, R.R. (1979) *Toward a Science of Accounting*, Houston: Scholars Book Co.

Sterling, R.R. (1988) 'Confessions of a failed empiricist', *Advances in Accounting*, 6: 3–35.

Sterling, R.R. (1989) 'Teaching the correspondence concept', *Issues in Accounting Education*, 4(1): 82–93.

Sterling, R.R. (1990a) 'Positive accounting: an assessment', *Abacus*, 26(2): 97–135.

Sterling, R.R. (1990b) 'Teacher, educate thyself', *Journal of Accounting Education*, 8(1): 1–16.

Stewart, J.C. (1975) 'The emergent professionals', *The Accountant's Magazine*, 129(825): 113–16.

Stigler, G.J. (1964a) 'Public regulation of the securities markets', *The Journal of Business*, 37(2): 117–42.

Stigler, G.J. (1964b) 'Comment', *The Journal of Business*, 37(4): 414–22.

Stigler, G.J. (1971) 'The theory of economic regulation', *The Bell Journal of Economics and Management Science*, 2(1): 3–21.

Sunder, S. (1991) 'Measuring research accomplishments', *Issues in Accounting Education*, 6(1): 134–8.

Sweeney, H.W. (1964, originally published 1936) *Stabilized Accounting*, New York: Holt, Rinehart and Winston.

Sykes, T. (1994) *The Bold Riders: Behind Australia's Corporate Collapses*, Sydney: Allen and Unwin.

Tabart-Gay, J. and Wolnizer, P.W. (1997) 'Business firms as adaptive entities: the case of the major Australian banks 1983–94', *Abacus*, 33(2): 186–207.

Tarnas, R.T. (1996) *The Passion of the Western Mind*, London: Pimlico.

Tawney, R.H. (1920) *The Acquisitive Society*, New York: Harcourt, Brace and Company.

Taylor, D. and Fisher, J. (1990) 'Educating tomorrow's accountants', *Charter*, 61(1): 78–9.

Tinker, A.M. (1985) *Paper Prophets: A Social Critique of Accounting*, New York: Praeger.

Tinker, A.M., Merino, B.D. and Neimark, M.D. (1982) 'The normative origins of positive theories: ideology and accounting thought', *Accounting, Organizations and Society*, 7(2): 167–200.

Tinker, T. and Koutsoumadi, A. (1997) 'A mind is a wonderful thing to waste: "think like a commodity", become a CPA', *Accounting, Auditing and Accountability Journal*, 10(3): 454–67.

Tinker, T. and Puxty, T. (1995) *Policing Accounting Knowledge: The Market for Excuses Affair*, Princeton: Markus Wiener.

Tomsen, S. (1992) 'Professionalism and state engagement: lawyers and legal aid policy in Australia in the 1970s and 1980s', *The Australian and New Zealand Journal of Sociology*, 28(3): 307–29.

Torstendahl, R. (1990) 'Essential properties, strategic aims and historical development; three approaches to theories of professionalism', in M. Burrage and R. Torstendahl (eds) *Professions in Theory and History: Rethinking the Study of the Professions*, London: Sage.

Trebilcock, M.J. (1978) 'The professions and public policy: the nature of the agenda', in P. Slayton and M.J. Trebilcock (eds) *The Professions and Public Policy*, Toronto: University of Toronto.

Tricker, R.I. (1983) 'Corporate responsibility, institutional governance and the roles of accounting standards', in M. Bromwich and A.G. Hopwood (eds) *Accounting Standards Setting: An International Perspective*, London: Pitman.

Tuohy, C.J. and Wolfson, A.D. (1978) 'Self-regulation: who qualifies?', in P. Slayton and M.J. Trebilcock (eds) *The Professions and Public Policy*, Toronto: University of Toronto.

Turner, B.S. (1986) 'Nursing, professionalism and job context: the vocabulary of complaints', *The Australian and New Zealand Journal of Sociology*, 22(3): 368–86.

Turner, B.S. (1995) *Medical Power and Social Knowledge*, 2nd edn, London: Sage Publications.

Turner, J.H. and Jensen, D.L. (1987) 'Recent episodes in the "oversight cycle" of accountancy self-regulation', *Research in Accounting Regulation*, 1: 35–50.

Tutticci, I., Dunstan, K. and Holmes, S. (1994) 'Respondent lobbying in the Australian accounting standard-setting process: ED49. A case study', *Accounting, Auditing and Accountability Journal*, 7(2): 86–104.

Tweedie, D. (1993) 'The accountant: a tradesman or a professional?', in M.J. Mumford and K.V. Peasnell (eds) *Philosophical Perspectives on Accounting*, London: Routledge.

Tyson, T. (1995) 'The archivist responds to the new accounting history: the case of the US men's clothing industry', *Accounting, Business and Financial History*, 5(1): 17–37.

Van Whye, G. (1994) *The Struggle for Status: A History of Accounting Education*, New York and London: Garland.

Vatter, W.J. (1964) 'Survey of accountancy education in Australia: report of Professor W.J. Vatter', *The Australian Accountant*, 34(8): 429–60.

Velayutham, S. (1996) 'Corporatization and the regulation of accounting services', *British Accounting Review*, 28(4): 351–68.

Walker, F. (1981) 'Regulation of the accounting profession', *The Australian Accountant*, 51(4): 235.

Walker, R. (1987) 'Australia's ASRB. A case study of political activity and regulatory "capture"', *Accounting and Business Research*, 17(67): 269–86.

Walker, R.G. (1993) 'A feeling of deja vu: controversies in accounting and auditing regulation in Australia', *Critical Perspectives on Accounting*, 4(1): 97–109.

Walker, R.G. and Robinson, S.P. (1994) 'Related party transactions: a case study of inter-organizational conflict over the "development" of disclosure rules', *Abacus*, 30(1): 18–43.

Walker, S.P. (1988) *The Society of Accountants in Edinburgh 1854–1914: A Study of Recruitment to a New Profession*, New York and London: Garland.

Walker, S.P. (1991) 'The defence of professional monopoly: Scottish chartered accountants and "satellites in the accountancy firmament" 1854–1914', *Accounting, Organizations and Society*, 16(3): 257–83.

Walker, S.P. (1995) 'The genesis of professional organization in Scotland: a contextual analysis', *Accounting, Organizations and Society*, 20(4): 285–310.

Walker, S.P. (1996) 'The criminal upperworld and the emergence of a disciplinary code in the early chartered accountancy profession', *Accounting History*, 1(2): 7–35.

Watts, R.L. (1992) 'Accounting choice theory and market-based research in accounting', *British Accounting Review*, 24(3): 235–67.

Watts, R.L. and Zimmerman, J.L. (1978) 'Toward a positive theory of the determination of accounting standards', *The Accounting Review*, 53(1): 112–34.

Watts, R.L. and Zimmerman, J.L. (1979) 'The demand for and supply of accounting theories: the market for excuses', *The Accounting Review*, 54(2): 273–305.

Watts, R.L. and Zimmerman, J.L. (1986) *Positive Accounting Theory*, Englewood Cliffs: Prentice-Hall.

Watts, R.L. and Zimmerman, J.L. (1990) 'Positive accounting theory: a ten year perspective', *The Accounting Review*, 65(1): 131–56.

Weetman, P., Davie, E.S. and Collins, W. (1996) 'Lobbying on accounting issues: preparer/user imbalance in the case of the *Operating and Financial Review*', *Accounting, Auditing and Accountability Journal*, 9(1): 59–76.

Weiser, H.J. (1966) 'Accounting education – present and future', *The Accounting Review*, 41(3): 518–24.

Wells, M. (1976) 'A revolution in accounting thought?', *The Accounting Review*, 51(3): 471–82.

White, A.R. (1967) 'Coherence theory of truth', in *The Encyclopedia of Philosophy*, New York: Crowell Collier and Macmillan.

Whitehead, A.N. (1933) *Adventures of Ideas*, Cambridge: Cambridge University Press.

Whitley, R.D. (1988) 'The possibility and utility of positive accounting theory', *Accounting, Organizations and Society*, 13(6): 631–45.

Whittington, G. (1987) 'Positive accounting theory: a review article', *Accounting and Business Research*, 17(68): 327–36.

Whittington, G. (1993) 'Corporate governance and the regulation of financial reporting', *Accounting and Business Research*, 23(91A): 311–19.

Whittred, G. and Chan, Y.K. (1992) 'Asset revaluation and the mitigation of under-investment', *Abacus*, 28(1): 58–74.

Whittred, G., Zimmer, I. and Taylor, S. (1996) *Financial Accounting: Incentive Effects and Economic Consequences*, 4th edn, Sydney: Harcourt Brace.

Wilensky, H.L. (1964) 'The professionalization of everyone?', *The American Journal of Sociology*, 70(2): 138–58.

Williams, D.Z. (1991) 'The challenge of change in accounting education', *Issues in Accounting Education*, 6(1): 126–33.

Williams, P.F. (1987) 'The legitimate concern with fairness', *Accounting, Organizations and Society*, 12(2): 169–89.

Williams, P.F. (1989) 'The logic of positive accounting research', *Accounting, Organizations and Society*, 14(5/6): 455–68.

Williams, P.F. and Rodgers, J.L. (1995) '*The Accounting Review* and the production of accounting knowledge', *Critical Perspectives on Accounting*, 6(3): 263–87.

Willmott, H. (1984) 'Accounting regulation: an alternative perspective: a comment', *Journal of Business Finance and Accounting*, 11(4): 585–91.

Willmott, H. (1986) 'Organising the profession: a theoretical and historical examination of the development of the major accountancy bodies in the U.K.', *Accounting, Organizations and Society*, 11(6): 555–80.

Willmott, H. (1990) 'Serving the public interest? A critical analysis of a professional claim', in D. Cooper and T. Hopper (eds) *Critical Accounts*, London: Macmillan.

Willmott, H., Puxty, T. and Cooper, D. (1993) 'Maintaining self-regulation: making "interests" coincide in discourses on the governance of the ICAEW', *Accounting, Auditing and Accountability Journal*, 6(4): 68–93.

Willmott, H. and Sikka, P. (1997) 'On the commercialization of accountancy thesis: a review essay', *Accounting, Organizations and Society*, 22(8): 831–42.

Willmott, H., Sikka, P. and Puxty, A. (1994) 'Barely afloat: the industrialization and self-regulation of accounting', *The Journal of Applied Accounting Research*, 2(1): 58–79.

Willmott, H., Puxty, A.G., Robson, K. and Lowe, E.A. (1992) 'Regulation of accountancy and accountants: a comparative analysis of accounting for research and development in four advanced capitalist countries', *Accounting, Auditing and Accountability Journal*, 5(2): 32–56.

Windal, F.W. and Corley, R.N. (1980) *The Accounting Professional: Ethics, Responsibility and Liability*, Englewood Cliffs: Prentice Hall.

Wise, T., Needles, B.E., Anderson, H.R. and Caldwell, J.C. (1998) *Principles of Accounting Australasian Edition*, Brisbane: Jacaranda Wiley.

Witz, A. (1992) *Professions and Patriarchy*, London: Routledge.

Wolnizer, P.W. (1977) 'Primary production inventories under current value accounting', *Accounting and Business Research*, 7(28): 303–10.

Wolnizer, P.W. (1983) 'Market prices v. cost indexation in accounting for steel inventories', *Abacus*, 19(2): 171–88.

Wolnizer, P.W. (1987) *Auditing as Independent Authentication*, Sydney: Sydney University Press.

Wolnizer, P.W. (1995) 'Are audit committees red herrings?', *Abacus*, 31(1): 45–66.

Wright, D.T. (1978) 'The objectives of professional education', in P. Slayton and M.J. Trebilcock (eds) *The Professions and Public Policy*, Toronto: University of Toronto.

Wyatt, A.R. (1991) 'AAA Presidential Address', *Accounting Horizons*, 5(4): 99–104.

Young, J.J. (1995) 'Defending an accounting jurisdiction: the case of cash flows', *Critical Perspectives on Accounting*, 6(2): 173–200.

Young, J.J. and Mouck, T. (1996) 'Objectivity and the role of history in the development and review of accounting standards', *Accounting, Auditing and Accountability Journal*, 9(3): 127–47.

Young, S.D. (1988) 'The economic theory of regulation: evidence from the uniform CPA examination', *The Accounting Review*, 63(2): 283–91.

Zald, M.N. (1968) 'The common body of knowledge for CPAs: some problems in analysis', *Journal of Accounting Research*, 6(1): 130–40.

Zeff, S.A. (1972) *Forging Accounting Principles in Five Countries: A History and Analysis of Trends*, Champaign: Stipes Publishing.

Zeff, S.A. (1973) *Forging Accounting Principles in Australia*, Melbourne: Australian Society of Accountants.

Zeff, S.A. (1974) 'Comments on accounting principles – how they are developed', in R.R. Sterling (ed.) *Institutional Issues in Public Accounting*, Lawrence: Scholars Book Co.

Zeff, S.A. (1978) 'The rise of "economic consequences" ', *Journal of Accountancy*, 146(6): 56–63.

Zeff, S.A. (1984) 'Some junctures in the evolution of the process of establishing accounting principles in the U.S.A.: 1917–1972', *The Accounting Review*, 59(3): 447–68.

Zeff, S.A. (1986) 'Big eight firms and the accounting literature: the falloff in advocacy writing', *Journal of Accounting, Auditing and Finance*, 1(2): 131–54.

Zeff, S.A. (1987) 'Does the CPA belong to a profession?', *Accounting Horizons*, 1(2): 65–8.

Zeff, S.A. (1989a) 'Does accounting belong in the university curriculum?', *Issues in Accounting Education*, 4(1): 203–9.

Zeff, S.A. (1989b) 'Recent trends in accounting education and research in the USA: some implications for UK academics', *British Accounting Review*, 21(2): 159–76.

Ziman, J. (1968) *Public Knowledge: The Social Dimension of Science*, Cambridge: Cambridge University Press.

Ziman, J. (1978) *Reliable Knowledge: An Exploration of the Grounds for Belief in Science*, Cambridge: Cambridge University Press.

Zimmerman, J.L. (1987, originally published 1980) 'Positive research in accounting', in R. Bloom and P.T. Elgers (eds) *Accounting Theory and Policy*, 2nd edn, San Diego: Harcourt Brace Jovanovich.

Index